Gillian Bridge

The Significance Delusion

Unlocking Our Thinking for Our Children's Future

First published by

Crown House Publishing Ltd
Crown Buildings, Bancyfelin, Carmarthen, Wales, SA33 5ND, UK
www.crownhouse.co.uk

and

Crown House Publishing Company LLC
PO Box 2223, Williston, VT 05495
www.crownhousepublishing.com

Page 87, extract from Quinlan, Donald M. and Brown, Thomas E. (2003) Assessment of short-term
verbal memory impairments in adolescents and adults with ADHD, *Journal of Attention Disorders* 6(4):
143–152 has been reproduced with permission.
Page 125, extract from Immordino-Yang, Mary H., McColla, Andrea, Damasio, Hanna and Damasio,
Antonio (2009) Neural correlates of admiration and compassion, *Proceedings of the National Academy of
Sciences* 106(19): 8021–8026. Available at: http://www.pnas.org/content/106/19/8021.full. has been
reproduced with permission.
Page 264, extract from *Tadworth Times* has been reproduced with permission.

Crown House Publishing has no responsibility for the persistence or accuracy of URLs for external or third-party
websites referred to in this publication, and does not guarantee that any content on such websites is, or will remain,
accurate or appropriate.

British Library Cataloguing-in-Publication Data
A catalogue entry for this book is available
from the British Library.

Print ISBN 978-1-78583-108-9
Mobi ISBN 978-1-78583-131-7
ePub ISBN 978-1-78583-132-4
ePDF ISBN 978-1-78583-133-1

LCCN 2016910207

Printed and bound in the UK by
Bell & Bain Ltd, Thornliebank, Glasgow

Dedicated to the shades of William

Acknowledgements

My wonderful children, whose unfailing support and practical help could only be equalled by my gratitude and love.

Ro, for her patient reading and re-reading and endless encouragement and belief in me.

My case studies and other clients and patients whose rich but complex lives brought life to this work.

Peter Young and Emma Tuck, my editors, for taking this book (and me) on, for taking on more than they had to, for making it a better work, and for demonstrating more cool and grace under pressure than this author sometimes did.

To you all – thank you.

And, finally, my five grandchildren, Dylan, Charlie, Edie, Izzy and Frannie – the future that this work is all about.

Contents

Introduction

> When we remember we are all mad, the mysteries disappear and life stands explained.
>
> **Mark Twain**

The Significance Delusion is a synthesis of research, ideas, facts and fascinating real-life anecdotes exploring our human obsession with meaning: 'What does it all mean for me? What do I mean to others?'

Although my early trajectory destined me for a career studying and teaching arts subjects, life, as is its way, pushed me in rather a different direction. But it could only have done that if I were complicit in some way. Although I had nothing more than personal experience, curiosity and naive scepticism to go on, I found myself unhappy with conventional explanations of the strange human behaviour and life happenings that I came across. For many, including the 'experts', odd things – loving people suddenly turning violent; good parents rearing troubled kids; clever, busy, talented people becoming addicts – could be explained away by stories about repressed desires, inherent badness, 'King Babies' and the like. I wasn't buying into any of that. I wanted to hear about deeper causes and probe into the fundamentals of behaviour. Finding few resources available, I did my own research into the scientific underpinnings of these problems. I had to learn how brains do what they do and how this manifests in observable behaviour.

Then I started working with clients and added genuine experience to the pot of knowledge I had acquired. And now I mostly work with people who are not average, whose brains seem to function in a different way from most others. All of which is enormously helpful for defining how more regular brains work. This, as I have discovered, is not actually normal at all, at least in species terms.

What I have found is that humans are essentially delusional. And that in order to thrive, they need to share a common delusion. This finding, the underlying explanations of how it all came to be and where it has taken us, is what this book is about. The key features are:

- Research into two key mutations which allowed our brains to develop long-distance connectivity and thus symbolic thinking, but also vulnerability to mental health problems.
- The search for Significance.
- The science behind the 'mutant human'.
- Optimum child care.
- The central place of language (and individual language use) in wellbeing.
- Survival skills for human growth.
- The current obsession with individualism that is compromising our ability to thrive.

There are three interweaving strands throughout the book: brain matters, child-rearing matters and self-versus-community matters. The overall ambition of the book is one I have chosen, in places, to call 'surthrival' – a portmanteau term that suggests not just surviving but thriving in the best possible interests of the individual *and* of the species.

Our brains are us, but it seems we are not quite all we might like to be. Despite having advantages previous generations could only dream about, we are still not as happy or fulfilled as we think we should be. By understanding brain function, by seeing how it 'makes' us behave in the way we do, by looking at the implications of the nature/nurture debate and by considering how society works on both an individual and a group level, we can get a better grip on it all and improve our own lives, plus those of generations to come.

We are the blueprint for that future, so it is vital to question, in particular, the ramifications of some aspects of contemporary ideologies on the mental health of both present and future generations. I challenge givens such as: the importance of happiness and self-esteem; the value of subjective experience and individual 'rights' over social cohesion. And I certainly hope my take will prove controversial.

I also hope it will prove compelling because there is a hunger for understanding. My audiences and clients frequently express the need to understand themselves, and they want to understand why so much seems to be going wrong with us humans, despite having more of just about everything we ever thought we wanted. The old explanations don't work; the 'truths' coming from experts are problematic because they have not had the direct experience. The worlds of research and of professional caretaking of society have been secret, special and siloed for too long. I believe most people, given the appropriate information, would prefer to think of themselves as responsible enough to make their own judgements.

Who am I? What am I? How am I? You will find the answers here. By the end of the book, with the help of my occasionally challenging, often quirky and usually humorous observations, you should be a whole lot closer to understanding yourself – which is good. And if you have or care for children, either personally or professionally, you will also be a lot closer to knowing how to promote their future wellbeing in the best way possible – which is better still.

This book takes you on a journey through time, history and the mysterious labyrinth that is the brain, visiting a number of strange cases and everyday conflicts on the way. Some are eternal dilemmas such as, how do we feel we're individual but remain part of society? Others are utterly modern – for example, what can we do about clever kids addicted to online living? How do we make them less sensitive and susceptible to the knock-backs of failure? By the end, having read this compendium of all the lifestyle advice that a well-adjusted human will ever need, you will know what it takes to thrive and survive as the bizarre creature with danger written into its DNA – the human being.

Chapter 1

Is Life Enough?

Do you leap blithely out of bed and celebrate the dawning of the new day? Do you turn on the news and find yourself humming 'What a Wonderful World'? Does satisfaction, like an Andrex puppy, run riot through your workplace?

I ask, because I'd love to meet someone who felt able to say 'yes' to all of those questions. That would be something of a first for me, and as a cynical old thing I could do with the morale boost. I sometimes feel that if I were an alien anthropologist, just landed here to take soundings on the earth's viability as a place to colonise, I'd be advising my leader to think twice before committing to the project:

Well, yes, it's got all we need to support life, for survival …

Al, I can hear a 'but' coming. What's your problem?

Well … but, the humans seem to be in a bit of a mess. Plenty of them and all that, but somehow not quite, how can I put it? Thriving. Even in the places where there's enough of everything to go around, like food, shelter, clothing, education; it just seems that it's never enough.

Al, tell me more. Give me some facts, some evidence.

Okay, take these news reports I've been reading:

- Desire for happiness that only leads to woe
- Unborn child feels a mother's stress
- Face up to it: children are in the grip of National Attention Deficit Disorder
- Top head slams hothousing
- British parents are too intrusive and 'baby' their children, says MP
- Babies of obese mothers at risk of heart disease
- Britain's health has fallen further behind other Western nations, says *Lancet* report
- Loneliness in old age 'deadlier than obesity'
- Guilt of the balancing act mothers
- Buggy children are unable to walk at three

- Children 'are growing more miserable'
- Too soft pupils will get toughened up
- Student mental ill health is 'under treated'
- One in ten young 'can't cope with life'

I don't know about you, Leader, but that last one just about scares the coprolite out of me. Ten per cent of the species likely to fail to function? Why risk it?

Al, you've got a point. Let's fire up the rockets.

It's all getting quite depressing. If we take that last report (which was produced by the Prince's Trust in 2015) a bit more seriously, we can see that we're on target for it to get even more depressing, because, based on the UK government's population projections, by 2020 we will have 1.3 million non-coping unhappy youngsters in our midst.

This is not only about how we parent our young and how badly wrong we seem to be getting it. Heaven knows, parents get it in the neck quite enough already. This is about how we *all* live our lives; it's about things that run through the warp and the weft of every single human life lived.

It's a species thing. It's about why there really is something funny about our species, something that, if we weren't quite so successful at surviving, should surely make us non-viable.

This book is about that strange anomaly and explains how that anomaly lies behind so many of our modern problems. It leads, almost inevitably, to consider our contemporary tsunami of discontent – which includes:

STRESS
respect ADDICTION yearning religiosity
OVER-CONSUMPTION
INTERNET FIXATION fear of death obsessions
sentimentality ANXIETY
hypochondria Munchausen syndrome emptiness
despair DEPRESSION
emotional confusion authority issues AUTISM
identity issues texting obsession
POSSESSION ENVY perfectionism over achievement guilt
EATING/WEIGHT ISSUES power/megalomania
NOVELTY/THRILL SEEKING
restlessness RELATIONSHIP ISSUES commitment
issues SEX ISSUES

status envy loss of motivation shame envy
CO-DEPENDENCY control issues
genealogy 'special and different' therapy/counselling
fixation emotional desperation UNDEPENDABILITY
ceremony and ritual fixation BOREDOM SELF-DOUBT
procrastination COMMUNICATION DIFFICULTIES
demotivation
FAME SEEKING Facebook and 'phoney' friendships
THOUGHTLESSNESS

These are some of the most common and troubling concerns that people suffer from today, even though not one of them can be said to have any measurable or quantifiable existence in what we call reality. These concerns and troubles have their primary and most powerful and disturbing existence deep within our own heads.

What's in it for you?

Well, first, you'll find out a lot about what it means to be human in this book, including the implications of some of the most recent and ground-breaking research into those very heads where so many of our troubles are located. And then you will find explanations for those problems that you might be experiencing, together with a whole raft of solutions for them. At the same time, you will have to hand a masterwork on resilience that will fit you with the skills to help bring up a whole generation of more fully rounded and functional human beings. What's not to find helpful and fascinating?

Am I, in fact, an alien anthropologist? Not quite. But I'm enough of an outsider to have a useful perspective, and enough of an insider to know what I'm dealing with. Having spent years working with some of the most extreme forms of human behaviour, I have a very useful back catalogue of materials to draw on.

I have worked with geniuses who have been well-regarded and in highly paid work, with geniuses who have ended up in prison and with yet others who have lived in a permanent state of confusion. I have worked with brain-damaged people who have had little apparent physical or cognitive function left and come to me barely able to communicate at all, and those who have only grunted or barked. I have worked with crack addicts who have carried on slicing open already stapled together arms and with prisoners whose scarred heads showed horrific evidence of having been cracked open by 'colleague's' spades. I have treated people so desperate for booze that they've sucked the final drops of spilt alcohol from the carpet and gym bunnies so desperate for fitness they've pounded the treadmill till they dropped.

I have watched as sink-estate mums blossomed into Shakespeare-mad lecturers and seen apparently charming young men suddenly turn and throw knives at innocent kids. I have worked with stratospherically successful CEOs and with people who haven't had a clue how to get themselves out of bed in the mornings.

And here's the thing: without exception, I have observed that those who were the most damaged (and they were by no means always the least successful) had something very specific in common. They shared a particular trait.

The magic Cinderella key

This trait, the one that helps to pinpoint and identify dysfunctional thinking and/or behaviour, also pointed me in the direction of a factor underpinning all three: the trait, the thinking and the behaviour. This, I realised, had potentially revolutionary implications. So I decided to call this underlying factor my magic Cinderella key because its impact on humans is both mysterious and transformative, and it seems to have been more or less completely overlooked by everyone. Also it unlocks the cells (a rather useful pun here) in our imprisoning brains.

I shall keep you hanging on a bit longer, though, before I tell you what it is. If I said what it was straightaway you might simply see it as a rather familiar figure dressed in rags, and your response to it might go something like this, 'What, that old thing! Why do you want to make such a fuss about *that*?' So let me introduce you to Cinders when I've dressed her up a bit more formally in the material of science.

What I can tell you now is that this magic Cinderella factor is bigger than poverty, social breakdown, loss of religion, the internet, commercialism and all of the other suspected causes of unhappiness and failure to thrive. And in its way, it's much more dangerous.

Danger in our DNA?

It is dangerous because it is deeply implicated in the way that we developed as humans. Although it may have been no more than an accidental occurrence, a mutation even, it came to define the way we thought about experience and reacted to it, and so, in a very real sense, it made our species the special one that it is. But, but, but … the downside of this evolutionary quirk (or hiccup, or whatever) is that it also made us much more vulnerable than other animals to the possibility that quite large numbers of us could fail to develop into fully functioning, thriving members of the species.

To understand why this is, in the next chapter I shall be looking at the way our brains evolved. But that is only one of the reasons; the others are:

- Sometimes the stuff that's inside our head is our own worst enemy. Know your enemy is a very good principle.
- Understanding how brains work (at a reasonably user-friendly level) will help to improve anyone's parenting skills.
- Our brains are us and this is both our history and our inheritance.

Chapter 2

Bounded in a Nutshell

Oh God, I could be bounded in a nutshell, and count myself a king of infinite space, were it not that I have bad dreams.

Hamlet, **II. ii**

The girl in the canvas sack

There were screams coming down the corridor, followed by anguished cries, 'I'm living inside my head. I can't get out. I can't get out. Help me. Help me.'

The dark-haired young girl who was doing all the screaming and shouting was dragged around a corner and into view, straitjacketed in a makeshift green canvas stretcher which two grim-faced men were failing to hold quite taut enough to keep her above ground level as they hurried her past me on their way to the treatment area.

In the days before gap years, many young people spent the time between A levels and university earning a bit of extra cash doing any available kind of menial work. If you lived in the 'lunatic fringe' around Surrey, you ended up working in one of the many vast Gothic mental asylums. The one I worked in was called Belmont, and has long since disappeared in the dubious pursuit of care in the community. My job in that Hammer Horror of a place was cleaning the ECT (electro-convulsive therapy) wards, where the intractable cases were sent, and on those wards I learned more about human heads than a shelf full of books could have taught me.

I stated that the magic Cinderella key was deeply implicated in the way we have developed as a species and suggested that to understand it, and see how it affects what we call our psychological wellbeing, there would first have to be some dressing up of a simple-looking idea in some fancy scientific clothing. This is where I ask you to follow some quite complex connections between developments which are in themselves all about complex connections. It will be worth it (I promise), and you will advance your thinking skills at the same time, because, as we shall see, advanced thinking skills are what you get when you can make complex connections. It's a win-win exercise.

The fancy scientific clothing

One of the most curious things about our heads is this business of being aware that we exist inside them. If I were to ask you to say where you think the centre of your self is, nine times out of ten you would point to an area just behind or slightly above the bridge of your nose. It is this sense of being located in a physical place, and that this place is inside our heads rather than, say, in our feet (not as daft as it sounds – they move us around) that is both the making of us and the undoing of us. It's that anomaly that I mentioned earlier: the aspect of human development that makes us so special is also the one that places us at risk. This is what that poor girl found out when she was being dragged, imprisoned inside her head, to the ECT machine that may, hopefully, have helped free her for a while.

Of course, not everybody has experiences as extreme as hers, but the more common issues such as stress, respect, addiction and all the rest of my list are every bit as much the negative consequences of having an internalised self.

So 'we' are there, located inside our head casings, for good or bad (for good *and* bad). And it is in those head casings that we have both our sense of self and most of our conscious experiences. I don't intend to spend much time on the idea of what consciousness is (there are entire research organisations dedicated to that) but, briefly, and to use a modern analogy, consciousness is a bit like a series of text alerts that keeps us up to speed on what's happening (internally and externally), focusing attention on any need to prioritise and prompting initiation of any action required by that data.

A sense of self is altogether different. Put very simply, it is the perception that all of the above is happening to an embodied being that is unique and distinct from the external world which surrounds it. This is something that, perhaps surprisingly, we share with flatfish. In fact, it could be argued that flatfish are rather more self-aware than dogs (making a nonsense of the hierarchies of sophistication usually applied to different species). Because flatfish can camouflage themselves very effectively, this implies some primitive sense that they 'know' there is a self which, under threat, needs to become less obvious to the outside world. Dogs often try to get the same result by pushing their snouts into a corner while leaving their backsides in full view of the world, which rather suggests that they may be several steps behind the flatfish on the road to *self*-awareness. After about the age of 2, human beings will at least make an attempt to get the whole of the body into their chosen hiding place.

The flatfish may demonstrate some primitive form of self-awareness, but I'm not about to suggest that they have any over-whelming sense of their own subjectivity or that they painfully internalise all their experiences as that poor girl did. To understand where that comes from, and how a sense that we exist is important in the grand scheme of things, we must go back at least two and a half million years to the time when we Homo sapiens split from our predecessors and began to develop what we call consciousness and, more specifically, self-consciousness. This is the source of our greatness and of our great difficulties. To keep faith with my Cinderella metaphor, I shall call what follows the original blank for the magic Cinderella key.

Believing in what's not really there – it's all about connections

When you think about it brains, in general, amaze us with their ability to direct distant bits of body about – like air-traffic controllers directing planes around the planet. But human brains are something else. They are three times the size of chimpanzees' brains (our next of kin), and with their 100 billion neurons and 100 trillion neural connections are able to add an extra dollop of meaning to anything they come across. It is this extra dollop of meaning which is all important.

About two and a half million years ago our brains began to grow much bigger than those of our more ape-like predecessors. It was also at about this time that we began to do something that only a very few other species can do (and then only in the most rudimentary sense) and that is to make use of tools. We did not, at first, actually make or shape them as such – that capacity developed a bit later – but humans learned to see in naturally occurring things, such as sticks and rocks, the potential to be something other than just sticks and rocks. This development was extremely important; it implied several things about the way our human brains were evolving:

- We were starting to connect seemingly unconnected data that the environment or experience was offering up.
- Doing this involved stir-frying the data inside our brains because these connections didn't exist outside in what might be called the real world.
- What we then experienced had to feel as real to us as what we experienced in the outside world – otherwise we would not have been prepared to put it to the test. The internal notion that a flake of rock might be useful to prepare a nice steak with (that's to say, it could be a knife) had to have convincingly sturdy legs.

However, something strange and different must have happened to our brains in the first place to allow them to make those connections between pieces of flaked rock, dead animals and a desire to eat them more conveniently and tastily. Scientific research is now beginning to show us how that something strange and different might have looked.

Jumping genes and a genetic 'mini-me'

Relatively recent discoveries from research into brain development are jumping genes and what I'm rather frivolously calling a genetic 'mini-me'. Although both need further investigation, they are already offering up some convincing explanations as to how our brains evolved from being concrete and immediate to becoming imaginative, flexible and rarely satisfied with what was immediately in front of them. Or, to put it another way, evolved from being happy cave-dwellers to become *Grand Designs* devotees. It may not come as a surprise that jumping genes and mini-me's are both about connections.

Explaining the huge leap forward that humans made purely in terms of these two genetic factors is speculative, to say the least. There will almost certainly have been other things involved in the extraordinary development of our cognitive abilities, such as fire, diet, absolute brain size (Neanderthals had big brains, too, but do not appear to have developed symbolic and imaginative thinking), upright posture and social group size. Even so, these two relatively recent discoveries do seem to be some of the prime candidates for 'most significant causes of our brains having become super-connected and ready to roll'.

The back-story

Ever since God was largely written out of the equation by Charles Darwin in 1859, people have been coming up with explanations of how we evolved. Recently there has been a focus on explaining the sophistication of human thinking and behaviour in terms of two major scientific advances: the recognition that particular regions of the brain have specific and specialised functions, the most advanced of which are unique to our species; and the understanding that we all have an individual genetic blueprint, the human genome.

The focus on brain regions and specific functions for example, taught us that we have limbic systems which are flight-or-fight hairy primitives given to strutting their stuff on a Saturday night, and that it is our frontal lobes (all-important executive regions which orchestrate behaviour) which we can thank for damping down those wilder limbic tendencies. Such straightforward explanations are useful (though overused in leadership coaching) but, as with most things in life, the story turns out to be not quite that simple. When we get to the more exacting specialisms, things are altogether more complex. In fact, many scientists now tell us that brain regions, per se, do not have specific functions; their job is just to process energy into electrical patterns which travel along our nerves.

The fact that certain pathways and brain regions seem to have become specialised in dealing with certain of those inputs over time is the equivalent of riverbeds and lakes having become specialised in carrying around particular inputs of water. Just as they can be bypassed and replaced by new channels, so new neural pathways and brain areas can take over the functions of those lost to damage or disease. This is known as 'brain plasticity'. Although the concept remains controversial for some (see Chapter 6), it does serve to explain why recovery from brain damage is so idiosyncratic. It's long been known that babies can have complete halves of their brains removed and still develop perfectly normal functions with what is left, so brain plasticity is an extension (although less comprehensive) of that facility into later life. Brain plasticity suggests that location of function is not, after all, totally critical to the way we process experience.

As well as looking to brain regions to explain the way we

function, the other great white hope of science in recent times has been the human genome, the complete set of hereditary information contained in our DNA. Until very recently this was seen as having the potential to provide the conclusive answer to who we are and how we came to be who we are. But, once again, it now seems that was overly optimistic and simplistic.

There is a whole new field of study called epigenetics which shows that genes are not always the fixed things they were once believed to be. It seems they can be switched on and off. Although they remain unchanged in themselves (as it was always assumed), their likely impact on our development depends on whether certain environmental factors have caused their activity to be turned on or off. For example, if a boy has not had quite enough food at a critical time in his development, any sons he then has are less likely than they might otherwise have been to die of heart disease. The health outcome that should have been inherited by them has been subtly switched, in this case in their favour, by their father's genetic response to external conditions (see Day et al., 2016).

Further evidence that the genetic blueprint is not the only thing influencing how genes build us is that even though identical twins share all their DNA, they can still suffer from different diseases and develop quite separate personalities and skills.

So, it seems that we need to look again at what might have made us who we are.

Joined-up thinking – the connectome

Current thinking tells us that it is connectivity rather than the actual ingredients of our brains that makes us clever. A cake is not a cake until all the ingredients have joined forces. No matter how perfectly formed a particular part of the brain is, it is nothing in terms of overall cleverness if it does not link up with everything around it. Connectedness, in this case, is like society. Every individual element is important, but we need the individual elements to join up in as many relationships as they can, passing on information far and wide and linking closely to other elements with which they can develop deep symbiotic relationships. The more extensive the networks and the richer the relationships, the more sophisticated and flexible that society can potentially be. For 'society' read 'brain'.

The following is an explanation of how that species-unique connectedness probably happened (for a fuller explanation of gene jumping see Gage and Muotri, 2012). Jumping genes, aka retro-transposons, have been known about in the plant world for a while, it is only more recently that their place in human brain development has been understood. It appears that these particular sequences of DNA have the unusual ability to make copies of themselves, and these copies, being mobile, take themselves off to other parts of the brain. Usually there is no obvious consequence to this globetrotting behaviour, but on occasion they arrive somewhere that really suits them and they then act like cuckoos, muscling in on their host cells and changing the behaviour of the host. If they have landed on cells in areas necessary to brain development, memory or attention, these jumping genes can subtly alter gene activation patterns and lead to the brain developing in slightly different ways from how it might otherwise have done if the genome itself were the only factor involved.

This doesn't explain why these genes are so jumpy in the first place, nor why jumping, per se, should lead to greater connectivity. No one really knows, but it might work as follows: new environments, novel experiences and exercise appear to result in more gene jumping in the brain. This, in turn, results in subtle changes in brain behaviour, and a plausible outcome is an ongoing virtuous circle of novelty, adaptability and brain development.

It is important to say that quicker and more flexible responses to incoming environmental information are only part of the effect of gene jumping. There are also negative consequences including severe brain disorders. Clearly, jumping genes, like all changes to the status quo, are a mixed blessing. Gage and Muotri suggest that such a risky factor has not simply died out because nature (being utterly pragmatic about these things) may simply be taking a punt on the benefits of enhanced flexibility outweighing any negative consequences. So what we get is greater adaptability – plus greater vulnerability. One of their most significant arguments in favour of the influence of jumping genes on adaptability and connectivity is that the lineage of jumping elements goes back approximately 2.7 million years – to the beginning of the time when our ancestors first started to prepare their steaks using those flakes of rock.

A genetic mini-me?

Perhaps even more important and exciting are findings from the Scripps Research Institute in California. These suggest that a mutation, an accidental copy of a copy of a single gene, which took place approximately 2.4 million years ago, may have turned our brains into the amazing hyperlinking machines that they have become today.

The original function of this serially mutating gene, the SRGAP2 gene, was to prompt brain development (specifically in the neocortex where sophisticated higher order processing takes place) by making neurons generate connections to neighbouring cells (see Reardon, 2012). However, it seems that the second slightly smaller copy attached itself to its granny gene, and like any piggyback rider slowed down its activity.

At first this may seem like a negative or retrogressive change, but the effect has been largely to the advantage of humankind. This is because, rather counter-intuitively, slowing down the functioning of SRGAP2 has given neurons more time both to grow thicker and longer (and so to become more effective at making connections) and to migrate further from their starting point. This has enabled them to connect with more distant parts of the brain (remember the society analogy). Research by Simon Neubauer and Jean-Jacques Hublin (2012), from the Max Planck Institute for Evolutionary Anthropology in Germany, supports the idea that this will have conferred an advantage. They concluded that it was the comparatively *accelerated* brain growth experienced by Neanderthal man which meant that the environment had less chance of impacting on their levels of brain connectivity, notwithstanding the overall size of their brains.

The overall impact of this accidental copying was that around two and a half million years ago human brains became much more connected up than the brains of other species. This inevitably led to an infinitely greater capacity to link up and process information from a variety of sources, both internally and externally generated. Over time that capacity would lead us to cross-reference and weave together inputs and concepts that in other species would have remained defiantly separate. Put simply, the SRGAP2c (as the copy of the copy is known) was a sort of Heston Blumenthal of brain development, the source of the most unheard of combinations of apparently unconnected elements – the snail-porridge-maker of the brain.

Returning to the girl in the canvas sack

How does this all affect the way that poor girl was experiencing life? We're getting there, but first let's look again at tool use – that development of the ability to see more in something than first meets the eye. It now makes sense that this ability is likely to be an outcome of the brain's new facility for making many more internally generated connections between the data it is processing:

Oh … a sharp splintery thing!
　Oh … a piece of wood!
　Oh, oh … what if I put one next to the other? What if one moved backwards and forwards? Oh, look, it's made marks on the other!
　I wonder what I can do with that … ?

This is what we call *symbolic* thinking – one thing standing for another, despite there being no immediate association between them. In this case a broken flint becomes a knife, which is by no means a natural connection for other species' brains to make but one easily made by a brain that is networking wildly.

Language, probably the most symbolic of our skills, is very like tool use insofar as there is no intrinsic association between the items we're referring to and the sounds and shapes we're creating with our voices and on paper or screen. The associations are only symbolic ones. That lack of any immediate connection is made even clearer when what we're referring to are ideas, concepts and emotions which have no physical presence in the first place. It's now relatively easy for a healthy (and connected) brain to see that these abstractions are created from flurries of brain connectivity that link one set of non-things with another set of non-things, and that they will (and can) only exist inside our heads. However, it will be less easy for people with certain types of mental disorder to understand that what they're experiencing in all that rampant internal cross-referencing is not actually real.

Which brings us back to self-consciousness, the way we differentiate between what is happening to several centillions of neurons all around the world and what is merely affecting a specific set of 100 billion neurons lying closer to home. Within that lacy web of dreams and pictures, fancies and thrills that is our brain, there also exists a vital system which operates like a corporate 360 degree feedback review: it tells it like it is and puts a bit of a brake on our more eccentric impulses. This system incorporates those bossy frontal lobes, a fascinating area called the anterior cingulate cortex (ACC) (which, at the risk of contradicting any earlier comments, does attention, pain, inhibition, motivation, self-awareness and a lot else besides[1]), all the motor and sensory areas that tell our bodies what to do and how we feel, together with the hippocampus which covers our memory for what we have previously said, done and felt (autobiographical memory). When all of these work in concert we become aware not only of our own bodies and our own pasts but also of our own inner processes, even as they are happening. It is that system which, operating optimally, gives us insight and self-control – et voilà, self-consciousness.

However, when some parts of that superb human-specific process fail to function (and we'll come back to the reasons why that may happen later) then a person can suffer all kinds of disturbing and essentially depersonalising symptoms ranging from a sense of fragmentation to becoming detached from their own sensations or totally enmeshed in them.

I can only assume, because I never encountered the girl in the canvas sack again, that in her case the last of those things had happened. Some aspects of that superb process had broken down and her internalising neural loop was acting like a stuck record, drowning out connections that might have told her that she was still living in an external body and having a physical life in an external world, as well as experiencing all those obsessive internal reflections on that life.

In a nutshell

Hopefully, this chapter has explained how evolution has worked to turn us from relatively simple reactors to outside stimuli into sophisticated creatures capable of shape-shifting what we call 'concrete' reality into intricate internalised webs of possibilities by means of flurries of brain connectivity. Unlike other species, when we take information into our heads it does not remain unadulterated but becomes amplified and even distorted by all that connectivity, as

---

1   Activity in its 'twin' region, the posterior cingulate cortex (PCC), has recently been found to be predictive of recovery from coma states (see Silva et al., 2015). See also page 251 and Appendix B on autism for further references to the PCC and its link to autism. It would appear that the cingulate cortex, as a whole, is critical to consciousness and, probably, to a sense of self.

though it were passing through a series of echo chambers, each of which causes more of that shape-shifting to take place.

Living inside our heads can be wonderful and enriching. We have concepts, emotions, dreams, imagination, ideas, schemes, plans, fantasies, romance and all the things which drive us on to create more and more of the complexity we now appear to crave. However, living inside our heads can also, as the girl in the canvas sack so poignantly showed, be a real drag. As we have lost the option of getting out and living more like the animals, so we may end up as prisoners in a surreal nightmare instead.

I said my magic Cinderella key could unlock the cells in our imprisoning brains, and although talking about brains as if they somehow locked us in may have sounded strange at the time, I hope it now makes more sense. In the next chapter I explore the mysterious and transformative nature of the key itself.

Chapter 3

Who Loves Ya, Baby?

It was the first day of a new term in the reception class. A small boy arrived by himself, one of few who had no mum alongside to cling on to. From the start he was fidgety and sullen and it wouldn't have taken a psychologist to see that he was likely to be alienated and troublesome. The reception teacher started the day by going around her little charges one by one, gently coaxing each into saying their name out loud. She arrived in front of the boy and asked him what his name was, but at that he seemed more than sullen – he seemed confused. She smiled kindly at him and tried again, 'What do they call you at home?' He thought hard, 'Shut up, George', he said at last.

At home he just wasn't *significant* enough.

But why should anything, or anyone, signify that much in the first place?

It's all to do with connectivity

Living inside our heads, connecting everything up, making new sense of things – it's all gone viral and our brains now seem positively to crave complexity. All the connectivity I described in the previous chapter – the connectivity between our neurons which ultimately separated us from our closest primate cousins – has now become so integral to what we are and how we live our lives that we seem to be completely unaware of what has happened to us. We assume that the need to see meaning or significance in things (that a hammer is for a purpose and is more than just a lump of iron attached to a length of wood) is utterly obvious and natural, rather than being a gift from our jumping genes and our mini-me SRGAP2 mutated gene.

To achieve anything like normal brain behaviour, our brains now have to be capable of amazing things, recruiting far-flung regions into sophisticated circuits involving all of the following: basic body mechanisms, breathing, heart rate, digestion, flight-or-fight responses

– all part of the autonomic nervous system; voluntary movements of all kinds – covered by the motor cortex; sensory experiences – covered by the sensory cortex; emotional responses – located in areas such as the amygdala, which in turn is part of the limbic system; higher order thinking – largely located in the frontal and prefrontal regions; and language and speech – which tend to be a bit dotted around but are primarily located in Broca's and Wernicke's areas. Then there are association areas, which basically bring stuff together and cross-reference it, giving us such skills as learning, memory, decision making, even writing. And, importantly, on top of all that, the brain has to achieve awareness of self.

Self-awareness is complex and involves many brain areas and systems, but one area is key: the anterior cingulate cortex. This is involved in a whole host of activities over and above self-awareness (attention, pain perception, novel word combinations, self-control, problem solving and long-term memory, to name but a few).[1] In particular, it is specifically needed to discount information – something which is at the heart of both tool and language use. This means that when we look at that flake of rock, we see it as it is, hold it and its attributes in mind, and then override all of that and allow another set of possibilities and imagined benefits (such as its being useful for cutting) to take over. The ACC facilitates our ability to see the potential in things. And being involved in self-awareness, it may even help us understand what we are capable of achieving (i.e. understand our own potential). What dog could possibly envision that?

Self-referral is a further extraordinary outcome of all these sophisticated brain circuits connecting previously unconnected things (before jumping genes, mini-me mutations and so on) in such novel ways. This follows from the involvement of the sense of self (the anterior and posterior areas of the cingulate cortex, for example) in complex associative circuitry, so that *we* become involved, even enmeshed, in all this brain traffic. *We* are the drivers caught in the midst of the vast circulatory system, the Spaghetti Junction that is our neural circuitry. We don't just care about how it's all flowing, we become reliant on it. Our futures as sentient creatures are being sculpted by what is happening at any given moment, even as it's happening.

The bottom line is that we are seriously concerned about how we

---

1   Under-activity in this area is associated with criminality, addictions, autism, loss of motivation and other dysfunctions. See appendices.

experience the world, just as we are seriously concerned about how the world experiences us. We self-monitoring and self-interested beings are emotionally connected to our inner processes and to the whirling traffic all around. A vital part of this system is the feedback confirming to us that we are indeed here and that we are indeed experiencing all of this. All of it has to have what we call meaning. To put it as simply as possible, we mutant humans now have to see meaning in life and have to *be* meaningful within it.

Two and a half million years of refining brain connectivity have led us to the point where meaning, looking for meaning, having meaning and searching for validation (the assurance that one, personally, has meaning) have become the main driving forces in human-specific behaviour.

Meaning arises from those extra connections in our brains. But there is something a bit more involved in the specificity of the connections that refer back to 'us'. There is an emotionally charged neural highlighter that serves to emphasise how necessary any such meanings we've concocted through all that connectivity may be to our wellbeing. And this highlighting effect is what we call *significance*.

Who am I?

Significance makes us special. It places us centre stage in the drama of our lives. Of course we're in the spotlight (whoever had a fantasy in which they were just part of the crowd?). We're never going to be the first to die in a disaster movie or be rhubarbing extras at the guillotine; we're always going to be the ones who are up against it, the ones with the issues, the ones with the gifts. Otherwise, why bother? We need to matter – it's central to who we are. We need to matter to ourselves and we need to matter to the world. Mattering – being significant – gives us (the illusion of) control.

What does it all really mean?

Of course we're important, that goes without saying, but we need to see significance in the world too. We need to see purpose, order, intention, a guiding light or hand that *means* things should be a certain way. That's why when even the most anti-deist of scientists talk about man's evolution they will still say things like, 'The purpose of this ...' or 'It's designed to ...', as if there really were some significance in the ordering of things rather than mere happenstance.

We really, really want things to be joined up, to make sense, to have meaning and significance, and we really, really, really need to feel significant ourselves. Significance is that mysterious and transformative force which we so easily overlook and which unlocks the door to a more imaginative and expansive life.

So let's hear it for Significance, the magic Cinderella key that unlocked the door to the lives we live today – for better and for worse.

If you're thinking, 'Is that it?' then, unless you're being ironic, something's got lost somewhere because this is quite the most essential factor in human life.

Why is it so important?

We come on to 'Who loves ya, baby?' because love is something nature conjured up to fulfil that need for significance and to help our brains keep up the massive pace of learning that has got us where we are today. These are mutually dependent requirements of modern brains arising from our quirky evolutionary past.

When Kojak, star of the 1970s TV series of the same name, asked the question, 'Who loves ya?', he asked it rhetorically; it was his catchphrase. But for the human baby the question may be a matter of life or death, and they need the information – fast.

There have been many recent studies (and good books) exploring the vital role that love plays in just about every conceivable way in babies' development, but here I want to show that it also has a specific and utterly vital role in the make-up and functioning of my own magic Cinderella key.

When we see a harassed mother cat giving her mischievous kittens a good ticking off or a mild-eyed cow licking its steaming, struggling little calf into life, it's only too easy to indulge in a spot of gentle anthropomorphism and assume they share our own parental feelings of frustration or concern: will this child make it? Will they grow up happy and fulfilled? Will they end up at university or in prison? (Who hasn't had that thought?) But, of course, deep down we know it's not really like that with kittens and calves, any more than that they will have savings accounts set up for them or wills made out in their favour.

That's because when a cat or a cow keeps its baby alive to the point of self-sufficiency, it's done a good enough job. It's been a good parent, period. If only we could say the same! For us there is all the business of planning for the future too, complete with savings accounts, extra tuition and remortgaging the house. If we simply kitted out our kids with the skills they needed to survive, the *Daily Mail*, the NSPCC and social services would all accuse us of bringing up feral children.

The extras we have to provide for our young amount to more than survival skills. Rather they are surthrival skills – meaning that, with them, our children will have the ability to thrive as well as survive. And, yes, I hear what you say, but most young animals don't need to do more than learn how to be a good enough mouser or milker in order to thrive as well as survive. For other animals, the two matters are much more closely linked than they are for humans. Remember that before we can be said to thrive we have to learn how to satisfy those other, deeper and more complex needs as well. This is a well-established idea – see, for example, Maslow's hierarchy of needs (Maslow, 1943).

Let me say it again. Our brains are pre-programmed to be forever ranging and searching about to link many more things together than other species' brains appear to be capable of doing. This mental adventurousness is now such a firmly established part of being human that we will feel a sense of incompleteness if we live in only purely physical ways. As the great man himself says,

---

What is a man,
If his chief good and market of his time
Be but to sleep and feed? A beast, no more.

Hamlet, IV. iv

Young humans need to be much more than sleeping, feeding animals. They have to learn more than simple physical behaviours. They must be constantly searching for significance, and to do that they must also learn to *think* like humans. As thinking is not as concrete a behaviour as, say, chasing or catching, it can't just be picked up – in the way that a cat learns to hunt through copying its mother – simply by imitating someone else's visible/discernable actions.

Eye contact

In order to think, at least in the early days, you first have to watch another person's mind at work. You have to see the cogs whirring and whizzing, and you have to learn how that special human knowledge of how one unlikely thing may connect with another unlikely thing works in practice. This means learning strange human codes: an upturned mouth (a smile) makes for nice things and good feelings; those long things waving in front of your eyes (your arms and hands) eventually make for grabbing, holding and, ultimately, for pushing food conveniently into your face. Finally, you have to learn that there is more to human life than merely what meets the eye. You have to learn there is what lies behind the eyes. You have to learn to make sense of other brains.

It seems that eye-to-eye interaction is part of the vital process of becoming an advanced thinker. This is because eye contact makes human babies want to engage with their caregiver's brain, and this in turn leads to quicker and more effective learning. It has been known for a long time that eye-to-eye contact stimulates the development of the parts of the brain that are involved in higher order thinking. More recently, thanks to research by Katalin Gothard at the University of Arizona (Gothard, 2014), there is also the suggestion that the part of our brain that processes emotion and social interaction may actually contain specific eye cells which encourage a sense of special connectedness between people as they gaze into each other's eyes (as lovers have believed since time began but, heigh-ho, these days we need scientific proof):

> Our eye-beames twisted, and did thred
> Our eyes upon one double string;
>
> **John Donne, _The Extasie_**

Gothard's work was carried out using rhesus monkeys. Primates (unlike other animals) are generally upright and so able to look into the faces of their babies while feeding. This seems likely to have led to all of us having closer bonds with our young than other animals.

Another important factor in the learning process, though not specific to humans, is the existence in parts of the brain of 'mirror neurons'. These neurons specialise in imitation. When we look at something happening our mirror neurons kick in and we have the impression of experiencing that action ourselves. If there is an emotional resonance in what we are watching, it's going to make us feel good. Eye contact seems to enhance this process in babies as they are more engaged with the person carrying out the action.

So we now have two very powerful explanations for why eye-related stimulation is so important for babies' development and why the expression 'seeing eye-to-eye with someone' takes on a rather special meaning. If we want our young to behave as we do, we should give them plenty of eye contact. It is for this reason that I find it very worrying to see parents pushing forward-facing buggies while texting or talking on their mobiles. How will their babies learn anything helpful from them in that way?

Recipe for a brain

Lots of things go into the making of a baby's brain. There's all the genetic information I described in the previous chapter, together with the influences which have either turned genes on or off (epigenetic factors). In addition, there's the chemical soup that floods the baby's environment when it's in the womb, the make-up of which is affected by mum's behaviour and lifestyle – factors like diet, alcohol, cigarettes, drug use, exercise, stress, anxiety and so on. Plus the world the baby is born into and the way it is taught by experience to interact with that world – environmental factors.

John Bowlby made a special study of one particular environmental factor – maternal care and its impact on babies' development. So keen was he to know everything there was to know about his subject that he trained as a psychologist, psychiatrist *and* psychoanalyst. He then 'got lucky', inasmuch as he lived through the Second World War, which gave him almost unlimited access to the thousands of children who had been abandoned or neglected through forces beyond anyone's control.

Bowlby's findings (which were controversial with feminists in the 1970s but now seem to have become acceptable again) boil down to the following points:

- Babies need to feel that they have a secure base – a sense that their caregiver (usually the mum, hence the objections) will always be there for them.
- This means not only that the caregiver is physically available but also that they are sensitive and responsive to the baby's needs, all of which will be greatly facilitated by plenty of eye contact.

- Babies with a secure base become children confident enough to be adventurous and enquiring.

But:

- When the caregiver is unreliable (physically or emotionally) or unavailable (maybe through absence or self-absorption) then the baby is likely to end up damaged in some way.
- Babies with remote, anxious or invasive caregivers, and thus with only a shaky foundation for life, can become withdrawn, timid, hostile or indifferent.

Therefore, the quality of those earliest experiences is one of the most influential environmental factors of all. Get it right and the child will be primed to encounter life with enthusiasm and curiosity. Get it wrong and the child will be primed to encounter it with, at best, uncertainty.

So much in love with us are we
that you could kiss you, and I could kiss me.
'We Love Us', The Smothers Brothers

Finally, a baby with a secure base learns about love through all of its senses: by being touched, by being spoken to and sung to, by being close to the milky fragrance of its mum and by seeing the look of love in her eyes. At first the baby does not distinguish between the different senses. It's thought that synaesthesia (the confusion of colour, number, sounds, etc.) may be the result of the normally developing distinction between them never taking place. Then, rather than experiencing specific sensations, the baby lives in a sort of all-enveloping sense cloud. For a well-loved baby, that sense cloud is a very special place to be; the baby shares it with the most special person ever, its mum.

The baby, even as it starts to detach and distinguish one sense from another, and to learn to reach out and touch, hear and see for itself, still does these things as an extension of mum, safe that there is no real break. It's not alone; everything is still mediated through those 'double string' eyes. They are still really one and that one is the most significant thing in the world – the only knowable thing, the only thing worth knowing. ('There's just me, you, and this darned world. And what's that there for, eh?') Interest in the world, and the need to find significance there, comes a bit later once the baby is well grounded.

So the answer to the question, 'Who loves ya, baby?', really should be apparent to the baby from the moment it comes into the world. The answer is mum herself. Or, with a nod to feminism and in the interests of modern conflicted mums, mum and/or a caregiver who can give the baby that same quality of care and concentrated attention. It genuinely does take that much commitment to make a truly successful human being – as in good at being human rather than good at being successful.

A quick résumé

- Evolution generated in us almost hyperactive neural connections which nowadays are primed to spread and chatter as widely across the brain as possible.
- Some of those connections incorporate areas specialising in self-awareness and sense of self.
- This development has set up an ongoing requirement that the self is, as it were, in the loop.
- Whenever any one of the evolutionary neural loops is compromised (which includes having an adequate sense of self) we are left incomplete, not fully human.
- Eye contact early in life, plus a sense of being well loved, sets up a positive dialogue between a baby's brain and the world outside it. The baby feels special and significant, and free to be, do and explore as much as possible.
- The well-loved baby has both its need to be of significance to others and its curiosity about the world beyond itself, together with that world's potential to have more meaning than first meets the eye, stimulated by the ways in which its mum forms the vital element in a neural feedback loop. She reads meaning into the baby's looks and behaviour, connects that all up with her experience, knowledge and, above all, love, then feeds the whole enriched mix back to the baby ('Oh, little one, that's only wind. It'll feel better soon. Mummy rub your tummy. There now, that feels better, doesn't it?').

That last point may not sound much, but there's a lot in there that will be very important for the baby's whole future: a set of expectations about how important its feelings and experiences are, a fundamental sympathy for its physical sensations mixed with practical help, and a message of hope and trust in the probability of positive outcomes in negative times. This apparently simple communication is going to stimulate a complex neural network. It's the beginning of the child's journey towards a world in which surviving and thriving become heavily dependent on such super-sophisticated mechanisms as self-awareness, empathy and belief in an enhanced future.

And, as ever, the harmonious interplay of complex neural loops is at the heart of our babies' developing sense, both of their own significance and of the significance that everything outside and beyond them will hold for them as they journey through life.

SIGNIFICANCE
meaning *importance* RELEVANCE
standing PURPOSE **noteworthiness** magnitude
intensity FAME **status** celebrity
SUBSTANCE **value** implication
meaningfulness **mattering** applicability
definition delineation *outstandingness*
connection relatedness connotation
CONSEQUENCE making sense **worth**
being worthwhile **attention**
BEING CARED FOR salience
feeling validated

Hyper-connectivity – cure-all or curse?

However, this brain busyness that drives us relentlessly on to greater breadths and heights comes with some serious downsides. The more complex and sophisticated a thing is, the more there is to go wrong with it. In the case of brain development, think Chantilly lace – fine, intricate, beautiful and a whole lot easier to rip and damage than denim or cord. There are consequences to the subtlety of our wiring, as there are consequences to the intricacies of the lace:

- If our brains are inadequately connected up then we may fail to develop attributes that are helpful for personal or social functioning.
- If our brains make too many connections between things then too much meaning and significance can be read into aspects of

life. For example, this is a major symptom of some forms of schizophrenia.

- If established neural routes get damaged by injury or disease, then individuals may be left unable to connect up experience in a normal way. For example, people with Capgras delusion may believe that relatives are imposters. This is because their familiar faces no longer generate the expected emotions, and so the obvious conclusion is that they are not the real deal.

We will look at some of the variety of things that can go wrong in the next chapter.

Chapter 4

Kaleidoscope People

When significance is compromised

A patchwork quilt of a woman walked out of the country pub, generating amused incredulity in the breast of the quietly well-coordinated woman (let's call her Susan) who was enjoying a white wine spritzer outside on the terrace.

'What on earth was she thinking when she put on that curious collection?' she asked the man she was sitting with. Let's call him Graham.

'Oh, that's easy,' he said, with the assurance of absolute knowledge. 'She thought, "I like this patterned orange blouse, I'll wear that. I like this long blue skirt, I'll wear that. I like this pink cardie, I'll wear that. I like these black shoes, brown bag and so on, I'll wear those." What she never thought was, "What does everything look like put together?" And, even if she had thought it, she could never have conjured up that picture of the final effect anyway.'

This, as Susan told me when we discussed their case, was an amazingly accurate and perceptive account of a kaleidoscope mind, especially coming from the man who, a short while later, and to her amazement, would be capable of a most extraordinary display of even more disjointed thinking (maybe it would be more accurate to say, even more disjointed processing).

There are two versions of their story, hers and his:

Susan's version:

Graham hadn't had full-time work for a while but was picking up odd jobs as a general handyman. Susan, a short while into a relationship with him, asked him to do some bits of work for her. She wanted him to pick up an extra length of hall carpet while he was getting some of the building materials he needed. He said that would be fine. She gave him a small sample of the carpet as a match and agreed to reimburse him on his return. When Graham had been gone for quite some time she wondered if there was a problem. At last she got a phone call from him. He said he was sorry but he couldn't find the sample she'd given him and would she speak to the salesman at the shop to confirm he'd chosen the right carpet. She said she would, but even as she was agreeing to do that, Graham changed tack and said, no, it was okay after all, he thought he could deal with it. And then he absolutely refused to let her talk to the salesman, even though the man was obviously standing right next to him. Graham didn't return to her house that day. When he did come back on the following day he neither brought any carpet with him nor made any reference to carpet at all. It was as though the matter had never arisen. Realising by then that the subject was going to be a resolutely no-go zone, a bemused Susan was left contemplating her uncarpeted hall and thinking her own rather less-than-happy thoughts about the relationship.

Perhaps surprisingly, given his apparent amnesia, some while after the event Graham was perfectly capable of giving me a breakdown (an appropriate word in the circumstances) of what had actually happened during those missing hours.

Graham's version:

Before going to the trading estate where the DIY and carpet stores were he had done a couple of other things and had somehow managed to lose the carpet swatch in the process - keeping track of things was not exactly a speciality of his. So by the time he went into the carpet store he only had a hazy idea of the carpet colour. He found one he thought was right, called the salesman to get the roll down, had second thoughts and decided to call Susan for confirmation. He did not want to get into any trouble for buying the wrong carpet. He felt awkward that the roll was already being opened up, so phoned her, having already given the go-ahead to the salesman. He then shut down the phone call mid-conversation to avoid having to deal with his overwhelming confusion.

By this time Graham was thoroughly wound up. Having paid and put the carpet into his vehicle, he wanted only to get away from the focus of his awkwardness. His exit from the trading estate was blocked by a vehicle waiting to turn right so he decided to undertake and sweep right in front of the slow driver. In the process he hit an oncoming van. By the time he had dealt with a furious van driver, offering cash in settlement of any damage claim (inevitably too much cash) the day was getting late. The altogether simplest way out of this unsettling and incriminating carpet situation was provided by a skip he drove past on his way home. Even though his own flat was shabby, with stained and threadbare carpets, he put the brand new carpet, which he had just paid for, straight into the skip and then happily drove off, unencumbered by the need to do anything more about any of what had just happened – except to treat it as if it had never happened.

As you can tell by the fact that he could fill me in on all of this later, Graham had not actually forgotten any of the details. They were quite simply unconnected to any of the contexts that would have applied with a normal brain, and so, to all intents and purposes, great chunks of it were unavailable for processing or recall at times that would have been appropriate.

Graham has Asperger's syndrome (see Appendix B). Although gifted with an extraordinary IQ, he has great difficulty in connecting things up, and therefore does not function as effectively as might be expected with this level of intelligence. This means that significance gets scrambled. For Graham, the overriding priority is always to avoid any sensory or emotional confusion that he will feel now, rather than to avoid the logistical confusion which will have its impact later. Unfortunately, this tends to lead to more confusion overall, an irony that is not lost on him at the purely intellectual level. Nevertheless, he remains unable to connect that awareness to his subsequent real-time behaviour. In theory, he realised that Susan might not have been happy to be left carpet-less, but he had subsequently noticed nothing amiss in her behaviour. The relationship is now over.

Asperger's syndrome, and autism in general, have a lot to teach us about how brains work and about how social relationships work. Graham's tale demonstrates how under-connectivity leads to problems for modern humans who depend on creating and understanding strings of associations between things. Connectivity between all the relevant areas and functions of the brain, is, as I stressed in the previous chapter, the foundation of significance. Any lack of joined-up thinking will lead to difficulty in understanding significance within the bigger picture. We need connections to make sense of the wider world. Connections are good. But sadly, as with chocolate, you can have too much of a good thing. Trying to see meaning in every spilt blob of paint and insisting they are relevant parts of the bigger picture can be hugely problematic.

In our socially normalised world, over-connectivity can be just as cognitively troublesome as under-connectivity. At the end of the last chapter I said that schizophrenia, an often devastating condition of fractured reality, was frequently characterised by over-connectivity. Schizophrenics with this profile find that associations overspill and pile up like randomly donated goods at a jumble sale until they can no longer distinguish those things which do actually have legitimate and logical associations from the things that don't.

For example, one young woman I treated, at first sight quite rational, genuinely believed that people she passed in the street had taken the trouble to wear clothes specifically selected to send specially coded private messages to her. One happy delusion was that people wore yellow, her favourite colour, whenever they wanted to let her know they were glad she was feeling better. Another young man I worked with, who saw multiple possibilities in everyday language, believed that the letter 'I' was capable of seeing into people's souls, and so he spent some time chalking warning messages on pavements, letting others know that the 'I's in all the newspapers were watching them, and that God knew everything they were up to.

It's easy to see how horribly confusing, frightening and illogical life in a social world can seem for untreated schizophrenics when they experience such indiscriminate over-association of external and internal data. Paranoia and psychosis are frequent outcomes for them. However, there's another aspect to this ability to see more in things than most other people do – and that is creativity.

His rather more controlled and contained use of the same kind of linguistic bohemianism that my young client indulged in led to the writer, James Joyce, being hailed as an artistic genius! Joyce's creative use of neologisms (invented words) and fondness for word salads (long strings of apparently unconnected words – the ultimate in over-association) were seen as part of a ground-breaking literary style rather than symptomatic of some kind of mental disorder. But can it just have been coincidence that Joyce's daughter, Lucia, spent years in asylums as a diagnosed schizophrenic? It sometimes seems that society has decided to draw a fine line between what it chooses to treat as lunacy and what it chooses to treat as creative artistry.

So both under- and over-connectivity lead to different, and usually compromised, processing. But for vulnerable modern humans the problems don't stop there. There are also difficulties with what might be called broken connections, when the previously established routes running between motor, sensory, emotional and higher order brain regions become damaged by injury or disease. This leads to a rather different kind of fragmentation.

With Capgras delusion there is a breakdown in the connections between perception and appropriate emotional feeling or emotional recognition. This results in people rejecting members of their family as imposters, simply because they no longer feel 'right'. But Capgras is only one of a number of strange manifestations of the fragmentation of connectivity. There are also disorders of personal identity and self-image that result in people believing themselves to be dead (Cotard delusion) or in them wanting to rid themselves of alien body parts such as their arms or legs (apotemnophilia). Then there's a condition, almost the antithesis of Capgras, which leads to patients wanting to claim complete strangers as their long lost friends (Fregoli delusion).

These are just a few of the bizarre problems that can arise when aspects of brain connectivity break down, when recognition no longer cross-references with emotional congruity or a sense of one's own embodiment no longer 'talks' to the sense of self, telling it that everything belongs together in one great big happy body/brain/feeling family.

This is the downside of mutant man's connectivity and significance. Anything so very complex and predicated on the one main driving principle of searching out associations between things that have no immediate, literal or concrete association is bound to be very vulnerable to the knocks and hazards of genetics, environment, disease and accident. After all, evolution is really asking us all to spend our lives in a kind of delusional state. Keeping this up requires not only a culturally shared hallucination but also strength of will, resilience and good powers of surthrival.

The best way I can think of to describe the outcome for those people whose mental wellbeing has been affected in any of the above ways, so they can no longer share the same hallucination or recognition of significance as the rest of us, is that their identities have suffered the kind of fragmentation that we see in kaleidoscopes. Their minds will have static moments of apparent lucidity and logic, even of glinting colour and complexity, but when they are shaken up that all falls away and their brains are incapable of holding on to a settled core of meaning, congruence or competence. Instead they enter a state of confusion, semi-chaos and shattered patterns. As things settle down another order becomes established and a short-lived display of multifaceted meaning shows itself off to any passing observer. But this lasts only briefly.

We tend to categorise these people as mentally ill or as cognitively dysfunctional. If they were to be isolated from society, many of them would be able to survive perfectly well at the purely biological level. Therefore we could not say they are altogether incompetent. Their problems often come from their failure to see the same significance in things that other people do. This is one of the main reasons that they can be so disturbing to be around. Other people feel left out of their mindset. Their failures are of connectedness, socially as well as neurologically. This means they are also failures of surthrival which, as we saw in the last chapter, requires us to think like other people do.

How do we come up with a culturally shared view of significance?

It used to be easy to come up with a shared view of significance. In the past, when people tended to stay put, non-negotiable seasons dictated when work had to be done and utterly intransigent authority (overlord, Church, state) dictated the things you were allowed to do. It was then a straightforward task to work out your priorities and where you fitted into the grand scheme of things. It was all pretty much immutable. In the Middle Ages and Renaissance there was even a comprehensive system for these matters called the 'great chain of being'. In that early form of list mania, everything was categorised and placed in its rightful order by medieval geeks, starting with God at the top (the king if you were only considering the state) and working down to the lowliest of the low creatures. In domestic households, the man took God's place, with his wife, children and servants following on behind. There were even hierarchies of importance constructed for angels, animals, plants and minerals. Nothing, simply nothing, was allowed to remain in ignorance of its place in the world or of its relative significance or insignificance. Which was kind of comforting.

This must have made it a whole lot easier to avoid the huge modern conundrums of, 'What does it all mean?' and 'Who am I?', especially as you could always blame a Mysterious God for any inexplicable phenomena. But while supporting people at one level, these solid, impenetrable and unchallengeable ethical and social systems left little room for individualism or social mobility, in comparison with today. By and large, once a peasant with a peasant's mindset, always a peasant with a peasant's mindset.

In our modern age, we now (seemingly) have the freedom to make many more of our own individualised decisions about matters such as what to believe, what to worship (gods, mammon, the Jedi?) and how to interact with others. Although theoretically this should help us to believe in our own significance as free agents, the overload of personal decision making can seem like a burden in its own right. This was one that medieval peasants did not have to bear. After they had sorted out the basics of food, shelter and warmth, the need to see significance in the world beyond them could be catered for in quite straightforward and utterly dependable ways. They found significance in God and in the ordered world around them, and having been indoctrinated in the understanding that most people were of little importance they accepted their personal irrelevance. However, that changed at the point of death when they were finally accounted for as individuals within the greater scheme of things. Then they would either be sent to sing with the angels if they had been good or, if bad, to be pricked and roasted by devils for eternity.

Life within today's social groups, at least in most Westernised cultures, is seen as a more personalised and subjective matter than it was in those times, as we like to believe we are free to make more individual choices about what our values and objectives should be. These were alien and dangerous ambitions in the past, and probably a misleading perception today. I will be returning to this topic later, but for now it is enough to say that this concept may undermine the realisation that we need a shared idea of significance to survive.

The search for significance within ourselves has become increasingly subjective. Nowadays we use far more self-focused (as opposed to self-aware) language, with terminology such as 'self-actualisation', 'maximising our potential' and 'because we're worth it' all part of the process. This has turned our *need* for inner validation into some kind of necessity or *right*, which, in a world of competing rights, makes it less rather than more probable that the majority of people will or could ever feel sufficiently valued and validated.

This supercharged self-referencing may have muddied the waters a bit and led us to feel that the search for meaning/significance is pretty much a full-time job – and, like the search for the Holy Grail, almost impossible to define, understand or realise. But, at bottom, despite our desperation to elevate our own role in the matter (burdening ourselves in the process), we still think things are significant if and when society at large says they are significant, and we still think we are of significance if our primary caregiver said (by word, look or deed) that we were significant. The rest is just contemporary self-importance.

The brain chemistry behind connectivity and significance

In the previous chapter we looked at the role of the primary caregiver in the creation of our sense of inner significance, and earlier in this chapter we touched on models of external significance in medieval and Renaissance societies. Now it's time to look at the subtly different role played by today's society in the formation of significance. But before doing so, we need to know more about the part played by brain chemistry in the whole affair.

Over and above the genes, neurons and brain regions and how they all work in concert to create the modern human brain, it is brain chemistry that ties the whole thing together. We need to factor that in, especially as brain chemistry has such a large part to play in pro-social and anti-social behaviour, as well as our ability to function as individuals.

Whether our brains connect up in ways that are appropriate, or whether they fragment in kaleidoscopic ways like Graham's, none of this happens without the movement of chemicals in the brain. These chemical neurotransmitters specialise in transporting messages between neurons – in effect, creating the flow that powers the connectivity of neural loops.

Different neurotransmitters are produced in specific cell bodies and have specialised roles. They take what might be called priority routes through specific regions and this allows them to influence key activities. For example, serotonin takes pathways which affect pain, sleep and mood; noradrenaline, pathways which affect physical and mental arousal and mood; and acetylcholine, pathways which affect attention, memory and learning. But having said that, neurotransmitters are usually multi-functional. These are all sophisticated and complex processes so there is much overlapping of both chemicals and brain-related functions.

What follows is a rather simplified overview of some hugely complex science, but it will, I hope, be enough to draw together (or connect up) some essential elements in my story.

Dopamine

Dopamine is one of two neurotransmitters that we are especially interested in here (the other is oxytocin). It is involved in a variety of functions, including speech, mood, memory and movement, but of particular significance is the role it plays in directing attention. This is vital for the selection of salience, relevance and importance in the environment within which we are operating – either within our own heads or in the world outside. It has some other pertinent characteristics:

- Dopamine is one of the main regulatory neurotransmitters for the anterior cingulate cortex, a part of the brain that specialises in attention (among other things). Between them they 'decide' what is significant enough for us to focus our attention and efforts on – in other words, dopamine motivates us and leads to goal-directed behaviour. It is the chemical for significance, the liquor of life. Paying attention and finding significance in things are not, per se, moral or healthy, and may lead to many different types of behaviour.
- Schizophrenia, a condition marked out by an over-abundance of significance, is also marked out by an over-abundance of dopamine at the biochemical level. Treatment for schizophrenia usually involves drugs that reduce levels of dopamine in the brain. This leads to a reduction in significance-related psychotic symptoms such as hallucinations and paranoia.
- At the other extreme, Parkinson's disease leads to the death of nerve cells in a part of the brain that usually produces dopamine (the substantia nigra), resulting in lower dopamine levels and thus to the inertia, depression and lack of motivation, both physical and mental, that goes hand in hand with loss of significance. Treatment for Parkinson's is usually either a synthetic version of dopamine, or a dopamine agonist, a dopamine substitute. As a potential outcome of over-treated schizophrenia is Parkinson-like symptoms, it is easy to see how the two conditions overlap.
- Dopamine levels need to be optimal for healthy functioning, so

dramatic changes in level are likely to lead to the breakdown or fragmentation of normality. There is no set level of dopamine that works for everyone. Much depends on the individual's overall arousal system, which is partly determined by genetic factors and partly by environmental factors. Although the baseline is essentially set at birth (maternal behaviour affects this), production of dopamine may later be enhanced by things like diet and exercise.

- Dopamine is involved in the production of language and speech, which may explain the variations of language and speech found in both schizophrenia and Parkinson's.
- Low levels of dopamine in salient areas of the brain are thought to be implicated in autism, which would explain the lack of cognitive and social connectivity and also the differences in language production.
- Seemingly counter-intuitively, low dopamine levels, rather than high ones, are involved in attention deficit hyperactivity disorder (ADHD). Dopamine is necessary for attention and people with ADHD cannot concentrate on any one thing for long.
- Bipolar disorder (formerly known as manic depression) appears to involve fluctuating levels of dopamine, leading to excessive enthusiasms and talkativeness (the highs) and depression, inertia and taciturnity (the lows).
- Production of this get-up-and-go and significance-related neurotransmitter can become enough of a reward that seeking it becomes an end in itself (see Appendix A on addiction).
- A curious side effect of boosting dopamine in Parkinson's patients has been that a significant number of them have developed obsessive gambling habits.
- Dopamine leads to novelty, reward and arousal-seeking behaviours rather than automatically to pro-social ones. It is a motivational chemical, not a moral one.

Dopamine's relationship to pro-social and anti-social behaviour is a complicated one, and the scientific jury is very much out as to the nature of its impact on either. But the part played by this fascinating neurotransmitter in social functioning is well worth investigating further. It could be that too much dopamine leads to violence, aggression and selfish reward-seeking behaviour, or that too little results in an inability to concentrate or to focus on the bigger picture (which would encourage the delaying of gratification) so that low-level disruptive behaviour seems to be attractive. Especially interesting is the extent to which levels can genuinely be affected by lifestyle choices.

Oxytocin

The second chemical of importance in determining our behaviour is oxytocin. If anything, this has an even more complicated personality than dopamine – it is a cuddle hormone with a darkly twisted side.

Oxytocin has often been hailed as the cure-all for many states involving lack of emotional engagement and empathy with others. This stems from some research done in 1992 which showed that prairie voles (of all unlikely creatures) with high levels of oxytocin receptors in their brains pair-bonded in almost human, monogamous, ways (see Wang et al., 1998). Although human behaviour is almost undoubtedly more complex and sophisticated than that of prairie voles, and although human monogamous lifestyles last rather longer than those of prairie voles, nevertheless there does appear to be some substance in the supposition that oxytocin may play a large part in bringing us into closer harmony with other people.

Oxytocin is produced when mothers go into labour and when they begin to breastfeed. It stimulates both these activities and so is very much associated with the developing bonds between mother and child. It promotes emotional closeness and is released when eye contact is made with another person. This helps to explain the usefulness of eye contact to the learning process, but it also perhaps goes some way to suggest why autism (in which the capacity for emotional closeness is impaired) is also marked by lack of appropriate eye contact.[1]

So far, so good. It looks as if oxytocin is a thoroughly decent neurotransmitter. There are also other indicators of its beneficial role:

● Many partners of Asperger's people report that in the early

---

1   I have known many Asperger's people make apparently perfectly normal eye contact. However, when they are asked to describe what they are seeing it emerges that they are looking for clues to people's probable moods and thoughts. For example, the 'wrinkles at the corners of the eyes' indicate that it's highly probable the person is expressing happiness. In other words, they are creating a database of usable information.

days of a relationship (presumably when attraction led to significantly higher than normal emotional engagement, and thus heightened oxytocin) the overall Asperger's behaviour was less noticeable – even misleadingly non-evident.

● When oxytocin is secreted into a brain that already has plenty of dopamine in the appropriate places there is a double benefit. Combine the desire for the closeness of pair-bonding with the focused pursuit of significance and what you get is an overwhelming desire to pair-bond with one significant other (i.e. romantic love).

This is all very positive and apparently pro-social stuff. As a consequence of some of these findings, oxytocin is now being promoted as a treatment for some of the social/emotional deficits of autism. However, it is hard to find convincing information on its efficacy because oxytocin doesn't easily cross the blood–brain barrier. Trials to date have mostly involved snorting the stuff nasally – not the most effective of scientific methods.

So what can there possibly be about oxytocin not to like? Well, bonding and empathy are not necessarily universally applied. According to research carried out at the University of Freiburg, Germany, it is the context in which oxytocin is generated that is all important (see Yong, 2012). As it makes you want to connect with your group, in any culture that doesn't encourage intimacy, oxytocin is only going to encourage pro-social behaviour that does not prioritise intimacy. Likewise, because it encourages us to look for salience (empathy is a form of salience), when we fail to find it in another person's appearance, attitudes, tastes and so on, it makes us more likely to feel antagonism towards them. In other words, oxytocin can lead us just as readily towards racism and xenophobia as it can towards caring, sharing and bonding.

This is definitely a topic requiring further examination in the context of several behaviours I will be looking at in Chapter 9. Now it's time to consider what society does both to make and break our connection with significance.

The fragmented mind

Graham's story illustrates both how a fragmented mind operates and the ways in which it fails to make sense of, and make sense to, societal norms. Kaleidoscope people (of all kinds, many of them apparently normal) have a limited overview of the bigger picture. Connections are made in different ways. Sometimes their sense of what is significant may be highly focused, fixing on detail or parts of a larger whole (autism), or it may be delinquent, fixing briefly on fleeting images that are barely processed before being discarded (ADHD). Regardless of the variety of ways in which the lack of coherence may betray itself, its causes come back to the same thing. They all relate to that person's inability to see significance in what the great majority of humankind sees significance in. Whether the underlying reason for this is down to genetics, disease or environment, and whether the neuro-biochemical markers of it involve non-functional brain regions, impaired connectivity or suboptimal neurotransmitter behaviour, the impact of that lack of a shared sense of significance will be similar: a compromised relationship to society, a lessened cultural empathy and a threat to surthrival.

However, a hugely important question for the twentieth and twenty-first centuries has been, to what extent does society itself have to take the blame for such social problems in individuals? Setting aside the question of whether society really exists or whether it is simply a collection of individuals that is no bigger than the sum of its parts, I want to look at what it is that modern society does that is so very different from what medieval society did. And, briefly (because it is impossible to do more than speculate from such a distance), to wonder if kaleidoscope minds are more likely to be an outcome of today's society.

It is hard to get any real evidence for rates of mental illness and cognitive dysfunction in the Middle Ages. There must have been many instances of birth defects and early accidental damage, but then there must have been proportionately high levels of premature death, and, no doubt, many mentally ill and damaged people were simply lumped together and categorised as 'the poor' or as vagrants. But madness itself was not totally undiagnosed as a condition. The Priory of St Mary of Bethlehem, founded in 1247 and later known as Bedlam, was specialising in housing (if not actually treating) mentally ill patients by the fourteenth century. However, it is said that in the early 1400s it held just six insane men. Undoubtedly, mental illness and learning disorders could be more easily and naturally assimilated into the noisy, smelly, multifaceted street scene of those days than they can be today, and so many troubled but quiet or unaggressive individuals would have gone unnoticed.

Those troubled souls could probably also be more easily incorporated into the worldview of the time. When God 'spoke' through his agents (priests) in strange tongues (Latin) it could only have been a short step in imagination to accept that intrusive voices telling people to behave in unusual ways were just another manifestation of God's strange and wondrous ways. Joan of Arc's visions and voices are now routinely interpreted as being aspects and evidence of temporal lobe epilepsy, but back then (1412–1431) she was accepted as a visionary by some of the highest people in the land – and nations went into battle purely on her say-so. Just imagine nations going to war on the whim of a deranged mind today!

Equally, any strange anti-social behaviour a person indulged in could simply have been dismissed as bad or morally degenerate and that person then written off as being consigned by God to hell rather than to salvation. And oddly behaving women could be accused of witchcraft, 'tried' and then burned at the stake for being possessed by the devil. So, all in all, it is quite difficult to get a firm fix on the true levels of mental and cognitive disorders during a time when there was such a multiplicity of ways to interpret what was going on inside the head. No DSMs handed down from on high for them.[2]

Today, in our more enlightened times, we have both manuals and statistics. We also have a tendency to blame poverty and social disadvantage rather than diabolical interventions for many cases of cognitive impairment and mental breakdown. The average medieval peasant was almost certainly both poorer and more socially disadvantaged than the majority of people today, but there is little real evidence that they expected as many as one in ten of their young to fail to thrive (see Prince's Trust, 2015); fail to survive, maybe, but fail to thrive once alive, less likely. If we want to understand their putative impact on human functioning, we need to look more closely at what poverty and disadvantage mean both in relation to significance and at the cognitive and biochemical level. This may be more of a chicken-and-egg situation than glib headlines and social engineering gurus have suggested.

A study by Dr Diana Martinez (Martinez et al., 2010) found that increased social status and social support go hand in hand with a higher density of dopamine receptors (dopamine-specific docking stations) in another part of the brain (the striatum, a subcortical structure) that, like the ACC, is central to reward and motivation. This makes it possible for that part of the brain to process more

---

2   The Diagnostic and Statistical Manual of Mental Disorders (currently in its fifth edition – DSM-5) is the standard classification of disorders used by mental health practitioners.

dopamine and therefore make a person feel more motivated. Dr Martinez observes:

> We showed that low levels of dopamine receptors were associated with low social status and that high levels of dopamine receptors were associated with higher social status. The same type of association was seen with the volunteers' reports of social support they received from their friends, family, or significant other. (Elsevier, 2010)

Dr John Krystal, the editor of the journal *Biological Psychiatry*, which published the paper, added:

> These data shed interesting light into the drive to achieve social status, a basic social process. It would make sense that people who had higher levels of D2 [dopamine] receptors, i.e. were more highly motivated and engaged by social situations, would be high achievers and would have higher levels of social support. (ibid.)

While this study does not go deeply into how the high number of dopamine receptors originate, it does suggest that they are pre-existing and that there seem to be few changes in density once the baseline has been established. The implication is that high achievers are born not made, and that it is their basic biology rather than any financial or social advantages that drive them on to still higher achievements – and then, of course, to still higher social status and levels of engagement. For them it becomes a win-win situation.

This seems a bit reductive, leading to the inevitable conclusion that there's not much we can do about any of it and that low-status people should just accept their lot – as peasants in the Middle Ages did. Are some people just born to be drones?

However, it may be a bit more complicated than that, given the following considerations:

- There are fewer medieval peasants around than there used to be – what changed?
- The study used only physically and mentally healthy, socially engaged volunteers and that is bound to affect the findings. After all, many very high achievers with apparently active social lives have strongly bipolar characteristics (Stephen Fry, Winston

Churchill, Ted Turner, to name but three) and they wouldn't have been let near the study. So who can say if they, with their fluctuating dopamine levels, would still fit the study's neurobiological profile of 'high achiever'?

● Even though they found little evidence for changes to the *density* of dopamine receptors, fluctuations of dopamine *levels* can be dependent on a number of other conditions and circumstances. Density of receptors creates the potential for higher levels of dopamine to exist but may not actually dictate the flow at any given moment. After all, even the most gung-ho of people have their down days.

● We don't really know if dopamine receptor density is adversely affected by setbacks.

● Do high achievers lose motivation when knocked back? If so, will affected people fall down the social scale, losing social support (and maybe dopamine receptors) on the way? Or, if receptor levels remain constant, are high-density folk more likely than others to pull their socks up and hit the road again after any setback? Because, being better able to process dopamine, they are also more likely to see the point (the significance) in forcing themselves onwards.

● Can an unexpected increase in social status result in higher dopamine receptor density? If so, could social engineering work to level people up?

There's the rub! If there is a relationship between high dopamine and high status, would high-status people still be satisfied? In other words, would they feel it was *significant enough* (would enough dopamine still be generated?) if they were on a social, financial and intellectual level with others? And would this be true now when (unlike in the Middle Ages) we place emphasis on nonconformity rather than on conformity? We choose to make nonconformity seem more significant and certainly reward it more highly. Could we ever satisfactorily level people up, or would others still feel more motivated to want to move up ever higher?

Some further hypotheses:

● The medieval world was small. People knew their place and felt they were of significance (however constrained) within that environment.

● Individuals had few other models with which to compare theirs. While maybe not socially successful, they could still function within a socially cohesive group. Mostly they were accepting of the status quo.

- The modern world is large. People are now less sure of their place and often feel socially insignificant.
- This is especially the case if they try to compare their lot with the world's most successful people – easy to do in a hyper-connected 24/7 media-dominated society. With often few chances of achieving what so many others may appear to have, perhaps many low-status and low-dopamine people fall into resentful acquiescence rather than either (medieval) acceptance, or proactive (high dopamine) efforts to achieve.
- Maybe acceptance is essentially a more benign condition than acquiescence. It's therefore less likely to lead to fragmentation of the processes that link significance, self and satisfaction.
- Resentful acquiescence is more likely to result in fragmentation and, therefore, kaleidoscope people.
- The modern world would seem to be geared towards loss of significance and, therefore, to reduced surthrival skills.

The Black Birth?

In the late 1340s, a series of outbreaks of plague began which, cumulatively, became known as the Black Death. The Black Death killed approximately 40–50% of Europe's population and turned the known world upside down. It also turned the accepted world order upside down for a while as the ruling classes were no more exempt from plague than anyone else. But still, somebody had to run things and so a small (well, quite large actually) social revolution took place.

Now, was it just the case that low-dopamine people were more susceptible to the plague (dopamine levels affect physical as well as mental wellbeing), or was it the case that people who previously may have been happy with their lot suddenly found themselves having to take on roles that would have been unthinkable before? Many lower-status people began to take on the behaviours as well as the roles of much higher-status folk. Peasants and even women (!) became landowners and estate managers – in a similar way that the upheaval of the First World War probably did more for the cause of universal suffrage than political action ever had. Serfdom more or less died out (at least in the UK) and there was an explosion of creative and artistic thinking that moved history along at a faster pace than would have been imaginable if the status quo had been maintained.[3]

Discuss: My contention about what happened can be read in this way:

- A radical challenge to orthodox thinking happens when the world changes more or less overnight.
- In response to changing conditions, new neural connections are made which join up whole new sets of possibilities.
- More symbolic thought is an inevitable consequence of all these new sets of possibilities.
- Likewise, the creation of new hierarchies of significance.
- Together, these lead to an increase in individual potential and to greater social flexibility and mobility.
- Entrepreneurship is enhanced and rewarded (which was very much the case after the Black Death).
- Dopamine levels will rise with rewards – maybe also as a consequence of changes in brain development.
- A virtuous circle of significance, higher dopamine levels and social engagement becomes established.

Basically it was a sort of big bang moment for social climbing! And potentially an argument in favour of some forms of social engineering, and against the idea that dopamine receptor levels at birth must define a person for life.

Before moving on entirely, though, there are a couple of related areas of research which feed into this line of thinking, even if only slightly obliquely.

The work of the neuroscientist and criminologist Adrian Raine (2013) has demonstrated that the anti-social brain shows lower than normal activity in the ACC. While his findings on dopamine are more nuanced than that might suggest, the connection with significance is strengthened. A brain that cannot focus attention well or build networks of meaning and significance is much less likely to see the point (and reward) in behaving in pro-social ways. It is also much less likely to think symbolically and less able to process complexity

---

3   Recent research by Sharon DeWitte (2015), a biological anthropologist at the University of South Carolina, has shown that, post the Black Death, the number of people who lived past the age of 70 doubled. Other research has shown that descendants of the survivors of the plague share certain beneficial changes in some immune genes. So it looks like we may be on to something. As DeWitte says, 'It is definitely a signal of something very important happening with survivorship' (quoted in Pappas, 2014).

– for example, to understand that one thing leads to another, that there is a wider context within which individual behaviour happens and that anti-social behaviour often rebounds on self and family.

In his Neighborhood Project, evolutionary biologist and anthropologist David Sloan Wilson (2011) has shown that people moving into an area and wishing to be pro-social will fit in with existing norms. If those norms are resolutely anti-social then, paradoxically, so will be their adaptive behaviour. His contention is that the overall environment has to be tweaked to encourage cooperation and to engage residents in the creation of communal projects. Oxytocin levels will rise with social connectedness and 'resentful acquiescence' will give way to more positive attitudes as people experience significance and rewards through the creation of social cohesion.

There is a wealth of research that indicates that the mental health of higher-status and proactive autonomous people is better than the mental health of low-status and resentfully acquiescent people. So, if we look at all the factors that I have been outlining in this chapter, it should be relatively easy to see the connections between society, significance, brain chemistry and personal fragmentation and breakdown.

Extreme individualism

For an individual to function well, they need to have a shared view of what is significant. This suggests that coming together in societies should be protective of coherent identity (although not necessarily of moral standards) as it encourages the development of these attributes. *If, however, for complex individual or social reasons, there is either a lack of ability to detect significance in normal ways or a breakdown in culturally shared values and expectations of agreement with, and engagement in, community behaviour, then the outcome will be what might be called 'extreme individualism'.*

For those with the potential to process dopamine effectively and efficiently, the outcome might ultimately be positive, even revolutionary, as for survivors of the Black Death. However, for those whose dopamine processing systems are fundamentally compromised, whether at birth or through environmental factors (which is to say that they will never have the capacity to link significance, effort, outcome or reward in a joined-up way), individualism is less likely to lead to the motivation to go it alone. It is much more likely to lead to fragmentation and the inability to be connected and coherent, even inside one's own head, never mind within the wider world beyond it.

Kaleidoscope people, like Graham, ultimately neither connect up with nor make sense of the shared delusion that mutant man creates. This is the delusion that there is such a thing as significance and that there is only one true version of it that we must all buy into. Kaleidoscope people live lives that might in some ways be seen as more authentic because they don't share our mutual fantasy that everything joins up, makes sense and has meaning. For them things are still, well, just *things*. And experience is still, well, just *stuff*. Some good, some not so good, some downright nasty.

However, in the best interests of surthrival, we really need to be encouraging as many people as are able to work together to create experiences that support the mutual fantasy – that sense of shared understanding and shared identity. To do this it's important that we understand the practical implications of the sentence in italics above. Therefore, we need to consider the following questions:

- What complex individual reasons might prevent someone from detecting significance in normal ways (in addition to autism and the other conditions mentioned in this chapter)?
- How might that person behave as a consequence of not being able to detect significance?
- What complex social reasons might lead to a breakdown in culturally shared values and expectations of agreement with, and engagement in, community behaviour?
- And how might that breakdown show up in social behaviours?

Once we've got that little lot sorted, we can then look at the ways in which we could make changes in both individual and social behaviour, and so help in the creation of a world in which we will ultimately all feel much more significant. And surthrive much better.

Because, notwithstanding the fact that our need for significance is a delusion, significance, as a driving force, does now also underpin our species' functionality.

Chapter 5

The 'I' of the Storm – Fifty Shades of Me

The individual and significance

I first began to question the prevailing attitudes to addiction and mental health disorders of many kinds when I attended an addictions conference. Its USP was that it had been set up to challenge conventional thinking on the subject. I listened with increasing disbelief to the same-old, same-old series of personal stories – nearly indistinguishable to me – with their emphasis on subjectively traumatic experiences ranging from physical abuse to existential crises. These were clearly seen as cogent, poignant and ground-breaking witness statements by the speakers, all of whom appeared to be fired up by an almost messianic zeal.

I don't want to sound altogether heartless – I was emotionally touched by many of the stories – but eventually I felt I had heard enough of them and needed to hear another, different, story about addiction. I thought I knew what it should sound like, believing that it might be much more significant in the grand scheme of life and survival, but I felt it was being overlooked, drowned out by the sound of 'me', so I stood up and asked, 'Given that many people here will have siblings who are *not* addicted, wouldn't it be more useful to be asking what *protects* people from addiction? If all these traumas affect so many people in the world (which they do), why are some of these people *not* addicts?' I would like to say the question was a show-stopper. It wasn't. At the time, it was responded to respectfully … but *afterwards*! Afterwards, I was bowled over by the number of people who quietly came up to me to say that mine had been the only really important question of the day.

And so began my years of researching Resilience, the protection that allows people to have bad experiences and not only survive them more or less intact but also to grow and thrive as a consequence of them, rather than collapse under them as addicts (and many other dysfunctional people) appear to do.

At the culmination of that research – having worked with

brilliant people's minds and broken people's minds; analysed the processes involved in developing brains and in damaged brains; deconstructed the language use of saints, sinners and villains; read the histories of psychology and neurology; and attempted to keep up with all the latest research into neuroscience – here are some of my findings. One of the most significant of those findings (apart from Significance itself and, anyway, they are all intertwined) is:

In the beginning (of Resilience) was the word.

Language, that great symbolic development in human brains, that internally created indicator of our relationship to the outside world, turns out to be not only a cornerstone in the actual creation of our relationship to the outside world but also one of the most significant players in the whole field of mental health and of Resilience in particular.

Before describing the fascinating work of a number of psycholinguists who have been researching the ways in which our relationship with our inner and outer worlds is both represented and formed by language, and how this affects our wellbeing, I'll take a closer look at the irony that underlies this heavy emphasis on the word 'me' by some of the most damaged people, such as those addicts that I have encountered. The irony is that there appears to be an almost inverse relationship between their levels of self-esteem and self-referral; the lower the apparent sense of self-worth a person feels, the greater the emphasis on personal experiences and personal feelings.

'I, myself and me'

These verbal affirmations of selfhood, 'I, myself and me', are both the unholy trinity at the heart of extreme individualism and a favourite saying of many drug and alcohol workers. The phrase used to come up a lot in the prison drug and alcohol teams I've worked with over the years. It usually came accompanied by a rueful look as an ever-hopeful but frustrated worker attempted to describe what might be going on in the head of the impossible prisoner who had come to them begging for help while maintaining an absolute resistance to change.

It might seem unfair to expose the desperate thinking of the addict – who is probably only just managing to hang on to life by their fingertips – to critical scrutiny and analysis, but it is illuminating. As it's essential to understand the ways in which people think before we can undermine unhelpful anti-surthrival thinking or underpin adaptive thinking, I shall risk accusations of unfairness and borrow the language of a couple of these imprisoned addicts to highlight the typical self-absorption of their thought processes. What follows are the exact words used by two of 'my' prisoners – both polydrug users, both repeat offenders and basically both permanently at war with what they saw as the totally unreasonable system.

Here is what they wrote when they wished to complain about the way they were being treated in prison.

Frankie

Every time I'm off the drugs I get this horrible feeling. I get really anxious. I get really nervous. I feel scared. I feel really ill … why can't you just understand what pain I'm in …

I mean I was wrattling [rattling - suffering withdrawal symptoms] the other day and I went to one boys cell and used a dirty needle and spoon filter because he had a wash in the spoon … but if the detox team HAD HELPED ME with my drug problem I would not have been in that situation. I would not of had to use a needle because I would not have been searching for gear because I would have had a script [prescription].

Simon

I get a TV mag every week and this week I never got one! Waz one sent coz I can't get wing staff to even open me for gym never mind … sort that out, also these gym teachers just never get me, even after 11 month of me being here. This is my 16th complaint about no gym. They lock me up all day with no work though I wish to work, coz they think I'm contaminated. I was set on fire by an idiot who is 6 foot and there to cowardly to even talk to. I was sacked for this arson attack, so I want work as I could make the prison the same in a day if I where that way inclined but luckily I am not. So I want work. I hate cowards.

Although relatively ungrammatical, neither piece of writing is completely illiterate, and as they were both quite regular writers of letters of complaint, they don't give out the impression that they were having difficulty in putting thoughts into words. No, these men wrote what they were thinking, and what they were thinking was all about 'me'. It would be only too easy (and maybe emotionally comforting) to think, 'Poor sods! Who wouldn't be self-absorbed under their circumstances? Who wouldn't want to blame just about everyone else but themselves for their situation?'

Maybe it would be better to challenge any knee-jerk tendency to find personal comfort in hypothetical and rhetorical questions of that kind, and to take instead a more hard-nosed stance and ask a more direct and potentially more helpful question – a chicken-and-egg sort of question that might propel us into thinking more radically and analytically about human behaviour: does adversity lead to solipsism, or does solipsism (and its causes) lead to adversity?[1]

In Chapter 1, I mentioned a particular trait that had helped to identify and mark out dysfunctional thinking and/or behaviour and which had pointed me in the direction of the underpinning factor that influenced all three. That factor, the magic Cinderella key, Significance, has already been brought into the equation and we've looked at it in some detail. However, the trait which I said I had observed in all the most damaged (but not always the least successful people) has not. This trait is an unhealthy preoccupation with 'I' (see Chung and Pennebaker, 2007; Pennebaker, 2011).

I, I, I, I, (love me *very* much) I, I, self-obsession, self-absorption, self-focus, self-interest, self, self …

Not only did I hear an awful lot of talk about 'me' from those addicts I worked with, whether in prison, in rehabs or at conferences, I also heard it from the disturbed or dysfunctional high achievers I was coaching, from those with mental health disorders and brain damage, and especially from those clients who *apparently* suffered from what is called 'low self-esteem' – a term that, ironically, implies a low prioritisation of self. What on earth was going on?

It was as though these people lacked a fundamental core sense that they *existed* in any significant or validated way (one which needs

---

1   Solipsism: the view that only the self is knowable or can be certain of existence. Colloquially used interchangeably with egotism.

to be originally created or endorsed in the primary, probably maternal, relationship – à la Bowlby). They had been left with a space, a vacuum, that had to be filled by the endless echoing sound of 'I'. This would act as a permanent reminder that they really were still there, even if only capable of feeling a shadowy approximation, a dulled sensation of their own existence.

Were all these people talking about 'I, myself and me' all the time because fundamentally they didn't really get their own significance? Was this due to compromised primary or maternal care? Would that also then mean that they were less likely to get other forms of significance too? This could easily result in extreme individualism, with its implied lack of personal and social coherence.

If this were the case, then there should be other clues in their communications which would provide external evidence of their internal cognitive organisation. It wouldn't necessarily be useful to ask any of them the direct question, 'What is going on?', because chances were, if they didn't fully sense their own experiences, they would be unlikely to be able to describe them or even know them at any conscious level. In other words, they would be the last ones to be truly aware of what they were doing, thinking or feeling.

To thine own self be true

My journey from language-based lecturer to expert in the field of language, cognition and behaviour was one that had taken me from an interest in language for its own sake, with all its beautiful and bounteous potential to let the human imagination take flight, to a very clear understanding that it was through language – the most magical, misunderstood but also most obvious marker of our difference from the other primates – that we could most easily and usefully access the mutant workings of a human mind.

Once I had twigged that this word 'I' was both a significant marker and a marker of significance (or lack of it), I then started to listen even more carefully to the contexts in which it cropped up so frequently. These would surely provide the cognitive landscape through which this compromised figure 'I' walked, at once so marked out and yet so lonely.

Here are just a few fairly typical descriptions of their experience of being themselves, given by people who seem in some way to be detached from any authentic subjective experience of being fully alive. Lacking the usual sensation of being tied to their embodied selves, of being separate and distinct from those around them, they nevertheless, despite such lack of sense of 'self', seem to be preoccupied with their own states:

- I feel I am that Mr Cellophane Man from *Chicago*, all see-through but removed from sensation. There's nobody there.
- I'm deep underwater, at the bottom of a tank. I'm looking up through darkness to distant light. Seeing everything through a darkened glass, wanting to knock, to make contact, but there's no real connection.
- When it all happened, when my marriage broke down, I felt I had disappeared.
- Why did I think you knew what I had done? Because I'm transparent; people can see through everything I do.
- But you knew that's what I thought and felt about you. You always knew what I was thinking. You knew from the start everything that went through my head.
- I've existed for twenty-nine years, though I've been alive for considerably less … [referring to his own childhood]. If you ever see that little boy, please tell him I love him and miss him. Please show him the way back home so he can be a part of my life again.
- Cutting [myself] was the only way I had any feelings. Nothing else felt like it was happening to *me*.
- There were all these voices, telling me stuff, all the time. I never knew if it was me talking or someone else.

This is evidence given by people who have all experienced substantial depression, anxiety and/or substance misuse. They are by no means all failures, either financially or in terms of career, but none of them has sustained any long-term relationships. At least two could be placed somewhere on the autistic spectrum. Even at the best of times the subjective experience of living has not been easy for any of them (although they may reflect on it endlessly) but, in line with what I would expect, what really throws all of them is having to deal with periods of crisis in their lives. It is then that their lack of personal coherence really lets them down.

Most people can negotiate and manage the easy times in life, times when we are in our comfort zones (although these vary widely from person to person; some people's comfort zones would send others into spirals of panic and depression), but when we encounter challenges we have to draw on our Resilience resources. Maybe this is why we assume that people with addictive and other mental health problems have experienced more bad things than average because their difficulties only emerge when they are failing to cope. Superficially, it's easy to assume a causal relationship between traumatic events, stresses, psychological and behavioural dysfunction, but establishing genuine cause and effect takes a much more skilful and forensic analysis.

If your day-to-day experience of living inside your own skin is as simultaneously challenging, self-absorbing and annihilating as it is for these people – who are all trying, and failing, to catch glimpses of their own shadows as they walk through life; all trying, and failing, to believe in themselves as agents in their own lives – then you will have few resources left with which to counter any external challenge. In fact, you will have a much lower than average awareness of the outside world in the first place. Because you have fewer antennae reaching out to it, you will be getting less sensory feedback from it and less information about it. This means you will be constantly fighting blind and constantly wrong-footed by it.

It seemed to me as if absorption in self was, counter-intuitively, the outcome of a fundamental *lack* of self, and that the language that came across as so very egotistical could, ironically, really be a marker of *lower* than average levels of resilience. This would account for the fragmented or damaged lives that so many apparent egotists seemed to live.

Case study: the search for the self

Perhaps one of the most famous and most easily accessed and imagined examples of this kind of dysfunctional mismatch between appearance and reality is Oscar Wilde.

As a man who managed to combine so many seemingly contradictory elements that he was almost a walking oxymoron, Oscar Wilde provides us with a perfect example of how all these discrepancies (levels of self-worth and self-referral yet disconnection from self, and so on) can be communicated through language use. Expressing himself in some of the most lovingly and beautifully constructed linguistic flourishes in the English language, he unwittingly shows us how it is possible to have the least self-knowledge while being the most absorbed in the study of his own life and inner processes.

De Profundis (from the depths), which demonstrates this almost perfectly, is the title of a long letter Wilde wrote while he was serving time in Reading gaol – for gross indecency with men. Ostensibly written as a form of *nostra culpa* (our fault) to his lover, Lord Alfred Douglas, but essentially a personal reflection that was always intended for public view, *De Profundis* begins with a description of Wilde's previous hedonistic lifestyle, its luxury, its critical successes and the relationship with 'Bosie'. Then it shifts tone to indict the selfishness of all that indulgence before finally moving into another stranger phase in which Wilde identifies himself with Christ, whom he claims lived just such an individualistic life as artist and poet as he himself did.

In this long, sombre and curious work, Wilde never unequivocally and completely condemns or regrets his own past, but instead gives us an at-first-sight wholly judgemental and self-lacerating summary of his downfall:

Tired of being on the heights, I deliberately went to the depths in the search for new sensation. What the paradox was to me in the sphere of thought, perversity became to me in the sphere of passion. Desire, at the end, was a malady, or a madness, or both. I grew careless of the lives of others. I took pleasure where it pleased me, and passed on. I forgot that every little action of the common day makes or unmakes character, and that therefore what one has done in the secret chamber one has some day to cry aloud on the housetop. I ceased to be lord over myself. I was no longer the captain of my soul, and did not know it. I allowed pleasure to dominate me. I ended in horrible disgrace. There is only one thing for me now, absolute humility.

Brilliant and insightful though this self-analysis might seem to be in all its Gothic wandering, Wilde entirely fails to fix clearly and forensically on the one thing that might have saved him all this heartache in the first place. Ironically, all the self-lacerating really achieves is to imply a kind of doomy masochistic relish for all the sufferings, and to serve as yet another example of Wilde's self-absorption.

Expressive and seemingly self-aware though his words are, Wilde's *De Profundis*, with its constant refrain of I, I, I, is really only another outpouring of the solipsism that is closely associated with depression, anxiety and failure to thrive. Conditions which so often lead to mental health problems, addiction and even criminality – that with which Wilde was charged.

It would be naive to respond by declaring that Wilde's behaviour wouldn't be considered criminal today, that he was in fact yet another victim (and maybe one of the saddest of them all) of the repressive sexual mores that lasted until very recently and that all his final troubles were the result of that. But it was not his sexual activities, per se, that landed him in court (in fact, his homosexuality was pretty well recognised and overlooked at the time); it was much more the same sort of challenge to authority demonstrated – although in rather less fluent language – by 'my' two prisoners whose words were quoted at the beginning of this chapter. Going against all advice, Wilde took on the system and sued Lord Alfred Douglas's father for libel over comments he had made about his sexual behaviour. Unfortunately, although both crudely and rudely expressed, they were accurate. It was a perhaps understandable own goal, one that had tragic implications for Wilde, but one which might have been avoided had he been less inclined to grandstand all the time.

In that extract from *De Profundis*, Wilde got close to the truest interpretation of his underlying problem in the words, 'I grew careless of the lives of others.' And, as it so happens, careless of the pronouns that might have suggested that he was aware of the lives of others too. The nearest he gets to referencing others is in that rather sweeping phrase, 'the lives of others' – an anonymous expression that itemises no particular individual life or, indeed, any particular individual harm that he might have caused any such individual life. Everything else in the extract refers back to himself, even his use of the impersonal 'one' ('what one has done in the secret chamber'), which acts like a barrier between himself and the responsibility that he appears to be assuming for things done 'in the secret chamber'.

Poor man, even in his attempts at self-awareness and assumption of personal responsibility for his earlier grandiosity and self-indulgence, he still gives the game away. Poignant though *De Profundis* is (his suffering in prison was both very real and very physical), a forensic reading of it only manages to reinforce the impression that he has really learned very little and is still inclined to grandstand his suffering. Given his time again he would in all likelihood plant himself firmly back in the path of temptations of various kinds. That he would have learned enough from experience not to do *exactly* the same things again is pretty likely – he was an extremely clever man – but it is equally possible that he wouldn't have been able to recognise it even if he was acting out in ways that were very similar to before. Self-absorption seems to make people particularly bad at monitoring and recognising their own behaviour – yet another irony.

Life in an echo chamber

So does Wilde fit my tentative profile of someone whose primary (probably maternal) relationship failed to significate or validate their existence, so leaving them to echo their own name endlessly through that empty space where a core self should have been established? As well as lacking in the resilience to cope with hardships? Well, to answer the last question first, Oscar Wilde only lived for another three years after being released from prison. He was abandoned by his friends (most selfishly and shockingly by Lord Alfred Douglas), went downhill fast and died in 1900 at the age of 46.

Wilde had been brought up by a mother who was eccentrically unconventional and attention seeking, and although he was said to be devotedly attached to her, when he was small he can never have had, or felt he had, all of her attention devoted to him. It was said, and may even have been true, that she dressed him in girls' clothes when he was little, because she was disappointed that he had not been born a girl (although it was not at all unusual for small boys to be dressed in frocks in the nineteenth century). What is certain, because it was central to her own life and self-presentation, is that she did imbue him with the belief that image, the way you looked and dressed, was central to your identity, to who you were and to what others felt about you. And who you were, as she also made very clear to him, was someone who was a cut above the rest of humanity. So, if Wilde was taught from the earliest times that others were less significant than him, but that even his own significance depended to a very large extent on outer forms, then it is hardly surprising that he grew up failing to detect significance, either his own or that of things in the world beyond himself, in what might be called normal ways, or that he ended up as such an extreme individual.

An 'extreme individual': a person so distanced from the normal and healthy development of a core identity and sense of interrelationship with others that they are left needing to fix their hazy sense of self by repeated references to 'I, myself and me'. And because they also feel that they (and their needs and concerns) have not been sufficiently attended to by others, or especially by one other, they are left needing to keep on reiterating their message, their story, in order to press home and validate their right to be heard.

Even Hamlet himself (the über standard-bearer for identity issues), at the very point of death, asks his friend Horatio to 'report me and my cause aright', scared that the truth of his life, as he sees it, will not be told. He is presuming that he and his life will have meant nothing – that he will have had no significance.

Challenging the echo chamber – and an unquestioned assumption

There you are, standing quietly at a bar, waiting patiently in a queue or sitting harmlessly on a train, when you are selected to be on the receiving end of a curiously dressed stranger's labyrinthine life story. Almost invariably, this story comes studded with references to people whose relationship to the storyteller is never fully explained but who are clearly somehow to blame for all their woes.

Eventually you escape and you wonder (if you give the matter any further thought at all) whether that eccentrically attired stranger is aware that the story you are most likely to take away from the hijacking is not the one they think they were telling you but an altogether different one about human inadequacy – their human inadequacy.

It's perhaps no coincidence, given the addict's inevitable lack of self-awareness, that nearly all addicts 'in recovery', particularly when attending meetings such as those run by Alcoholics Anonymous (AA), are encouraged to do something similar to that of the eccentrically dressed stranger. That is, to repeatedly go over their personal stories, their experiences and feelings with their group of fellow addicts – something known as 'sharing' with the meeting – to become, in effect, like so many versions of Samuel Taylor Coleridge's Ancient Mariner:

Since then, at an uncertain hour,
The agony returns:
And till my ghastly tale is told,
This heart within me burns.
I pass, like night, from land to land;
I have strange power of speech;
That moment that his face I see,
I know the man that must hear me:
To him my tale I teach.

The mariner is condemned by some strange internal force to tell and retell, at great length and to a total stranger, his story of wrong-doing, loss of faith and redemption. Coleridge was himself an opium addict and doubtless would have agreed with the following AA statement: 'in God's hands, the dark past is the greatest posses-sion you have – the key to life and happiness for others'.

If you read through the whole of *The Rime of the Ancient Mariner* you will find passages that could have been the original inspiration behind the AA quotation. To add weight to the point that testimony, bearing witness or sharing (or any other of the names used to describe the process that Hamlet called reporting 'my cause aright') feels as though it must (even should) be beneficial to those whose lives have gone awry, here are some other extracts from an AA book of daily reflections (2004):

> The legions of recovering alcoholics stay sober by sharing with fellow alcoholics. The way to my recovery is to show others in AA that when I share with them, we both grow in the grace of the Higher Power, and both of us are on the road to a happy destiny. (p. 129)
>
> No longer is my past an autobiography, it is a reference book to be taken down, opened and shared. (p. 131)
>
> Later I shared my life in order to help the newcomer find his place with us. (p. 133)
>
> It is easier for me to accept myself if I share my whole life. (p. 143)

Telling the tale over and over again, fixing on the man, woman, child or group who 'must hear me' is clearly meant to be, and is firmly believed to be, one of the most significant parts of the process of recovery in AA and other 12-step programmes. But is it? Is talking about yourself, expressing your feelings, telling your tale repeatedly really the panacea for all mental ills that any number of therapies, including AA, Narcotics Anonymous and other similar programmes have been assuming for so many years now?

My contention is that this fixation, this obsession with self and one's own story is an indication of lack of self rather than an expression of what, at first sight, seems to be a firm belief in self. While self-focus may be a useful indicator of underlying problems and should be recognised by mental health professionals and therapists as such, it is unlikely to operate as a tool to promote better mental health. Prioritising self and self-related concerns may in fact result in higher levels of anxiety, depression and so, ironically, in worse mental health. This is a possibility of which mental health professionals and therapists should be fully aware.

Just one more thing …

Like the TV detective show, *Columbo*, I am now, finally, going to offer some evidence of this apparently ironic and contradictory state of affairs. I am going to look at the research of James Pennebaker and Cindy Chung and particularly that written up in their paper titled 'The Psychological Functions of Function Words' (Chung and Pennebaker, 2007) in order to substantiate my point.

Pennebaker and Chung have been conducting research into the relationship language has with a number of aspects of both physical and mental health. They have come to the conclusion that it is often the small words we use that have the most to say about us. Pennebaker has even written a book about pronouns (Pennebaker, 2011).

Of their joint work, Chung says, 'Function words (e.g. articles, prepositions, pronouns etc.) … tend to be more reliable markers in detecting personality traits and psychological states than are regular content words (e.g. nouns, regular verbs, etc.).' This, she suggests, is partly because they are less easily manipulated. She adds that she uses statistical patterns to 'track topics over time, across cultures and in multiple languages', so their findings should be about as objective as is possible, given the huge complexity of their undertaking.[2]

The main findings in Chung and Pennebaker (2007), which are quite lengthy and intricate, can be summed up as follows:

- Function words inhabit Broca's area in the left frontal lobe of the brain (frontal lobes being high functioning areas where advanced social skills happen).
- Making the connections implied in the use of function words (those devoid of any concrete references) requires both advanced symbolic thought and social knowledge. Their use indicates the existence of advanced social skills.

---

2   See videolectures.net/cindy_chung

- Referring back to the work of Scherwitz et al. (1977), Pennebaker and Chung remind us that Type A personalities (ambitious, driven, impatient, aggressive) use first-person singular pronouns more frequently than other personality types.
- As testosterone injections suppressed volunteers' use of non-'I' pronouns, it may be that testosterone steers people's interests away from other people as social beings. (Many studies show links between autism and testosterone, so there may be an overlap with anti-social, or at least lack of pro-social, autistic traits here – my inference.)
- The use of the first-person singular pronoun is associated with negative affective states such as depression, and continues in affected people even after depression is lifted. (My question is whether depression is correlated with self-absorption in the first place?)
- Females tend to use the first-person singular pronoun at a consistently higher rate than males. It is unclear whether this is because they are more self-absorbed, traditionally hold lower-status positions or tend more towards depression.
- Suicidal poets who eventually committed suicide used more first-person singular pronouns than those who did not. Overall, suicidal poets' language was more self-referential than non-suicidal poets' language.
- The more people attend to and then make references to others, the healthier they are. Use of more third-person pronouns is linked to more adaptive coping which, in turn, results in better overall health.
- Those writing about emotional traumas who switched away from a high use of 'I' pronouns showed greater improvement in health.
- With wide-scale social upheaval (Princess Diana's death, 9/11 and so on) comes a general increase in the use of first-person plural pronouns and a decrease in singular ones. (The study supports my contention that times like the Black Death lead to an increase of what might be called 'social sturdiness'.)
- Sadness (as opposed to feeling depressed), especially at times of social/emotional upheaval, results in bonding and better health for less inwardly focused people. It is accompanied by the greater use of 'we' and lessened use of 'I'. This shows that pronouns are markers of social connectedness and may be able to predict health outcomes for an individual.
- The truthfulness of statements can be ascertained by the use of

first-person singular pronouns (i.e. owning what is said) in combination with excluding words such as 'but', 'except', 'without' and so on. These imply the cognitive complexity that goes with truthful recollection.

- In terms of status, when two people interact the higher-status individual is likely to use fewer 'I' words.
- As people get older they tend to use fewer first-person singular words but use more excluding words, suggesting that they have become less self-focused and better able to distance themselves from their topics, and able to make more distinctions and speak with greater cognitive complexity. This assumes continuing good cognitive health.
- Attempts to change people's cognitive architecture by forcing change of use of pronouns has not proved successful in trials to date.

All of which is quite fascinating as well as being largely supportive of my hypotheses.

The following study provides much more nuanced evidence. Pennebaker and Chung (2011) looked at a claim that has been made by a number of psychologists and therapists in recent years, which is that expressive writing – writing about traumatic or emotional events (offloading, in effect) – is beneficial for both emotional and physical health. After much investigation they concluded, in a rather sceptical vein, that expressive writing was not a panacea and that the overall effect size of writing was at best modest.

This finding may be endorsed and even supplemented by yet another study carried out by medical researcher Werdie van Staden (1999, 2003; cited in Priest, 2011). He took transcripts of forty psychotherapy sessions for each of twenty patients, half of whom had done well and half less well, which had been recorded in the 1970s. He then compared sessions for first-person pronoun usage, expecting to find (against the slightly later evidence of Chung and Pennebaker) that an increase in first-person pronoun usage would be correlated with the better outcomes (this is the expectation of most talking cures). In fact, what he found was that both groups showed a small increase in first-person pronoun use. But this study used historic material, so there could be time and culture differences.

Obviously perplexed, van Staden finally explained this by looking at the ways in which first-person pronouns were being used. He realised that there was a distinction between the worse-outcome

group whose use of 'I' was associated with a sense of relative inca-
pacity and what he terms 'loss of agency' (often now called
'self-efficacy'), and the better outcome group whose use of 'I' was
associated with the stronger positioning of assumption of agency, '*I*
did so and so', '*I* am responsible' and so on. The recovering patient
is one who no longer sees themself as being on the receiving end of
life – that is, as a victim.

All of which tends to endorse my contentions and undermines
the dearly held belief that a greater focus on the self is good for
what has long been known as 'self-esteem'.

I don't want to hear it …

So how does that square with the sentiment expressed in the recovery movement's booklet, *The AA Service Handbook*?

Although we are the *victims of the illness*, we have no profound
knowledge of either its cause or its 'cure'. (Alcoholics
Anonymous, 2013: 12; my italics)

Is it possible that the use of such language as 'victims' and 'illness',
together with the idea that telling and retelling one's personal story
must be therapeutic, will serve only to reinforce the sense that an
alcoholic, drug user or other 12-step practitioner is on the receiving
end of life and needs to big up their right to be heard? In all probability this cognitive positioning may have played a major part in
establishing the problem in the first place.

Is a recovery programme just another formulation of the
problem – an alternative crutch for those whose surthrival skills
were never properly developed in the first place, rather than a
re-education of the thought processes involved?

And I'll thcream and thcream
if I'm made to …

A few years ago I had an experience that rather suggested this. I
shared a platform at an educational conference with a man who had
once been a famous journalist and had then gone on to become an
equally famous drunk. However, at the time of the conference he

was dry, in recovery, and we were both there to debate the problem, for schools and for parents, of teenage drug and alcohol use.

I wanted to give the parents, who formed a large part of the audience, some message of hope. The possibility that their child may descend into some kind of druggy hell is one of the most feared nightmare scenarios that parents have. My wish was to inform them, fairly objectively, about the various factors involved in substance-using behaviours – the neurobiology which makes some people more prone but not absolutely condemned to what we call addiction, plus the instrumental environmental factors which often constitute the triggers for addiction, but may, even so, be optimised to support even prone types to develop resilience and so avoid any descent into said druggy hell. The leading scientists in the field now widely endorse the view that addictive behaviour is caused by the combination of some kind of genetic predisposition allied with environmental factors. There is a lot of research showing that children who have the right kind of all-round care in their early years are much better able to withstand pressures and temptations of all kinds – from chemical to social and behavioural.

I wanted the parents to know that they weren't powerless, that their children weren't about to be hijacked by some kind of indis-criminate and diabolical demon, and that they were able to influence how resilient their children were likely to be – that is, how good their surthrival skills were. My famous co-speaker got very steamed up about it and in the debate that followed spoke quite angrily, rejecting most of what I had said out of hand. However, later on, when everyone else had gone, leaving just the two of us in the hall, he turned to me and apologised for his aggressive stance. As I hadn't really felt that he had been aggressive towards me per-sonally, I said 'no need'; but then he said something that has stayed with me, which sums up a problem inherent in, and at the heart of, the recovery agenda: 'You see the trouble is, I can't afford to believe you.'

By which he meant that the success of his recovery programme was dependent on his belief that his drinking had been the result of some indiscriminate and diabolical demon; that he had, through no known fault of his own, developed the disease of addiction; and that his recovery would only take place if he handed over the reins of control to a Higher Power. If he felt that *he* was in any way to blame for his addiction then, inevitably, he would spiral out of control again. Plus, presumably, he would be burdened with the weight of responsibility for his own previous bad behaviour. Everything I had said went pretty much contrary to the beliefs to which he was clinging. He couldn't afford to give headspace to that challenge, so instead he drowned out the sound of it with angry rejection.

This has not been the only time I have witnessed such passion and such an angry repudiation of the scientific stance by those who are in what might be called the recovery position. In fact, the recovery movement and the scientific community are sometimes in such fundamental opposition that at another conference on addiction that I attended, I saw two men – one an addiction therapist and the other a psychiatrist who specialised in treating addiction – literally square up to one another. They had to be firmly coaxed apart.

I do find it sad that it takes abandonment of personal responsibility to recover from one's habit. I also doubt that a recovery predicated on fear is the way to a freer life. This often leads instead to a lifetime spent balancing on the edge of a chasm, terrified that one false move will tip you over the edge. The research on language use, which doubts the helpfulness of focusing on 'I, myself and me', and which implicitly questions the victimisation of self by means of language use, would appear to support my doubts about that particular approach to the problem of substance dependence.

Words, words, words

On the other hand, how we feel, our mental and physical health, depends on the way we refer to ourselves, how we represent ourselves to ourselves and where we place ourselves in relation to the world and people beyond ourselves. To a large extent we need words to be able to do this. Words make us and words make the world what it seems to be to us. I don't suppose that an elephant, given the power to mull the question over, would describe the world in quite the same way that we humans would. That is largely because we think about the world in much the same way that we think about ourselves – that is to say, in words.

Put simply, the more words we have access to and understanding of, the more sense we can make of the world and of ourselves. However, single unrelated words are not much use (unless you're 2, that is, in which case 'no' seems to have the power to do pretty much anything). As Chung and Pennebaker's work implies, words – and, counter-intuitively, function words rather than nouns and verbs – help to create those complex relationships between things (including ourselves) that make us special and human. In other words (try to imagine *that* idea being expressed any other way!), words are the highest expression of hyper-connectivity that we have. The more ways we have with words, the more ways we can be connected and the more über-human we become. But as we have also seen in this chapter, the less connected we are and the less significance we feel within ourselves or see in others, the less our language will express connectedness and the more it is likely to echo to the rising sound of 'me'.

Now that we've looked at some of the ways a person might be prevented from detecting significance in normal ways, in the following chapters we will explore some of the many ways a person might behave as a consequence of not being able to detect significance.

But first I'm going to tell the story of a client who first lost and then found language again, about how she behaved as a consequence and what she felt about the difference.

Chapter 6

The Lost Girl and the Bamboo Man

Lost and found

Imagine being 12, clever, full of curiosity and already alive to the idea that your life lies ahead of you – an adventure that you can't wait to enjoy, full of possibilities and promise. Then imagine all those possibilities, all that promise, destroyed in one overwhelming physical catastrophe as your body catapults through a car windscreen, head (and brain) bouncing over the car bonnet, coming to a stop on the ground – your life changed forever.

Three years later, you are still unable to walk, feed yourself, make conscious decisions about what your body does or where your body goes next. But, worst of all, you have no speech – you can't talk, not a word, not even your own name – so you can't even make a claim to your own identity. Who are you now? Who can you be when so much of yourself has been stolen from you?

Such was the tragic condition of a girl I'll call Sophie with whom I was about to work. She was unable to do very much at all physically and was quite unable to communicate orally, managing only to talk to the outside world with the use of a Lightwriter (a device with a keyboard that allows a user to type in words which are then both displayed on a small screen and turned into synthesised speech). Frustratingly, one of a Lightwriter's intended benefits, the use of predictive speech (which saves the user from having to make too many keystrokes) can create a problem for someone whose brain has been as severely damaged as Sophie's; it creates ambiguity of meaning. So, with very limited and compromised access to the contents of her brain, I was at first uncertain as to whether Sophie had any real cognitive ability left in her at all. Her typed communications, such as they were, came in short bursts, easily became two-word abusive ('fuck off' being one of her more expressive and fleshed-out communications) and her attention span was almost non-existent. Within a few minutes of meeting anyone, Sophie would either fall asleep, head drooping in the most uncomfortable looking positions, or, frustrated or angered by something that had been said or that was not (by her) sayable, she would start banging her chair with her usable (left) hand and kicking out quite violently with her usable (left) leg.

I mention the side of her body which was still partially working because it is more than a little significant in this context. This is because our brains are arranged in two hemispheres, left and right, and, notwithstanding what I said about brain region specialisation in Chapter 2, in terms of their function, our brains are largely organised hemispherically. The left side of our brain controls the right side of our body, and vice versa. So, from what I have said you can detect that Sophie's brain damage was mostly in her left hemisphere, which had two quite appalling consequences for her, over and above the obvious that brain damage completely messes up your life.

One outcome of left hemisphere damage is its effect on mood. Although the research is both complex and often contradictory, there seems to be sufficient evidence to show that left-brain damage affects networks that are essentially positive and optimistic ones (and leads to depression), whereas right-brain damage has relatively little negative effect on mood (see Davidson, 1998). In fact, in some cases of quite severe right-brain damage a patient can seem almost indifferent to their limitations, while left-brain patients suffer much more depression and negativity than would seem proportionate. This may be partly a consequence of the left hemisphere being rich in dopamine systems (dopamine being the neurotransmitter for attention, significance and, to an extent, mood). So, Sophie was pretty miserable most of the time, not only because she was brain damaged but also because of where the damage was situated.

The other harmful effect of left hemisphere damage is that, for normally organised (in terms of brain function) right-handers, which Sophie had been before her accident, language is located on the left side of the brain. For left-handers these things are a bit more variable, as language may be in the left hemisphere (as for right-handers), it may be in the right hemisphere or, more usually, it may be spread out across both hemispheres. This last possibility has two consequences: the downside is that left-handers can be more compromised in terms of language processing. They are more likely to be dyslexic, to stammer or to have other related problems. The upside is that having language spread rather more around the brain means that 'two-hemisphere' left-handers are less likely to lose all speech should they have the misfortune to suffer a brain injury or have a stroke. So, not all bad news, eh!

It wasn't so good for Sophie. Having been a normally organised right-hander before her accident, she had lost all speech and was left with only the simplest forms of vocalisation, such as grunts, sighs, cries and so on. Sometimes these could be almost unbearably poignant to hear. For example, having written on her Lightwriter one day that she had always bottled up her true feelings (something I was told she had never expressed before), I asked her how she really felt and she painstakingly typed out the one word, 'heartbroken', and then let out a piercing wail that was as moving as it was despairing.

I'm glad to say that within a month she was using these vocalisations to articulate her name, and at the end of four months she was not only able to greet me in complete and properly articulated sentences, but was even cheeky enough to be saying things like 'Hey, get a move on' when things weren't going fast enough for her!

Claiming back her own identity through the use of her name was, I firmly believe, the crank handle that started the engine of her speech and language recovery. In his poem, 'The Naming of Cats', T. S. Eliot talks of 'The deep and inscrutable singular Name'; a team at the University of St Andrews in Scotland (King and Janik, 2013) has demonstrated that even dolphins, some of the smartest creatures on the planet aside from humans, have their own unique signature whistle by which they can be individually identified. So it seems that both artists and academics agree that to have a unique way of referencing oneself, a personal calling card as it were, may well be both integral to being a sophisticated thinker and to the creation of a strongly individual sense of self.

From the day that Sophie was able to say (with much coaxing and many strange facial contortions) her own name to herself, she definitely began to think in more connected ways and to link her current perceptions of what was going on with properly verbalised memories of the past. The words she was now able to use gave her the tools she needed to cobble it all together.

While Sophie may never have the full physical or cognitive capacity that she might once have achieved, and while her life will always be substantially compromised, she can now at least give full voice to her current feelings, thoughts and hopes. She can argue, debate, sing and gossip. She can articulate ideas that are complex and personal. She can negotiate rather than hit out, and ask people to change the subject or go away rather than fall asleep. She can chat people up, learn new subjects, self-talk herself into a better frame of mind and follow verbal instructions more easily.

Sophie has unrestricted immediate access to language again. She has the power of direct speech, the power to shape other people's responses to her in sophisticated ways and the power to shape her own responses to life again. When asked what had been the most important part of her recovery to date, she said, without a moment's hesitation, 'Getting my speech back.'

Only connect

One of the most interesting aspects of this process, from a professional point of view, was to how great an extent Sophie's memory and cognitive function in general was dependent on speech, or rather on language. It is very much a chicken-and-egg epic as to whether we are able to have any of these sophisticated functions without language. One of the ironies is that without the use of language it is very hard to find out what, or indeed how, someone is thinking.

Advanced imaging techniques may one day be able to tell us with greater certainty how all of that works, but as of now I cannot provide a definitive answer to that centuries-old question. However, I can offer you the perceptions of a girl who has been closer to the answer than most of us would ever wish to be. Even so, as she was amazingly able to recognise for herself, by the time she could talk about her previous condition she was already bringing language to bear on her own memories – and maybe by means of language post-rationalising, construing meaning or even confabulating[1] (not that those were her exact words!) what she had actually experienced at the time.

Sophie's witness, though, was that she had been somehow aware of how she felt – miserable and very frustrated – all the time she was lying immobile and uncommunicative. She said she thought she could remember what people around her were saying but she was rather vague about it. Overall, what seemed clearest to her was that she was uncertain as to whether she had experienced any verbal thoughts throughout those three long years. Whereas, once she had speech back (and with it an infinitely greater power of expression – she had never used the Lightwriter to express anything complex or sophisticated), she had no doubts at all about the way she experienced her inner ruminations – she experienced them in words.

---

1   Confabulation is the fabrication of imaginary experiences to make up for a lack of memory. It is usually an unconscious process, often a consequence of dementia or brain damage, including alcoholic brain damage.

Not only had her fast developing verbal capability given her the capacity to think in more complex, abstract and sophisticated ways, but it also appeared to affect her mood. Of course, it would be almost impossible to differentiate the positive effect of regaining greater control over her own environment and being able to communicate with those around her from the dopamine stimulating effect of left hemispherical activity.[2]

So language, or at least its most obvious marker, speech, was generally a huge factor in Sophie's recovery process. Being better able to follow instructions helped her to comply with exercise regimes, and the language/dopamine/motivation nexus seemed to have a positive effect on things like her posture too. Then there was a remarkable improvement in social awareness, one which was reflected in Sophie's own use of increasingly pro-social language.

Let me repeat something. If, for complex individual or social reasons, there is either a lack of ability to detect significance in normal ways or a breakdown in culturally shared values and expectations of agreement with, and engagement in, community behaviour, then the outcome will be what might be called 'extreme individualism'.

Nothing could be more extremely individual than a brain-damaged patient. Okay, there will be certain deficits in common among those with brain injuries, depending on the type and location of the problems, but no two injuries are exactly alike. And the underlying personality and intelligence will also impact on how an injury plays out for the individual patient. But when we talk about individual behaviour we usually mean something along the lines of 'distinctive', 'edgy', 'cool' or even 'eccentric'. However, I am using the words 'individual' and 'individualism' slightly differently to mean separate from others, not forming an integral part of the generality of society. 'Separate, special and different' to use another expression common to many of the drug and alcohol workers I have worked alongside.

With that definition in mind, it is easy to see that brain damage will leave most patients with fewer of the pro-social resources that

---

2   The relevant language centres are in the left hemisphere, which is mediated more by dopamine than the right hemisphere, plus language appears to be mediated by dopamine in its own right. It is well known that depressed people have less desire to talk, and talking therapies are usually shown to improve mood – allowing for all the first-person pronoun material discussed in the previous chapter. As I've mentioned before, talkativeness is associated with the highs of bipolar disorder, and many different types of people have experienced the 'word high' that comes with talking passionately, fluently and expressively.

link people into community groups. They will often be unable to think things through, exercise restraint, manage and organise time and resources, pre-plan, work cooperatively or communicate effectively. This leaves many of them frustrated and lonely for much of the time. There is also another feature of many (though not all – again, it depends on the nature and location of the injury) cases of brain damage, and that is that it becomes harder for brain-injured people to imagine (create an internal impression of) and realise (make concrete and real) the worlds and minds of other people. The consequence of this devastating loss is that they find it much harder to feel and show empathy and understanding, and this makes social and emotional relationships very much harder for them – and very much harder on the people they have been close to pre-injury. Thus, brain-damaged people are quintessentially extreme individualists. An inevitable consequence is that they lack the ability to detect significance in normal ways as they have lost the ability to see any particular significance in the lives of others.

Sophie was like this when I first met her. Clearly, she knew I was someone separate from her, but she gave no indication that she had even the smallest interest in my actual existence or in the existence of anyone involved in her care. She asked no questions, did not respond to any small talk and gave her limited attention only to matters of direct and immediate concern to herself.

It took some time, but the breakthrough came when, as I walked in one day, she turned and asked with a note of genuine interest in her voice, 'How are you today?' This was her first expression of social connectedness and of her understanding of another's existence and need for recognition. So began her journey towards a much fuller life, a life that holds the possibility of networks and of cooperative efforts that will not only give her the emotional and psychological reward of belonging, but also keep on providing the mental stimulation that deeper engagement with other people brings.

Looking back at the previous chapter's material on pronoun usage, you can easily see how a change from self-absorption and self-referral to a general curiosity about the world beyond the self naturally leads away from a fixation with 'I' and towards greater use of pronouns such as 'you', 'he', 'she', 'it' and so on. Hopefully, it is now easier to see that when a person has no sense of Other nor any markers for Other[3] – words that do not create and mark their existence – then it is inevitable that the outcome will be anti-social, or at the very least demonstrate a lack of pro-social behaviour. (Sophie's actions when kicking out and all the rest can't really be described as anti-social as she had very little true awareness of what she was doing.)

Having said that, an awareness of the existence of Other is only the jumping-off point for truly pro-social behaviour. Once you've recognised that Other is out there, whether it's a person, an event or even just the day-to-day negotiations and navigations that people have to cooperate with to make the world go round, then you also have to see how it all relates or connects up. You know a person not only by the fact that they're in front of you but also by the way they look, sound, act and so on. It's the same for everything out there – you have to monitor it and connect it up, you have to identify it and relate it to everything else. Name it, frame it and hang it in the gallery of life.

John Donne knew it all along:

No man is an Iland, intire of it selfe: every man is a peece of the Continent, a part of the maine;

Meditation XVII, *Devotions*
Upon Emergent Occasions

But it is fast being recognised by the world of scientific research that there is an interdependence between us and our fellow men, as well as between us and our actions and words, and these are the building blocks of all our relationships, both internally and externally constructed. The words we use are the pointers to and markers of significance – that which our hyper-connected brains, with their attention-maintaining dopamine systems, fix on as important.

Older and wiser – unless …

It follows that the more complex the language, the more complex must be the connections made within the brain; the referral systems are more labyrinthine, the networks more sophisticated. Although this may not sit happily with many modern educationalists, it is one

---

3   Other, written with a capital letter, denotes that which is beyond the self – which could be other people or simply the outside world in general.

argument in favour of teaching complex grammar – clauses, sub-clauses and all. It is also the case that good language skills are good for our health.

Chung and Pennebaker (2007) found something to encourage us all, which is that ageing brains work a bit differently from younger brains, and that the older people get, the less self-absorbed and the more future-aware they become. Now, there are sad exceptions to this rosy and benevolent picture of an ageing populace, and these are the people who suffer from dementia. The brains of dementia victims are much more likely to fixate in quite self-absorbed and paranoid ways on what other people are doing *to* them, and they will be unable to project far into the future, instead clinging on to memories of what happened years before. In their imaginings, childhood often seems closer than what is happening in the here and now.

Dementia is a catch-all term; one of its most common forms is Alzheimer's disease which is marked by plaques and tangles in the brain which effectively destroy various working areas. It is no coincidence that language is one of the areas earliest affected by Alzheimer's because it is language that makes manifest the complexity and sophistication of thought in the first place. Once the complexity and sophistication are compromised, so too will be the language. There are only a very few particular conditions (among them autism spectrum disorder, which I cover in more detail in Appendix B) in which language may appear to be more sophisticated and imply more meaning and understanding than is really the case.

It is still not proven that good language skills help to prevent dementia but the evidence is building fast. It has yet to be determined whether this is a purely mechanistic effect, as language areas such as the anterior cingulate cortex are heavily involved in many other higher order cognitive processes too, or whether it is because language is, in itself, an armour against cognitive breakdown.

Recent research from three institutions is representative of findings from around the world:

- *Shakespeare and Wordsworth boost the brain.* Research carried out by Professor Philip Davis at the University of Liverpool reveals that reading complex and challenging prose and poetry acts as a 'rocket booster' to the brain, stimulating electrical activity and leading to a virtuous circle of self-reflection, engaged memory, emotion – and further reading. 'Translating' the works into more accessible modern versions (i.e. 'dumbing down') had no such effect (educationalists, please take note).[4]

- *Bookworms show less mental decline as they age.* A study carried out by Dr Robert Wilson of Rush University Medical Centre (Wilson et al., 2013) suggests that taking part in mental exercises, such as reading and writing, from childhood on, is necessary for brain health in old age. In a study of 294 elderly people, which concluded with a physical examination of their brains after death, he showed that the brains of those who had engaged in mentally stimulating activities throughout life showed fewer physical signs of dementia than those who had not.

- *Childhood cognitive ability correlates with rates of dementia.* Research carried out jointly by Edinburgh University and McGill University in Canada (Karama et al., 2014) has shown that the cleverer a young person is, the less risk they have of developing dementia as they age. Participants' IQs were tested at 11 and then their brains were scanned at age 73. The higher the IQ, the thicker the brain cortex – the area that 'contains' the most sophisticated functions. The researchers believe that two-thirds of the link between later cognitive abilities and cortical thickness could be accounted for by differences in childhood IQ levels.

In the beginning was the word ...

These three items of research taken together leave few doubts about the desirability of leading children gently, or even kicking and screaming, into the world of books, and in particular into the world of intellectually and grammatically challenging books. These are the ones which contain complex ideas expressed using elaborate clauses, creative word combinations, lively expressions, novel notions, rational cause and effect and challenging language. They help children to connect up as many neurons as possible from as many different brain areas as possible; they take their neurons on

---

4   Researchers at Washington University demonstrated that the frontal lobes, and particularly the anterior cingulate cortex and major language areas in the left hemisphere, showed furious activity when novel noun/verb combinations were tried out (Raichle et al., 1994). This activity dampened down after practice at those combinations, when new regions, particularly the insula, were activated. This tends to suggest that all 'challenging' language tasks have a stimulating and therefore protective effect on the brain – including on the ACC, which as we've seen is essential for so many elements of higher brain function.

exciting journeys of exploration and discovery, energising and invigorating them and kick-starting their growing brains into enjoying a process that will bring benefits to the end of their days – at the same time as saving the country billions in health and social care costs.

So, reading and writing in complex ways can help our brains to grow and remain strong. They also save us from having to sniff one another's bottoms or do any of the strange things that other animals do to suss one another out. These human-specific ways of marking, monitoring, capturing and expressing significance also function as fairly reliable indicators of what's going on in a brain, of its essential composition and way of thinking. In other words, our language systems allow us to access information about other people's character and likely intentions towards us far more cleanly than if we had to ferret it out by pheromone analysis.

If you can use and follow sophisticated verbal structures, and your references and connecting words suggest awareness of others, relationship with others and an understanding of complex cause and effect and consequence, then you are a pretty sophisticated and well-evolved human. Other people should be able to detect that from your language use alone. However, not everyone can do this. So we come back to the question of extreme individualism as the consequence of an inability to detect significance in what might be called normal ways.

If language in a normally organised brain reflects what is being thought about at the time of speaking or writing, then it follows that a person's way of thinking, their fundamental system for organising experience, will show up in their choice of words. Chung and Pennebaker's (2007) exploration of pronoun usage has already demonstrated this to a large extent, but there are other ways of showing the complexity or otherwise of mental processes. These might be through the use of sophisticated syntax or sentence structure which indicates that a person can not only think about all the twists and turns and possibilities of a situation, and the thoughts or feelings that come with it, but can also quickly marshal all of the possibilities into a communication that conveys more than a simple personal reaction, such as 'Oh, that's great!' or even 'Fuck off!'

Additionally, the truly sophisticated thinker can demonstrate core consistency. That is to say, they communicate a unifying set of principles of thought, taste and action which are rarely at odds with one another and which inform and guide the overall behaviour, attitudes and language use of that person. It is this unifying set of principles which indicates joined-up thinking and offers evidence that a person is what they claim to be. It is also, from my experience, one of the best indicators that a person is likely to be reliable.

Only disconnect

We've all said it, haven't we, of someone who seems a bit flaky, a bit troubled, 'They're all over the place ...' Well, it's their being all over the place in their thinking that I'm talking about here. That appearance to others of being all over the place is the external evidence of an internal lack of core consistency. There are other expressions that seem to describe that state of incongruence rather well: 'Not walking the talk', 'Etch-a-sketch people' or even 'All mouth and no trousers'.

These phrases all describe individuals who give out a particular image of themselves through the way they present themselves, the things they say, the claims they make about themselves and their capabilities, but who then fail to deliver on the implied promises, expectations or undertakings. Rather worryingly, psychopaths are pretty good at doing all of this. But it's not just psychopaths (whatever that media-hyped word really means) who mislead with their apparent persona and their spoken or written communications. It's also individuals whose crimes may seem very small beer in comparison but which still cause a lot of confusion and distress in people's day-to-day lives. These misdemeanours appear with yawning regularity in the columns of the popular press – usually because they have involved some credulous individual in a marriage scam or in a financial enterprise that has turned awry, leaving the victim both embarrassed and heartbroken.

We know that most people occasionally misremember and have false memories. The cognitive psychologist, Elizabeth Loftus, in her seminal studies on eye-witness testimonies, has shown how easy it is to use language to manipulate memory (Loftus, 2004). She did this by inserting a word with strongly emotive qualities, such as 'crashed', into a question about an apparently clearly remembered road accident. Once this word was incorporated into the memory, the speed at which the accident was remembered as having taken place suddenly increased. She also demonstrated how easy it was to persuade someone of the existence of an event in their own life that had never taken place – even getting them to describe it. (This effectively demolished a whole recovered memory industry.) And most of what she achieved was done with language.

Language is a symbolic system linked to things that are not necessarily either in front of us, external or even verifiable in the first place, so it is just waiting to do service as the handmaiden of falsification or confabulation. It is only because we are given a rulebook when we are very young that we use language to serve the truth – most of the time. Small children have very few qualms about creating bogus worlds which give them great pleasure. It is as much through their innate desire to belong as through any intrinsic sense that there really isn't a dinosaur called Bert in the back garden that they cross-reference inner experience with outer experience. So they sign up to what I call 'culturally shared values and expectations of agreement with, and engagement in, community behaviour', even if only at the simplest level, by finally concurring with the majority vote as to the existence of Bert.[5]

But not always. Some people never develop a strong relationship between what might be called factuality and the things that they say. It's not so much because of false memories as such (though that may be a factor) or because they are what we term 'liars' (which suggests conscious deceit), it's more because language works a bit differently for them. For these individuals, language is nearly as creative of reality as it is descriptive of it, and this can lead them into trouble. Communication will inevitably be compromised and there will be a distortion of reality because they will be unable to distinguish between memories based on things that can demonstrably have taken place and memories based on fantasy.

The Bamboo Man

An empty man is full of himself.

Edward Abbey

I called him Bamboo Man for two reasons: he was obsessed with growing bamboo and he was fundamentally hollow inside – lacking any of that core consistency essential for joined-up thinking.

When I first met him he came across, as he did with everyone initially, as being very friendly, open and approachable. He seemed generous, being (self-reportedly) in the habit of taking gifts of home-baked goodies around to his neighbours and (again self-reportedly)

5   The Restoration dramatist, Nathaniel Lee, on being consigned to Bedlam in 1684, expressed this truth plaintively but pithily, 'They called me mad, and I called them mad, and damn them, they outvoted me.'

of taking on the task of helping new neighbours find their feet, linking them up with tradesmen (his mates, 'no worries'), cutting down overgrown boundary hedges, mowing verges and so on. Only it turned out he had history with neighbours and with quite a few other people as well. His history included a spell inside for assault, threats of violence, acts of criminal damage and various kinds of nuisance behaviour, such as loud late-night parties and the persistent growing of intrusive roof-height bamboo against neighbouring properties and boundaries.

I soon discovered that he had a very tenuous grip on factuality and only a partial grip on the accuracy of the words he was using at any given time. He reacted far too quickly to what others said for there to have been time for him to have either processed the content or monitored his response. He tended to use other people's words as a springboard for his next claim about himself. It quickly became apparent that everything he said or did was to serve one purpose – himself.

For example, he undertook to cut back a new neighbour's hedge for them on the understanding that he would follow up by cutting down the vast bamboo screen he had grown on his side, 'Because they (the previous owners) refused to cut their hedge and it shut out my light, so I grew it to get my own back.' However, as soon as he had been allowed to reduce the hedge to the height he wanted, he denied all knowledge of having made a reciprocal arrangement and allowed his bamboo to carry on growing until it reached roof height – notwithstanding that it was then his own greenery that was shutting out his light.

His behaviour regularly demonstrated an erratic but self-defeating selfishness. Eventually most of his dealings with people went sour, often ending with him using threatening and abusive language against them, if not worse. He was 'fortunate' enough to have found himself a very co-dependent partner[6] (with a house and a job) who continued to believe everything he said, despite each separate and cumulative piece of evidence to the contrary. She even reputedly overlooked the fact that he had attacked one of her own children. So he carried on indulging himself in ways that not only

---

6   Co-dependency – an expression often used about a partner's relationship with an addict. It implies that the relationship is more important to the co-dependent party than any of their own (healthy) needs. They will go to great lengths to satisfy their partner's needs while overlooking their own, but rarely achieve a more satisfactory outcome than to fulfil their own need to be needed. In other words, having a deficit from childhood, it is their only way of experiencing the sensation of being significant themselves.

drove his neighbours to distraction but also, ultimately, only served to bring disasters down on his own head.

The lack of core consistency behind all of this was demonstrated by the mismatch between his claims and his actual behaviours. Some of his claims were quite clearly fictitious, others more subtly so.

- He said he had taken a prestigious course in landscape gardening but showed none of the skills you might have expected – butchering trees instead of lopping them.
- He claimed he had recently owned a substantial property but moved in to live with a housing association tenant.
- He declared himself to be a disciple of Japanese art but showed no interest in an expensive book of Japanese prints.
- He professed to be addicted to gardening but bought all his plants fully grown, apart from some lettuces which he just allowed to bolt. His garden was full of thousands of pounds worth of plants but his drive and patio were strewn with weeds, broken bins, broken chairs and mounds of building debris.

One area in which he was consistent was in his tastes. However variable and inconsistent they might otherwise have been, these were invariably hyper-stimulating and immature. He loved intrusive noise such as sentimental fifties music played very loudly, multiple sets of giant wind chimes (part of his ersatz oriental phase), raucous laughter, garish clashing colours in garden planting schemes and fixtures, and bright lights such as an arena scale spotlight and a Christmas galaxy of LED lights spewed randomly over house front and lawn.

He also – which should come as no surprise – ate too much, drank too much and chain smoked (of course, he took no responsibility: 'It was her fault, I'd given up till I met her'). Above all else, what particularly interested me was the way his verbal communications were also strangely excessive in that they flipped between verbosity and silence.

He seemed to be incapable of maintaining any real dialogue at all. He either dominated conversations, talking about himself, or became silent, blatantly inattentive to anyone else's communications. Even when he spent time alone with his partner there appeared to be little attempt at any conversation other than about simple practical matters, and even these mostly consisted of her agreeing with all his recommendations. Drink would loosen him up, but then he seemed compelled to shout or shriek things in very short phrases – in effect, the vocalisations of an uncontrolled kiddies' playground. He had the round unfeatured face and big-bellied unsculpted torso of a toddler, complete with jutting under-lip which, when not laughing over-exuberantly, made him look almost permanently aggrieved. He was a sort of overgrown infant, physically as well as mentally.

Inability to detect significance in normal ways

Bamboo Man's stunted development went back to childhood. He had experienced family problems from early on but it wasn't clear what they consisted of. He would only acknowledge great difficulties with his father, a man whom he eventually physically attacked, so it seems likely that the difficulties involved a certain amount of disciplining (it would be too ironically neat if it had involved caning). It is also probable that he thought his mother weak, unwilling or unable to come to his defence. This, in later years, translated into his need for a willing, slavish, compliant woman, whom he could dominate (and enact a form of 'soft' revenge on) in turn. The evidence that his attitude to women was compromised became clear as soon as he was not able to control their behaviour. Then he resorted to bullying, haranguing and childish name-calling – 'Spoilt brat', 'Who wears the trousers?', that kind of thing.

His name-calling, like most name-calling, was the result of that inability to engage in any real form of dialogue, the kind that might have allowed him to rationalise and negotiate situations better, either with adversaries or friends. This arose from the different way his language system worked – he had very little short-term verbal memory. Verbal memory allows us not only to hear and retain what others are saying to us, but also to hear our own inner processes and thoughts, as well as to direct our own future actions. In a conversation we need it to help us hold in mind and simultaneously juggle the various verbal, bodily and emotional sets of information coming from other parties as we formulate plans, intentions and responses of our own, based on what we are also able to tell ourselves about our own inner states. Verbal memory function is related to verbal ability, so different people do all this at different levels. It can vary from:

Shit! Keeping schtum, but looks fucking furious. Not scared
- yes I am. Better scarper.

To:

Tight smile, tight grip, too. Not happy, though words at
odds. Said 'Yes', meant 'No'. Must have annoyed him with
last comment. Uh, oh, can feel that pit of stomach thing.
Makes me over-compensate. I'm going to talk too much -
better make my excuses …

We take this process for granted but really it is one of the greatest
wonders of the world!

Verbal memory is strongly associated with inner speech, which
was brought to the attention of modern researchers by the work of
Communist-era Russian psychologist, L. S. Vygotsky. Psychologist
and writer Charles Fernyhough, from Durham University, tells us
that 'Vygotsky hypothesised that this "private speech" develops out
of social dialogue with parents and caregivers. Over time, these
private mutterings become further internalised to form inner
speech' (Fernyhough, 2013: 32). He adds:

Sure enough, long after his death, fMRI (functional Magnetic
Resonance Imaging) studies have linked inner speech to the
left inferior frontal gyrus, including a region called Broca's
area, which is known to be important for speech production.

It may also be that verbal thought can allow communication between other cognitive systems, effectively providing a
common language for the brain … and inner speech gives us
a way of taking control of our own behaviour, by using words
to direct our actions … So we know that inner speech has a
role in regulating behaviour … Inner speech may even help
us to become aware of who we are as individuals. (ibid.:
33–34)

Then, quoting Canadian psychologist Alain Morin, from Mount
Royal University, Calgary, he adds:

Inner speech allows us to verbally analyse our emotions,
motives, thoughts and behavioural patterns. It puts to the

forefront of consciousness what would otherwise remain mostly subconscious. (ibid.: 34)

In other words, playing around with the concept of who we are, for which good short-term verbal memory will be necessary, is part of that complex process of being fully human, especially as this implies having the ability to attend to information and select from it – to detect significance.

Clearly, an inability to do any of this will have serious consequences for an individual. Because inner speech, with all its attendant benefits to the mutant human's need to connect things up, is dependent on retaining a memory of the words that have just been used, it follows that problems with this kind of verbal memory will lead to all manner of difficulties with life. Donald Quinlan and Thomas Brown (2003: 143) say of ADHD patients:

These patients complain of chronic difficulties holding in mind what they are planning to say while they wait for someone else to finish speaking and remembering what they have just been told or what they have just finished reading. Short-term verbal memory problems can cause significant impairment in school, work, social relationships, and other aspects of daily life ... often does not follow through on instructions and fails to finish work ... persistent failure to hold in mind what one was asked to do or what one had set out to accomplish, especially if instructions or goals have multiple components ... working memory also functions as the computational 'file manager' of the mind, selecting and retrieving from long term memory information and plans needed moment-by-moment for current tasks. Working memory is a critical element of those 'executive functions' which constitute the management system of the mind.

All of which goes a long way towards explaining many of the Bamboo Man's problems, from his inability to maintain any kind of dialogue with the outside world, to his inability to use his experience of past social disasters to inform the verbal and behavioural actions of his future and so avoid making the same mistakes over and over again, to his lack of self-control, his lack of education, his lack of self-awareness and his inability to follow through on work undertakings or, in fact, on any undertakings. It creates a rather sad picture – although one no less annoying for his neighbours. However, it does not help us to understand why he had this deficit in the first place.

Graham, our kaleidoscopic wunderkind in Chapter 4, also had a short-term verbal memory deficit. In fact, being a wunderkind, tests proved that he managed to combine having an extraordinarily high IQ with having no discernible short-term verbal memory at all – but then, that's wunderkinder for you – always got to be extreme achievers. Although Graham, too, had little ability to follow a conversation or to remember his own verbal instructions to himself, he had enough innate intelligence in other fields that he managed to compensate for many shortcomings by being able to 'do everything from first principles' at quite a fast rate.

Bamboo Man did not enjoy the same level of intelligence, and nor did he have the same reason for his memory deficit (Asperger's) as Graham. Whereas someone with Asperger's may have quite a large amount of activity going on internally but suffers from connectivity difficulties (both neurologically and socially), someone like Bamboo Man has had what might be called their 'inner content' compromised from a very young age. As they are more reliant on inner speech than a person with Asperger's, once that inner speech fails to develop fully a Bamboo Man type person has less to work with than someone whose speech was only ever going to be secondary to other mental processes. Bamboo Man's silences were the result, quite literally, of his having nothing to say, rather than the result of his being unable to express his inner workings through speech. Attention is necessary for the detection of significance, significance is necessary for meaning, meaning is necessary for content and content is necessary for (most) speech. Likewise with dopamine, as it is a mediator of both language and attention. As we saw from Quinlan and Brown's work, Bamboo Man's ability, or inability, to attend is in all likelihood the cause of his short-term verbal memory problems. All the other symptoms I describe go hand in hand with those.

So why would a background like Bamboo Man's lead to him to end up with so few cognitive and linguistic resources and so many problematic behaviours? A clue is in the similarity of his attitudes and behaviours to those of Sophie when I first met her. Both were incapable of exercising self-control when frustrated or angry, both had problems with short-term memory, and therefore with long-term memory (after all, you need to store ideas in the short term before they can be committed to the long term), neither showed any genuine interest in the world, or in the lives of others, and neither was capable of forward planning or carrying their stated intentions into a realistic and realisable future. As a consequence of all this, both were confabulators, making up semi-plausible versions of their own pasts. They were also fantasists, setting up idealised versions of what their futures might hold, including what plans, tasks and undertakings they would carry out and how they would behave.

Sophie, however, had not always been like that. In fact, as her recovery took off, she began to regain many aspects of her old self. Her original self was academically clever; intellectual achievement is now thought to have an impact on how well a brain-damaged person recovers from injury. Although brain plasticity is still a relatively controversial area, as early as 1904 the American neurologist, Charles Mills, theorised that:

- If destruction of speech centres is incomplete, part of a convolution may learn to do the work of the whole.
- If centres on one side are destroyed, corresponding regions in the other hemisphere may take on function.
- If channels of communication are cut or blocked, new pathways may be formed.

So the theory can hardly be said to be new, and it was that theory I worked with when helping Sophie to regain her speech. However, there are still practitioners I have come across who are convinced that there are severe limitations to what can be achieved in the realms of speech and language and that even this will be time limited – two years being their cut-off point. Sophie's paediatric neurologist stated that it was highly likely that she would never regain any speech; fortunately for Sophie I didn't work with her in what might be called conventional ways and so I could ignore conventional wisdoms.

In Sophie's case, the preserved areas of high original intellect stood her in good stead, and this is why she is different from Bamboo Man. Once her recovery had started, she was quick to build on each stage of progress, even though her memory was (and always will be) severely compromised. One indicator that she retained some of her old abilities was that having told me a story of some complexity involving people whom she had met and places she had visited, she then stopped, seeming to mull this over, and said, 'Or perhaps I've just made that up.' This to me suggested that she was redeveloping a capacity to connect up what might be called her creative inner images with attention (in this case directed towards her inner processes), her own autobiographical past, her short-term verbal memory (she had to remember what she had just finished saying), context, self-awareness and, essentially, plausibility. Quite sophisticated stuff for a girl with as much damage as she had sustained. This was somewhat more sophisticated than Bamboo Man had ever seemed to manage, because he appeared quite unable to question the credibility of his own stories or even to remember the essential content of them. Instead, he would usually deny having said the exact thing that another person had recently heard him say.

'But you said …', uttered with some disbelief, is the anthem of partners, families, co-workers and those who have problems with verbal memory. This is one of the most distressing, disturbing and frustrating aspects of a number of brain conditions and it can lead to accusations of lying, deceit and criminality. Unfortunately for all concerned, the probability is that the cause of verbal memory problems, as in Bamboo Man's case, is, in effect, brain damage. In Graham's case it was all part of his Asperger's, which although not brain damage as such, means that his brain was working in non-standard ways. In Sophie's case, poor verbal memory was the result of straightforward brain damage. In other cases, especially those related to alcoholism and drug use, it is again a matter of brain damage as those behaviours result in damage to several areas of the brain. For Bamboo Man, as perhaps in many cases of ADHD, it is a form of brain damage caused before the brain has properly grown. In other words, it is developmental damage, taking place in the womb rather than later on.

It is, of course, possible for people to have problems which are very similar in nature to the ones just described, but which are either the result of genetic disorders or of progressive diseases such as Parkinson's. I do not wish to suggest that all disorders of memory and verbal processing that are not the result of brain damage are down to maternal environment and behaviour. However, quite a few will be, and mums, who usually want to do the best for their children, will need and want to know how all this works.

Stress is as stress does

All abusive relationships and all unhealthy behaviours will impact on babies and children in a great variety of ways. In Chapter 3, I described the importance of mums bonding closely with their babies and giving them lots of attention, especially eye contact, to help them feel significant. The impact of the prenatal environment on a baby's neural wiring is also hugely important. Whatever a pregnant woman does, however she feels, what she eats, what she drinks, smokes and ingests in general, all of these things affect the ways that the baby's brain gets wired up.

I'm not going to go into great detail about that here, but I do want to mention one of the things that occasionally gets overlooked – stress. Stress and the related problem of anxiety are killers of human potential. And what could be more stressful than being in an abusive relationship – whichever way the abuse takes place?[7]

Maccari et al. (2003: 119) first show how adult vulnerability to heart disease can be programmed by pre-birth stress. They then go on to observe:

> However, in extreme conditions like stress and/or under-nutrition, offspring of stressed mothers during pregnancy displayed short and long-term physiological and behavioural abnormalities such as reduced birth weight, increased infant morbidity, locomotion and cognition retardation and increased anxiety or sleep disturbances.

They refer to many other adverse adult consequences as well, and indirectly relate much of this to the effects of stress on the development of the foetus's amine systems – which takes us back to dopamine.

The large number of studies which catalogue the problems arising from prenatal and early years exposure to stress – which vary from vulnerability to addictions, lowered IQ, raised anxiety, learning disorders, depression, premature sexualisation, hyperactivity, low self-esteem and physiological impairment – nearly all point towards two significant things which are adversely affected by stress and which may be affected interdependently. One is the prefrontal cortex. This is known as the executive control area of the brain as it appears to do all our higher order thinking, such as forward

---

7   It is so often assumed that abuse, mental or physical, is a one-way street (i.e. male on female). This is by no means always the case. One alcoholic male prisoner I worked with (who was neither big nor strong) was 'in' for domestic violence. I asked whether his wife was also alcoholic. The answer was yes. I asked if the violence was one sided. The answer was no. When asked why he had said nothing about his wife's attacks on him, he replied that he would have felt like a fool. The moral, as far as I'm concerned, is that we should not be partisan and that abuse is abuse, whoever is responsible for it. We need to discover the often complex reasons behind this behaviour, rather than engage in ideological witch-hunts, especially if we wish to help the children of these relationships.

planning, self-control, decision making and so on. The other is the dopamine system which has a direct influence on the prefrontal cortex.

We know from researchers like Yutaka Tanaka and David L. Bachman (2000) that dopamine is necessary for verbal memory retrieval, and from Mark D'Esposito et al. (1995) that the prefrontal cortex plays a critical role in working memory and that dopamine, possibly in its role as a prefrontal cortex specific neurotransmitter, is also critical to working memory. (Although it appears that an optimum level is required, rather than a high level. As with bipolar disorder, too much can be as dysfunctional as too little.)

So, given that, it seems highly likely that someone with Bamboo Man's background – which almost certainly included an abusive parental relationship, probable violence, definite parental stress and probably many other negative factors – will have been irreparably adversely affected, pre-birth, in terms of cognitive potential, partly because the neurobiological foundations for concentration, attention and short-term verbal memory will already have been compromised. Studies suggesting that an enhanced post-birth environment (especially one that includes good education) may somewhat mitigate negative pre-birth factors are immaterial here, as his relationship with his family clearly remained poor and he gave no indication of having any interest in learning. In any case, I have found little research evidence to suggest that compromised verbal or working memory can be substantially improved even with dopamine treatment (which works relatively well for Parkinson's and in some cases of brain damage) if the impairment is from birth rather than developing in later life.

At the individual personal level this is not a very encouraging picture, but at another level, as I have discovered, it is very encouraging indeed. To bring about recovery in a damaged brain, one that was already functioning quite well before the injury and which had established routes for successful cognition (an embodied memory of function), is difficult enough. But helping to 'bring on' an older brain that has never developed certain key capacities and processes in the first place is proving to be much more difficult, if not almost impossible. The best that can be achieved through all the therapies that are being used, including chemical ones, is to quieten brains down enough to allow for behavioural training and for more acceptable habits to be learned. But, as our consistently high prison population shows, there are many thousands of intractable cases out there – far too many for such interventions to be practicable for all.

On the plus side, however, what is fast becoming clear is that real permanent changes in a whole population's behaviour really should be possible, if only we could get the important messages through to potential parents early enough.

This is about the rest of us too

In this chapter we have looked at some of the specific ways that people behave when their brain function is sufficiently compromised that they cannot detect significance in normal ways. This leads to a failure to see meaning in people and things beyond themselves, and a failure to understand how external factors and personal behaviours relate to one another. Essentially, we have seen that the outcome for them adds up to what might be called a *compromised core consistency* – a lack of connectedness both within and without, which results in a lack of joined-up thinking and some pretty flaky behaviour.

However, I can see that the behaviours I have described may seem too extreme, what with my talk of ADHD, confabulation, violence and so on, to sound in any way relevant to the rest of the normal world (because we're all much more normal than the people I've been writing about, aren't we?). Therefore, I am going to add a coda which covers rather more workaday examples of compromised core consistency, of unjoined-up thinking and behaviour. Some of these might come as a bit of a surprise to those readers who have never seen themselves as being anything but fine and dandy – no cognitive inconsistencies here, thank you kindly – but please just go with the flow for a while.

It might also come as a bit of a surprise when, in the second half of the coda, I highlight the cases of people who were not only very successful in their fields, but were also held up as standard bearers of society's gradual journey to empathy and emotional enlightenment. Especially as I am essentially accusing them of being not only a bit flaky (maybe no real surprise there) and lacking in necessary core consistency, but also as being potentially far more damaging to the cognitive coherence of those they touched than might seem remotely plausible. How could such emotionally alluring people possibly be damaging? I leave you to judge, and hope the coda may be something of a challenge and a wake-up call to anyone who thinks they may have been in possession of too sleepy and uncritical a brain.

Chapter 7 returns to the main thread and takes a closer look at the question posed earlier: what complex social reasons might lead to a breakdown in culturally shared values and expectations of agreement with, and engagement in, community behaviour? (Without which, of course, there is much less chance of surthrival for any one of us.)

Coda: Our dotty unjoined-up world

'Do what I say, not what I do'

Possibly the granddaddy of them all is the double standard of 'Do what I say, not what I do.' It's one of the easiest and most understandable self-deceptions to fall for; I can't believe there's a parent alive who hasn't been guilty of this at one time or another. But though it might seem relatively harmless to tell your child off for being rude to his or her grandparent when you have either directly criticised them yourself in the child's hearing or shown that you are perfectly okay with rudeness yourself, by, say, giving the finger to another motorist, it is anything but. What this behaviour does is to scramble a child's sense that there is consistency in the world. This then makes it more likely that they will develop an ad hoc morality and have lower levels of resilience than a child who has a greater certainty about how the world works.

The principle of consistency around language and behaviour, what we say and do, applies to a huge range of things, from working hard, to being an unfussy eater, to not being self-serving. One of the most glaring violations of this principle that I have ever come across is also one of the most telling. A recovering alcoholic, who was only recently out of rehab but who was already in training as an addiction therapist (something worrying there?), was describing to a recovery group meeting how her son appeared to be developing an obsession with weight training. She told the group how her (oh so aware and empathetic) response to his fixation had been to say, 'For goodness' sake, just stop it and get a life!' I won't count the ways that this spoke volumes about so very many issues.

'No, I'm fine thank you'

This is about minimising or denying that which is glaringly obvious to others. Addiction often falls into this category, as do many other problems which are in the course of developing. For example, in many households (especially middle-class ones in which certain behaviours just don't seem either credible or permissible) there is a rush to deny the possibility of any kind of weirdness in the family, such as:

- Excessive alcohol use: 'It's the end of a hard week, of course he/she's going to need a drink or two to unwind.'
- Mental health problems: 'Oh, I don't think we should interfere, they've always been a bit eccentric, that's all.'
- Problems at school: 'For heaven's sake, they're young. Let them have their bit of fun.'

To a child (or an alien anthropologist) watching as a grown-up spills another drink or knocks over another side table, as a scared-looking face peeps warily around a semi-closed curtain or as an adolescent falls over vomiting in the street, all this minimising can seem like pretty peculiar behaviour in its own right. And not a bit joined up with the belief that we're an advanced species with socially responsible inclinations.

Sentimentality

A sentimentalist is one who desires to have the luxury of an emotion without paying for it.

Oscar Wilde

Although not in an uncomplicated relationship with 'normal' himself, Wilde could usually be relied on to detect the sweet smell of self-interest in others. Sentimentality is really a very straightforward case of self-interest, even when it looks like concern for the wellbeing of others. As Wilde suggests, it is a form of emotional self-indulgence that brings no responsibilities.

How does sentimentality manifest itself? And what harm does it actually cause? Well, first, and this one is truly insidious and possibly deadly, there's the sentimentality that coos, squeaks or gruffly asserts, 'I love my kids to bits' (only too often, and sometimes only too literally). I've had conversations with thousands of prisoners and there's hardly one, female or male, who hasn't said those very words to me. But then ask them why they have not behaved in ways that would have kept them in closer contact with those kids (i.e. safely and legally at home with them) and it quickly becomes obvious that their love is of the emoting rather than the active kind. It goes with the need for a packet of fags being greater than the desire to send their child to school with enough lunch money. This type of senti-mentality, which is actively encouraged by afternoon confessional TV and prime-time soap operas, is genuinely scary because it rewards the pleasure circuits of the brain at times when the brain's owner is doing nothing of any real value, and nothing to benefit their children or society. It rewards self-indulgence rather than effort and achievement on behalf of the family.

There's an impolite but graphic phrase I use that neatly sums up the motivation and the reward behind sentimentality of this kind, which is 'having a great big emotional wankfest' – in other words, putting personal emotional gratification before rational and prag-matic good. There are too many possible excuses for such sentimental self-indulgence to list them all, but here is a selection:

- The sentimentality that anthropomorphises animals by treating them like people, 'Ah, who's a clever little fellow, then, looking out for mummy coming home?', which often leads to spoiling and overindulging them rather than taking good practical care of their species-specific needs.
- The sentimentality that finds most fulfilment in the emotional afterglow of generosity – being keener to buy the latest overhyped toy rather than taking the time and trouble to go out for a walk with a small child and pointing out natural phenomena on the way, thus feeding their curiosity and building their long-term resourcefulness.
- The sentimentality of the 'person with a conscience' (often young and idealistic) who finds it more rewarding to give money to a beggar on the street 'for a bed for the night' (and so feeds an addiction) than to take the more hard-nosed option of refusing money but encouraging them to visit a drop in centre – which might just save that person's life.

Two hundred years ago, Jane Austen wrote about this topic in her novel *Sense and Sensibility*. How many people who have read the book or loved the film will have thought about how much of it still applies to the dilemmas of modern life?

Laissez-faire, or just plain lazy minded?

The laissez-faire problem, which is quite closely related to the previous one of sentimentality, even exercised the great Hamlet himself. In act IV, scene iv of the play he is busy beating himself up for not having taken action against his uncle, the man who murdered his father, and who, in any other more traditional revenge tragedy would have been done away with long before now by the aggrieved and avenging son (sixteenth-century family life being much like *The Godfather* in tights). He ruminates as follows,

---

Now, whether it be
Bestial oblivion, or some craven scruple
Of thinking too precisely on the event –
A thought which, quartered, hath but one part wisdom
And ever three parts coward – I do not know
Why yet I live to say, 'This thing's to do';

Like so many of us, Hamlet prefers prevarication to dealing directly with the issue at hand. But at least he has the honesty to recognise that he might just be sugar-coating the reality which is that he is afraid to act. Afraid of the act, afraid of the consequences, basically afraid of the unknown and uncontrollable outcome of action.

'Thinking the matter over' is a preferable short-term solution, one that allows Hamlet to feel he is taking everything into consideration. And this is often how we justify inaction over matters that affect us, especially when we don't want to disturb the imperfect yet familiar status quo. We tell ourselves that someone else will be dealing with it (Baby Peter?); that it's not our business (sexual grooming in Rochdale?); that we shouldn't judge (alcohol use, drugs, petty crime, relative issues of morality?); that this is just how things are today (anti-social behaviour, litter dropping, abusive language?) and we walk away or turn a blind eye, safe in the knowledge that we have thought things over and chosen the sensible option …

Fine, just as long as we don't mind being challenged when a child (or alien anthropologist) asks how we can walk away but still love playing the part of the action hero when we're gaming. Or how we can walk away but still tell our children to stand up for themselves in the playground, to act on their beliefs and not be afraid to speak out about bullying.

To thine own self be true

And while we're on the subject of Hamlet, 'This above all: to thine own self be true.' These words spoken by Polonius, the aged politician, are often taken up by mavericks, self-starters, karaoke singers of 'My Way' and people who generally like to believe that they paddle their own canoes through life. Earlier in this book I used the expression literally, asking people to know themselves as they really are, but many of those who hijack Shakespeare do not realise that he was, to say the least, being faintly ironic when he made the elderly windbag voice these words. Polonius has less insight and less personal scrupulousness in his actions than just about anyone in the whole play, including the usurping king, Claudius himself. At least Claudius is capable of self (serving) knowledge. Unlike the devious and manipulative Claudius, Polonius remains totally ignorant of the consequences of his actions, not least because his idea of himself is so completely at odds with the reality of his behaviour that he has no way of joining the dots and predicting the outcome of his actions. Having unwittingly caused chaos, he dies precisely because he has not been true to himself. He has not acted in accordance with his own deceitful nature and fails to recognise that if he sets up a web of espionage, eavesdropping, disguise and trickery (he even stoops so low that he sets spies on his own son) he is just as likely as anyone else to be hoist with his own petar. And so he famously dies, stabbed through the arras he has been hiding behind, as he spies upon his own assassin.

Low self-awareness

Less harmful (probably) than Bamboo Man, less tragic than Polonius, but as lacking in self-knowledge as either, and therefore as incapable of modelling what he promoted (he couldn't walk the talk any more than many politicians) was the man I met on a course for executive trainers who literally embodied the difficulties of having very little self-awareness in an almost comical way.

A dozen of us were meeting for a seminar one wet winter's evening. He and I almost collided on the pavement outside the seminar building as the giant umbrella he was using as a weather shield prevented him from seeing anyone in his path. In his polite attempt to make amends by ushering me through the door before him, he not only flung the door far too hard backwards so that it hit me on the rebound, he also semi-inundated me with the rain from the umbrella he was simultaneously shaking and closing within the same doorway. As we started to take our places around a large conference table, he then knocked over his chair, followed, in the act of putting his briefcase down, by his water glass, which created a nice little flood among the tidily arrayed brochures and notepads on the desktop, and finally he emptied the contents of his unsecured briefcase over the lot. Once everything had been mopped up and rearranged we finally went around the table introducing ourselves to each other, variously, as media trainer, communications expert, style guru and so on, with my umbrella man referring to himself as – an international crisis management expert! Hmm …

It was a comical enough episode, but he did, rather worryingly, work at quite a senior level in the Middle East, among other global arenas. Let's just hope that lack of joined-up thinking where his own body was concerned didn't translate into an equal lack of awareness about other people's capabilities and intentions.

Respect, man

'Respect, man' is another double standard that would confuse the innocent child or alien anthropologist. A number of young men in our inner cities have actually been killed for failing to 'show respect' for another person. Could a language lose more meaning than this, when a word that implies consideration for the rights of others is used as an excuse for taking away someone's fundamental right to live? Of course, what is really meant by respect in this particular context is fear. It's just that the people using the term are themselves fearful of being brutally honest with themselves about their own motivations. They minimise, through a perversion of language, the cruel, primitive or self-serving codes by which they live.

One of the most unpleasant, and at the same time pathetic, examples of this kind of doublespeak that I have ever come across was in the seg, or segregation unit, of a prison in which I was working. The sex offender on whom I was carrying out an assessment kept asking me about the power of codeine, questioning if it could make you do strange things, because, as he put it, he only did 'silly things' when he was taking codeine for back pain. I said that I doubted a painkiller intended for general use would be potent enough to desensitise anyone to such an extent. His crime? The serial raping of his own daughter.

Language, the great provider of meaning, and perhaps the ultimate 'get out' clause of meaning, too.

Bullying

Once we humans get the bit between our teeth on an issue, we can really gallop off. The default position nowadays is that if someone *feels* they have been bullied and claims that they have been bullied, then that must indeed be the case – no question, they have been bullied. As we have no working definition of bullying it can be used with impunity. It can even, ironically, be used to bully into abject silence anyone who is querying the truth behind an accusation of bullying.

One college student who didn't get his own way over an issue of dress (he regularly went to classes wearing a beanie pulled down low over his eyes and a lecturer refused to teach him unless he removed it during class time) accused his lecturer of threatening and bullying behaviour. The matter was investigated at some length, with co-students being questioned (the incident was a public one and the lecturer was completely exonerated). The lecturer's counter-claim that the student had come up to her privately after class and threatened to have her dismissed if she didn't let him have his way, and that in addition, based on considerable other evidence, she believed that he had severe mental health problems, was completely ignored. A good lecturer gave up the profession in disgust and a profoundly disturbed young man, a serial complainant about bullying whose evidence was never called into question, was found dead some years later in a lonely bedsit. His body had lain there, unnoticed and unmissed, for three weeks.

To suggest that some victims may have problems of their own and that contemporary 'issues' can get in the way of a better understanding of human behaviour, and may sometimes lead to dark consequences, is not to imply that bullying isn't a real and deeply damaging experience for thousands of people (of which the Bamboo Man or the urban agenda of 'respect' are evidence). It's just that it's never enough to use a single concept word as a simplistic diagnosis of a problem. We need to join up our thinking with a whole lot of evidence, otherwise we run the risk of misunderstanding genuine cause and effect and thus of failing to pre-empt problems.

There is also sometimes a hint, in that single issue way of dealing with difficult social behaviour, of the same self-serving emotional gratification ('We've done the right thing, aren't we wonderful?') that I talked about in the section on sentimentality.

Case study: Diana, Princess of Wales

This brings me to what may be a very contentious topic indeed: Diana, Princess of Wales. Much has been written about her and there are so many complicated emotions about her short but troubled life that I only want to take a quick look at the aspects of her story that resonate with my general theme.

Emotional self-indulgence, sentimentality and doublespeak

Diana and her siblings were clearly negatively affected by the break-up of their parents' marriage and by the subsequent behaviour of both mother and father. All the children of that marriage, by report, have had emotional problems that betrayed themselves either through their relationships with food (anorexia and bulimia) or with partners (her brother has been married three times and Diana's problems in this area have been only too well advertised), and it is very easy to sympathise with their situation. Essentially they were the victims of poor parenting. The consequences to them were that they were left with a compromised sense of significance, poor coping skills and a desperate need for emotional validation. However, understanding and sympathising with the emotional and psychological background of someone's flawed behaviour does not necessarily mean condoning and encouraging it, and yet condoned and encouraged it was both by certain sections of the press and by Diana's most fanatical, partisan and sentimental followers.

Given her childhood experiences, emotional self-indulgence was at the core of Diana's behaviour throughout her life in the public domain – it even formed a key part of her appeal in a time that put sentimentality first. What could have been more worthy than a glamorous and beautiful but doomed romantic victim (think of that Taj Mahal photo opportunity)? Certainly not the rather dull royal family with its code of duty before emotion.

Looked at with a hopefully unsentimental eye one can see that Diana and her brother were both working to an agenda that put emotional indulgence and avoidance of personal responsibility to the forefront and duty to scrupulous integrity rather towards the back. Both claimed that the British Royal Family was cold and wholly and uniquely responsible for all that had gone wrong for Diana. Both credited themselves with having not only far bigger hearts but also far more honourable intentions. And yet, in reality, both appear to have been operating to double standards. Charles Spencer had apparently been quite neglectful of at least one of his own spouses, and Diana somehow managed to square her heart-break at Prince Charles's infidelity with an apparent emotional insouciance whenever she became the 'third person' in another woman's marriage. Whose hearts? Whose honour?

Then there was the matter of loving her children to bits. No doubt at all, Diana loved her sons in her own way, but she was the child of quite impressively thoughtless parents herself. Given the first principles of caring (outlined in Chapter 3), you would have to ask, what or whom is a young woman thinking of when she throws her body downstairs while carrying a new life inside it? Likewise, when she parades her victim status for the whole universe to emote over, seemingly careless of the effect this might have on the emotional development of her children? Yet she always claimed that they were her first and only real concern. Rather as most of my prisoners did.

Finally (poor woman), there is the aspect of Diana's life that relates to a much earlier theme, which is to do with the meanings implicit in language use, particularly the ways in which pronoun use can indicate the way a brain models the world and how relationships within it work. In her last interview with *Le Monde* (Cojean, 1997) Diana said the following things:

I feel close to people, whoever they might be. We are all the same, to begin with, on the same wavelength …

This is why I disturb certain people because I am much closer to people down there than people higher up …

[I have] really close relations with the most humble people.

Despite Diana's protestations, this language is not only resolutely hierarchical, it is also resolutely self-referential in its repeated use of the first-person singular and its relegation of all others to an anonymous group of 'people'. Other giveaways of the lack of core consistency which allowed her to believe one thing of herself while expressing another, and which no doubt helped contribute to her mood problems and impulsive (not to say, compulsive) pursuit of new relationships, can be found throughout the interview she gave to Martin Bashir for Panorama ('that' interview), in 1995. There are shifting tenses which betray her vagueness as to where an idea or episode belongs in time. There are inappropriate conjunctions suggesting that some ideas don't click together securely. Then there is her habit of objectifying people; she refers to 'drug addicts, alcoholism, battered this, battered that', in spite of her repeated assertions that the lives of individuals are really important to her. She also routinely uses locating language, even while protesting that she never thinks about the position of anything, and maintains that she has been 'put in', 'placed in', 'found myself in' unwanted situations, despite other statements she makes declaring that she feels both strong and empowered.

There was a tremendous disparity between the intended message, the substance of what she actually said and the way in which she said it. To some extent this could have been the outcome of Diana having been coached into conveying a message which was not authentically hers. This is often a dead giveaway if you know what you are looking for, but the average person doesn't and so they can easily be drawn into sharing such delusions.

As I keep stressing, true core consistency, achieved when someone has a strong sense of self and an authentic vision of how things fit together (a strong set of neural connections which are regularly reinforced by experience), is expressed in coherent, consistent and joined-up language as well as in autonomous and joined-up behaviour.

Poor Diana. Hers was a tragic example of how incoherent and fragmented, but also how egotistically toxic a person can become when early experiences fail to provide the appropriate conditions in which protective core consistency may grow and flourish.

Case study: Charles Dickens

Another person who for many years was seen, pretty much uncritically, as a force for social good, an emotional benefactor even, was Charles Dickens. He was the man who, almost single-handedly, changed attitudes to Christmas, social deprivation and considerations of morality in Victorian England, and so, by extension, morality in modern Britain. His legacy was universally admired and applauded, and it would still be a brave and churlish person who took significant issue with it. Or maybe an alien anthropologist.

The alien anthropologist might suggest that Dickens was, in fact, also responsible for a sentimentality about the plight of the young that has ever since impacted on the way that child development has been viewed and on the presumptions made about the effect of particular approaches to child management. For Dickens (at least in his novels) there was no doubt that some kind of exposure (however tangential) to sound, solidly middle-class mores should lead almost axiomatically to an innocence in children that, given the reality of the non-existent or abusive parenting his youthful creations experienced, would have been highly improbable.[8] How likely is it that Oliver Twist, raised in an orphanage in conditions of extreme deprivation, would have developed into so benign, so open and so naive a child? The truth is that he would have been much more likely to end up damaged, difficult and ungrateful, and behaving much as Dickens himself actually did in adult life.

The reason that Dickens is so unreliable as a psychological, if not a social, commentator is that in his writing, as in his life, he (like a number of other people) never really moved away from his emotional and psychological comfort zone. This was all about redressing the wrongs of his childhood and getting retaliation on his own very irresponsible, feckless and selfish parents. (His father bankrupted the family and was sent to prison. Meanwhile, his mother insisted that Charles, aged 11 or 12, went to work in a blacking factory and tried to force him to remain working there once their finances had actually improved.) He got his retaliation in by very creatively turning nearly all the parent figures featured in his novels into monstrous caricatures who, either foolishly or semi-malevolently, betray their children's trust.

His abandoned child victim heroes, with the exception of a few more nuanced ones who appear towards the end of his writing career, such as Pip in *Great Expectations*, are always innocent middle-class spirits, with conventional sensibilities and an almost complete lack of guile. Their completely unprovoked sufferings lead them eventually to becoming both champions of the oppressed and the highly principled husbands of virtuous (if often childlike) brides. The good are nearly always rewarded (excluding the most poignant,

---

8   Both 'lower order' children and 'high born' ones are allowed far greater latitude in terms of character deficiencies and dubious moral codes than are his resolutely middle-class ones.

who usually die) and the bad are nearly always punished (including the most sexually voracious, who usually die).

However, what we know now, but which many Victorian readers did not know, is that Dickens was himself a rotten husband. He emotionally abused and then abandoned his loyal wife, the mother to his ten children, and lived a double life with his much younger mistress. He was also a demanding, critical and unforgiving father to several of his own children, particularly his sons.

The moral behind this story is that when a creative person is made to feel invalid, or that they are of little or no significance, when they are young, they are very likely to try to validate themselves through their work. They do this by putting their own dilemmas and sensibilities at the heart of their imagined worlds; in a sense, parenting their younger selves rather better than their true parents ever did. The unconscious nature of this process seems to allow for even greater evangelism on the part of the writer, as it's often so much easier and more permissible to feel all fired up with righteous indignation on behalf of others than it is on one's own part. The unconscious evangelising agenda may even be an important part of the creative process itself, designed to extend the writer's significance far and wide.

The question that perhaps we should be asking is whether buying a worldview, or even a set of social or psychological principles, from people with such personal, perhaps narrow or even misguided purposes (even if unconsciously), is a safe thing to do. This seems an important question when the people trying to influence our responses and thinking are so very good in the language department (remember Elizabeth Loftus and her work on eye-witness testimony in Chapter 6).

Dickens was hardly alone in resolving deep trauma to the sense of self through his art. Perhaps even more misleading has been the impact such trauma resolution has had on some of women's deepest desires.

Case study: Jane Austen, George Eliot and the Brontës

At the heart of the so-called romantic fiction of women writers, such as Jane Austen, George Eliot and the Brontë sisters, is not the sugary fantasy beloved of movie-goers over the years. When you dig more forensically you find that theirs is not so much the story of passionate love for a romantic hero, as the story of gaining a sense of significance for themselves by dint of gaining mastery over the hearts of the men who otherwise controlled the authors' lives (in their cases, usually fathers and brothers, not lovers), thereby ultimately gaining greater control over their own historically circumscribed lives.

This is quite complex, and may only be of interest to literary geeks, but novels from *Pride and Prejudice* to *The Mill on the Floss* and *Jane Eyre* all have male pride as one of the central driving forces of the narrative, and they all feature fathers who fail their daughters. (Well, Jane Eyre's father is dead which is definitely a kind of failure to perform appropriately!) All, in one way or another, feature the emotional and/or physical humbling of the male. Brothers get physically harmed in both *The Mill on the Floss* and *Jane Eyre*; in the latter her brother (Richard Mason) is cannibalistically attacked by Bertha, the wilder and physically more overwhelming alter ego of the heroine. In all these novels, both situation and tension are only finally resolved once the male 'hero' figures have actually prostrated themselves psychologically and/or physically to the 'heroine' women. Significance gets bought at quite a high price for the male, but maybe a price that women felt they had been paying for generations.

These actually rather odd and deeply implausible works have had a huge influence over the thinking and expectations of generations of women, old, young and younger still. They still do. I know of at least two young women, one German and one Italian, who threw up everything in their home countries and came to study in English universities after having had one single exposure to Andrew Davies's 1995 serialisation of *Pride and Prejudice*. Intellectually they were far too bright to believe that a man could make them feel that significant, but that didn't stop them quietly nurturing the fantasy that Mr Darcy would be here, waiting to make sense of their lives.

I think it can safely be said that all three authors did become people of great significance in the end, but what was their true legacy? A shelf full of wonderful reading or several generations of women who firmly believe that their deep need for significance is best met by one single consuming relationship with a man?

Even today, a number of authors still seem to exhibit an unconscious drive to 'write' the wrongs that have been done to them. They wish to take control of the uncontrolled forces of the past and use this process to achieve a very personal sense of evangelising for the good of the future. It's not only through creative writing that this process can be worked out; two non-fiction writers, both very influential in their spheres, spring readily to mind: Gitta Sereny and Alice Miller.

Case study: Gitta Sereny

Gitta Sereny has written highly controversial biographies of the Nazi monsters of evil, Albert Speer and Franz Stangl, of the youthful child murderer Mary Bell and at length about the child murderers of Jamie Bulger. In most of her writing she concludes that there were causes other than what might be called original sin or natural evil for the killers' actions. She worked hard to attribute their behaviour to social influences and to abuse in early life (as is so often the case, never really addressing that vexed question about why other people with similar backgrounds failed to turn out in quite the same sadistic way). This has made for some very angry readers. The persistence she has demonstrated in her attempts to reclaim these people from the simplistic verdicts of evil and sinful which society has placed on them seemed to spring from more than just an objective compulsion to discover pragmatic cause and effect. Rather, it seemed to have its roots in the very complicated relationship that she had with her own pre-war Jewish childhood and adolescence in Vienna.

Sereny's father died when she was young and there were suggestions of maternal abuse. So it's possible that she was going to be more comfortable attributing her own early romantic attraction to the charisma and pageantry associated with the Nazis, and a later repudiation of her own Jewishness, to infant trauma rather than to some autonomous self. It's also possible that by taking on or even taking over the stories (Speer, Stangl, Bell and others) of an evil that seemed to be beyond any human control or influence, she experienced the same sort of frisson that a person might feel when breaking in a wild stallion – the frisson of being more than others: more capable, more in control, more significant. No doubt, she also reclaimed some kind of sense that she could understand and handle the darker side of her own life (and her own psyche).

To make up for a neglected childhood, Diana, Princess of Wales achieved the love of half the known world. To make up for an abandoned and impoverished childhood, Charles Dickens brought sentiment to child psychology and created a universe of innocent and improbably unbrutalised orphans who only awaited a cheery-faced saviour to become fully fledged Liberal Democrats. And to make up for an emotionally dark and complex past, Gitta Sereny reconfigured monstrousness, if not into beauty then at least into a psychological rather than a moral scar on the body of humanity.

But what about my final example of someone who was as remarkable for the awfulness of her own childhood experiences as she was for the influence she had over a generation (at least) of parents around the world? What was psychologist, Alice Miller, making up for?

Case study: Alice Miller

It is a matter of record that Alice Miller split with the psychoanalytic movement and wholly repudiated its principles. However, in a preface to a later work she writes that it then took her fifteen years to escape from 'the labyrinth of self-deception and *self-accusation*' (Miller, 1978: viii; my italics). Although the details appear to be sketchy, it seems that this Polish Jew, whose father died in a Warsaw ghetto, carried with her throughout her life a most awful burden of guilt, because by changing her identity and passing herself off as a Christian at her own mother's insistence, she had lived freely outside the ghetto and survived the war.

One of her books, *The Drama of Being a Child* (Miller, 1995) was tellingly subtitled *The Search for the True Self*. She regularly and repeatedly asserted both that childhood trauma was endemic and that disguise and denial of the bleak truth of childhood was behind most of the psychological problems of the day. This, in itself, would be a perfectly understandable stance if she had based her analysis of certain types of aberrant human behaviour around the sad facts of her own life, but she didn't. She spread her net much wider than that and conjured up a wholesale abuse of childhood itself, evidenced by numerous examples of what she called 'oppressive' coercion.

One particular example of oppression which Miller used to prove her point seems to sum up both the essential monomania that comes with the territory of righting the wrongs of one's youth and the simple wrong-headedness of applying one's own sense of grievance to the business of training another generation in child-rearing practices – another generation that has a wholly different background and set of emotional criteria. In *Banished Knowledge: Facing Childhood Injuries* (1988), she describes a situation in which a young mother sent her 3-year-old son to stay with her own mother. He returned upset and aggrieved. On both grandmother and child being questioned, it appeared that he had been put out at being gently reprimanded for helping himself to seconds of his favourite pudding without first asking permission. His grandmother wanted him to learn good manners and to consider the possible needs of others before he gratified himself.

The mother (and, by extension, the extraordinarily indignant author herself) saw this thwarting of his desires and his will as 'toxic pedagogy' and as an abuse of the power an adult holds over a child. Both of them regarded this small boy's development of self-generated self-control and courtesy around food as an inevitable adjunct of the maturing process, and believed that expecting him, in the meantime, to restrain his impulse to eat whenever and whatever he wanted, was also to expect him to submit to:

> an incomprehensible law that takes away my appetite, puts me under stress, and gives me feelings of guilt and shame, a law in whose hands I am totally powerless. Depending on later development, the result can be lifelong digestive troubles and a variety of eating compulsions and cravings that lead to anorexia or bulimia. (Miller, 1988: 154–155)

His grandmother, who had herself presumably lived through the war, obviously did not believe (as the title of that chapter firmly states) that 'the child sets limits', nor that all children, when not subjected to the poisonous restrictions of adults, will happily apply natural laws of restraint, courtesy and consideration for others to their behaviour.

Leaving aside the outcome of years of Miller's own pedagogy, which many people would say has now resulted in a very unhappy generation or two of youngsters who are unable to exercise any such self-control (and also leaving to the next chapter the marshmallow findings which suggest that the ability to exercise restraint from a very young age will lead to many more, rather than fewer, mental health benefits), it is interesting to consider the rationale of Miller's attack on what she calls 'pedagogic parenting'. In this chapter she reflects on her own childhood, saying that:

> I understood yet again that the tragedy of my childhood lay not only in my being afraid to offer resistance, but above all *in the impossibility of my realising what was happening.* When I entitled my books *For Your Own Good* and *Thou Shalt Not Be Aware*, little did I know how much of my own history was embraced by these titles. (ibid.: 154)

I would go much further than Miller and say that little did she ever seem to realise how much of her own guilt about changing her identity, and so surviving (for her own good?), shaped and coloured her need to blame the parent figure, in general, for the guilty feelings of one particular child. Her subtext is that if a parent imposes their will on a child, even if 'for their own good', then that child should never have to harbour feelings of guilt about the outcome. Or, as it might be, 'I, Alice Miller, am in no way accountable (however badly I feel about this deep inside) for the deaths of my family members, while I survived, because this survival was forced on me by unreasonable adult pedagogy, for my own good and against all my instincts and inclinations.'

Connecting the dots

Perhaps that sounds overly harsh and critical, but better to be critical than to buy in to easy but illusory beliefs. It's the equivalent of hoping that a Sunday lie-in might actually do you as much good as an early morning run. Recognising true cause and effect, being consistent, following through, being scrupulous about motivations and subsequent behaviour, staying on message with oneself – these things all take clear thinking, a good bit of effort and quite a lot of courage at times. But most important of all, in the context of this book, they are all the outcome of joined-up thinking, rather than dotty and significance-seeking processes, and they ultimately lead to better outcomes all round.

Miller's impassioned rejection of toxic pedagogy and the enforcement of food rules on children may have made sense to her and to a generation that bought into the principle that children should make more autonomous decisions about their food intake, but does her argument that children know what's best for them (and by implication, what works best for the future of the world) still make sense? Especially in the light of the Mumsnet statistic which, in the same month that the Institution of Mechanical Engineers said that half the food produced worldwide ends up as waste, tells us that only 12% of parents have a rule that their children eat everything on their plate?[9]

Then there's the US research which shows that burnout from over-empathising with hospital patients is actually driving nurses

---

9   See Institution of Mechanical Engineers (2013) and the Mumsnet Family Meals Survey at: http://www.mumsnet.com/food-content/family-meals-survey-2013.

from the profession (Klimecki and Singer, 2012). Is this equally a tribute to the contemporary prioritisation of 'emotional sharing' over practical actions; an emotional imperative that loves kids to bits or wants to be a queen of people's hearts?

At present, we appear to have an almost blind faith in the power of emotion, that semi-house-trained polecat, to produce only good intentions and good outcomes. That's already very unjoined-up thinking. But when that faith is married to an evangelising tendency the end result can be positively (well, negatively, actually) delusional and damaging. Among the astonishing variety of people in the last century who followed spiritualism – the belief that the spirits of the dead freely roamed the earth and could communicate with the living – was Sir Arthur Conan Doyle. Apart from being the creator of the most famous analytical mind in the history of literature, he was also medically trained. Nevertheless, he was so zealous in his commitment that he was known as the 'St Paul' of spiritualism, and he encouraged his many followers to share his strongly emotional belief that loved ones killed in the First World War could and would return to communicate with them. Was that a kindness or a delusional cruelty?

Joined-up thinking may often, at first sight, seem hard, which in a way it is, not least because it belongs largely in the left hemisphere, which likes sequences better than it likes emoting. Ultimately, joined-up thinking may lead to better or even happier outcomes than thinking which deals on an ad hoc basis with the needs of the moment, especially when these are emotional needs. Only when we work through some of the probable implications and consequences of our attitudes and actions can we make more informed decisions. These decisions are also far more likely to be more emotionally and socially responsible.

On occasion, dotty thinking can be delightful. It can be maverick and motivational. But because it doesn't operate within a frame of reference, or submit itself to checks and balances by very many external influences, it can also be quite severely delusional. Joined-up thinking, on the other hand, while sometimes seeming somewhat deterministic, at least has the merit of connecting us rather better to the shared delusion that is at the heart of mutant man's evolution. And it is ultimately the sharing of the delusion that results in our best chances of surthrival. Which brings us back to the main thread of the book …

Chapter 7

Sharing the Delusion

What complex social reasons might lead to a breakdown in culturally shared values and expectations of agreement with, and
engagement in, community behaviours?

A Tuscan cautionary tale

San Gimignano is a typically gorgeous Tuscan hilltop town, famed
for its dramatic skyline of fifteen medieval towers, its wines, its sun-
shine, its glorious views across cypress-dotted hills and ice cream so
good that former Prime Minister Tony Blair once wrote a letter
praising it to the gelateria owner (he keeps the letter in a frame).
What's not to like about such a romantic place?

Well, perhaps very little today, but in his book to accompany the
TV series *Francesco's Italy*, Francesco Da Mosto (2006), architect,
historian and filmmaker, suggests that we might have thought very
differently about San Gimignano had we lived there in the thirteenth century – unless we had been members of its powerful and
power-hungry elite.

In the thirteenth century, San Gimignano had seventy-two towers, not the mere fifteen we see today. These towers were built as the
totems, the signatures, of the powerful families which had both
strong commercial interests in the town and a penchant for showing
off their wealth and their power.

Tuscans had long built defensive towers against neighbouring
towns. This was quite normal because towns in Italy were, in effect,
like competing foreign states. But in San Gimignano the practice
had turned in on itself. The great families of the town ended up not
only competing for business far more fiercely against each other
than against neighbouring towns, but also building towers that went
ever higher – more to impress or intimidate one another than for
any rational defensive reasons.

As well as being highly visible signs of personal supremacy, the
towers were also, clearly, an implicit threat to the rights and

resources of the rest of the townspeople – the ones who didn't have the influence or the wealth to build towers of their own. Not only did they cast a shadow over the town by their very existence, but they also made it abundantly clear that most of its civic rights were reserved for those who could, metaphorically, shout the loudest.

Of course, the town's energies were dissipated by all this effort and expenditure. Over time, most of the towers collapsed, but not before the wealth and the welfare of the whole place had been compromised by this absurd quest for supremacy, this pursuit of individual advancement over the common good.

Da Mosto contrasts San Gimignano's rather dark and territorial past with the more gilded history of Siena. Another medieval Tuscan town, Siena had a radically different approach to the organisation of its society – not least because it actually *had* an approach to the organisation of its society. San Gimignano's development, such as it was, happened by means of family rivalry and vested interest. But Siena, in the thirteenth century, was far more organisationally advanced; it established an elected body, the Council of Nine, to run the city. The council had to be re-elected every two months, which had the very great advantage that it was almost impossible to corrupt and so was able to institute reforms in the general interest rather than for the benefit of vested interests.

The council appears to have been enlightened in many ways, providing for both welfare and education. As part of its drive to eliminate factions, it also insisted on the removal of all family insignia throughout Siena and on the demolition of all pre-existing totems of personal power, including Siena's own fortified towers. And perhaps even more significantly, the civic authorities specifically expected citizens to identify more closely with the society they belonged to than with their traditional family groups. To this end, instead of the architecture of the town being intimate and shadowy, as in so many medieval towns throughout Europe, it was cleverly designed to draw pedestrians into an increasingly wide series of streets, which finally turned towards a great *civic* open space, the Campo. Unlike most Italian towns which would have a great cathedral as the town's centrepiece, Siena's Campo had a vast public building, the Palazzo Pubblico. As Da Mosto (2006: 95) writes, 'Siena was designed with the idea that each citizen would be constantly reminded that he was just one small part of a greater whole.'

The systematic attempt to create a city of peace, stability, good governance and prosperity worked well for several centuries. It worked far better and much more fairly as a society than San

Gimignano ever could, given its individual family power bases and their accompanying practices of intimidation and self-promotion, until, eventually, the plague, that great scourge of the Middle Ages, killed roughly two-thirds of the population. Death, in the end, levelled everything in both these towns.

Are we all tribal now?

Of course, the best we could hope for now, if we wanted to avoid the problems listed in Chapter 1, is for the earth to become a seven billion strong version of thirteenth-century Siena, but that just isn't going to happen. It's all a question of proportion. Siena worked not only because the behaviour of its citizens was planned, organised and controlled but also because it was capable of being considered, more or less, as a single community of interest and operation. With the best will in the world it would be difficult for most of us to think of seven billion as any form of single unit.

It could be argued that the families – which Siena wanted to disempower and which San Gimignano was intimidated and overwhelmed by – were also single units of a sort, with a shared interest and operational structure at their heart. But the problem was that the shared interest was too exclusive – too many other people had to be recruited to support the system, without equal benefit to themselves. Shared values, shared interests and shared benefits – or at the very least a belief in those things (as the prerequisites of any agreement with, and engagement in, community behaviour) – are at the heart of a successful society. People must have faith that there is a greater good than that which applies to their immediate circle of interest or blood ties.

Or, to put it in the context of this book, people must believe in both the significance of the greater community to them and the likelihood that they can, personally, feel more significant within that community than without (in both senses of the word). Only then can they put tower-building ambitions to one side and redirect their energies and their trust into the wider community – the greater good.

My big question now is, have we, in much of our advanced world, forsaken the greater good for more local, personal/emotional and tribal interests? Are we too busy building higher and higher towers to notice that there are rather a lot of figures wandering around in the shadows on the ground?

The towers, the towers

Special interest groups, protest groups, subgroups, religions, sects, clubs, political parties – these are the tribes of today. They represent tribal interests and they give us that sense of belonging to something bigger than ourselves, which is so necessary for surthrival. Far from emulating Siena, though, they're more like the tower builders of San Gimignano, bigging up each interest group they represent higher than the next one, competing with one another for influence and resources. I'm sure many of them would argue against this loudly but they tend to fragment rather than support the interests of the whole. However, given some of the reports we read online and in print, it's hardly surprising that so many people feel that they get more support and satisfaction from belonging to these rather narrow groupings than from the so-called 'wider community' – which, despite politicians' apparent support, has somehow managed to allow the following outrages to happen:

Body lay in managed flat for five months (*The Telegraph*, July 2013)

'At least in Auschwitz I have friends. In here I have nobody' (an elderly Polish patient's last words before she dies at the scandal-hit Stafford Hospital – *Sunday Times*, February 2013)

Widow of 81 starved to death after council forgot about her for nine days: It did nothing when care agency was shut by police (*Daily Mail*, February 2013)

In the coda to Chapter 6, I wrote about a young man who was so alienated from other people that his dead body lay undiscovered in his flat for several weeks. In his case it was at least clear that he had few friends left and there was no one to look out for him. The truly weird thing about the first of these three headlines (apart from the fact that the flat was supposedly under the management of a social landlord, Twin Valley Homes) is that we read part way down *The Telegraph*'s report:

They also found a Christmas tree, and mouldy food, suggesting that her body had been there for some time.

Her sister … said she had tried to call 62-year-old Mrs Sharples in *November* but failed. She then telephoned Twin Valley Homes … to ask them to check on her. (my italics)

Speaking at the hearing, she said, '*Me and our Margaret were very close*. I knew there was something wrong.' (my italics)

Mrs Sharples' body was not found until April – the following spring. In what conceivable universe does that constitute being 'very close'? It is not necessary to live next door to someone to remain in closer contact than that.

Still, as we've already seen, people are remarkably adept at deceiving themselves, especially when it's in their interests to do so. In this case, the probable cause of neglect, the real culprit, was the growing belief that some (maybe most) things are best dealt with by specialists. So Mrs Sharples' sister did not see it as part of her sisterly remit to take on a professional's job. No doubt, she expected it to be taken care of in 'the community' by appropriately trained and qualified staff.

It all comes back (inevitably) to significance, to what we see as the meaning of our place in life and in the wider world. When we subscribe, or are subscribed – by birth, culture and so forth – to a group, whether that group is a national one (a country), what might be called a cultural one (a political or religious group) or even a variant of a cultural one (subgroups like eco-warriors, football fans or goths), then we *become* significant, both by belonging, per se, and by actively subscribing to its norms and activities. We find significance in its tenets; by following them we feel validated. Thus group culture should always be good for our surthrival.[1]

However, there is a corollary to this: dropping out of a group is very bad for us. If people have no inclination to link to subgroups, and their local 'wider society' does not function efficiently or caringly enough for them to appear on its radar, then those such as Mrs Sharples will continue to be let down. We need to encourage the development of systems which keep people enmeshed and interdependent, with mutual benefits accruing all round as we work for the *common* good. In other words, enlightened societies benefit from using the Siena model.

---

1   There are important questions being asked about the benefits to society of the hormone oxytocin (which helps us to feel more closely bonded to small groups). More on this in Chapter 9.

My parking hell – another cautionary tale

Well, I exaggerate a little. It was more annoying than hellish, but it was illustrative all the same. One Sunday morning I parked my car on a single yellow line in a side street in a small Surrey market town, somewhere I'd parked before. There was already a car there when I arrived, so I had no reason to think anything had changed and blithely went off to the shops. I wasn't away long but on returning I found a yellow sticker on my windscreen demanding £35 within a month or £70 thereafter. I'll spare you the details of my immediate response. I expect we have all shared that moment of dawning real-isation and the accompanying frisson of bloodlust.

I thought the fine unreasonable as it had not been made plain that new parking restrictions applied. To be strictly accurate there were signs indicating when parking was permitted, but these did not draw particular attention either to themselves or to the fact that they were replacing previous ones which had allowed Sunday parking. Once I'd calmed down a bit I decided that my best course of action was to be courteous and throw myself on the council's sense of reasonableness (!). I wrote to them begging forgiveness, said it would never happen again and pointed out that I had been ignorant, not contemptuous, in my behaviour, and would they please overlook it this once, and bear in mind that small towns didn't need to drive away what goodwill they still had – nor hapless but harmless shop-pers who hadn't read every local authority notice in the local papers.

The council rejected my plea, largely on the grounds that I should have known the change in policy as it had been in place for several months, and in any case I should have read the parking signs properly. They added that I could take the matter further, but then I would lose the option of paying the reduced fine should I still be found liable. So I paid up. I then rang up the local parking officer to complain. I explained again that I hadn't known of the change and thought they were being draconian.

This is where my tragic story becomes relevant. He responded by saying that my plea was groundless, especially as the single line pol-icy had been in place for ages. I responded that months was not quite ages. Then he acknowledged that he wasn't actually familiar with the specifics of the situation in the town as he was only an interim manager and had just arrived from Bristol. His job was completely divorced in any meaningful sense from the location in which he was implementing policy. Consequently, he had little knowledge of local conditions (while still expecting me to be thoroughly familiar, please note) and he was also on a career trajectory that involved moving from place to place, so there was no expectation that he should have either an interest in, or even an overview of, the specific needs of the area.

He was, in other words, a *specialist*, a parking specialist. His area of concern was making sure parking, in whichever area he happened to find himself, followed certain set procedures. He was doing a specialist's job, and although it was nominally a public interest job, the main significance of the job, as far as he was concerned, was probably twofold: it was a career move and it was about parking protocols. Either way, it had very little to do with the wider needs of that local community. Enmeshed? Interdependent? Mutual benefits? Common good? No.

High streets have died this way. It's about living according to the high-minded (high-handed?) principle that only specialists have the appropriate qualities plus the right to take certain responsibilities on to themselves. This is not just how communities die, but also the way lonely and marginalised people like Mrs Sharples die. You can't really blame her sister for simply knowing her place.

At some points in history, when communities were more self-determining than they are today and when people were either less bullied into conforming with laissez-faire principles or were more certain of a grass-roots cultural consensus, individuals felt freer to intervene – 'to poke their noses in' as someone like Arthur Seaton, Alan Sillitoe's anti-hero in *Saturday Night and Sunday Morning*, would have said. Their main aim was not popularity but a sense of doing what was right, however restrictive and judgemental that might sound in these more enlightened times. And they were not afraid to do what they thought was right. Now, after years of Arthur Seaton insisting that that sort of behaviour is a breach of other people's freedoms, and the professionalisation of keeping the peace and other related social controls ('We don't want the public endangering themselves by getting involved – leave these matters to the experts'), we are not only scared of popping our heads above the parapet, in case we are either getting in the way or judged to be judgemental, but we also live with the consequences of no one expecting us to get involved. Old ladies die hungry and alone, gangs steam with impunity through packed railway carriages, small children are daily brutalised, injured and killed by their parents, and yet no one sees (or pokes their nose in). Are we all looking the other way?

Design for living

The more we specialise, split interests, divorce society's elements one from another, create subsections, factions, areas of separate operational, financial, ethical and cultural concern, the more we lose sight of the common goal, the common good, and the more towers we build. It's a self-perpetuating fragmentation of society, as the less significance we get out of the wider society, the more likely we are to join narrower ones. And there is another possibility: lacking the availability of either a large and like-minded community or a warm and embracing subculture, then total alienation may set in. The outcome, doubtless, of the complete dopamine-less inertia that comes with feeling there is *no* significance in life at all: we belong nowhere, we mean nothing and we have no focus of interest.

Different ways of working

The difference between the two extreme positions – of having a common goal or no clear goal at all – is almost comically demonstrated by the diametrically different ways two historic factories operated. Factories are good analogies of society because, before they have even a reasonable chance of producing any kind of satisfactory outcome, they are completely dependent on people's commitment to working together and towards a common end. What follows are the stories of the yin and yang of the production line.

The first factory achieved that satisfactory outcome to quite a large extent. This was Etruria, Josiah Wedgwood's eighteenth-century pottery works in Stoke-on-Trent. It was one of the earliest buildings specifically created for the mass production of high-end goods. At Etruria, Wedgwood ran an innovative system designed to turn a single craftsman industry (in which the whole process of production from conception to finish had been carried out by one skilled person) into a series of separate activities. Although not the first to do this, it was certainly one of the most efficient and successful.

Briefly, he managed to mass produce goods which were as highly artistic and well executed as individually crafted goods. These goods had much wider public appeal and made money. He achieved this largely by paying constant and close attention to every part of the process, from the technicalities of the clay and the slips, to the design process itself, to the management of the workers and the marketing and sale of the goods. By being so closely involved and monitoring everything meticulously, he must have created the impression that each part of the process and every person responsible for it *mattered*, and that it and they were both significant and necessary to the end goal. Many of them would have felt that his micro-management was a bit oppressive. But feeling that you are significant is not necessarily the same thing as feeling that life is easy and comfortable – just ask any teenager if they're entirely happy about their parents continually asking what they're up to. Nevertheless, such attention does make them feel cared about, connected and, ultimately, that they are a valued and valuable member of their family. Concern means that you belong.

Wedgwood also kept his factory on message by keeping the finished product (the shared goal, the overall good, the vision) to the forefront of everyone's minds. He achieved this by recruiting the very best modellers to produce the finest blueprint models of his designs, so that all workers, at all stages of the process, knew exactly what the finished product should look like and knew exactly what they were aiming to achieve (which, of course, was the best). Unlike my parking specialist, Etruria's workers still had a sense of overall purpose, even while they were carrying out their specific specialist tasks.

Even Wedgwood, though, with all his commercial flair and insight into the absolute necessity of workers committing and conforming to a common goal, found he had problems with the modelling artists' desire to be special and different. They were nearly the undoing of the whole project, as he wrote to his business partner,

Oh! for a dozen good & *humble* modellers at Etruria for a couple of months ... for I will have no more *fine* modellers here, though I seem to wish for them, they would corrupt and ruin us all. I have been oblig'd to part with Radford. The hours he chose to work would, by the example, have ruin'd ten times better men than himself. (Farrer, 2011: 171; cited in Forty, 1986: 36)

Wedgwood finally resolved the problem of these resolutely maverick modellers by instead commissioning designs from the best designers outside his works, thus retaining the advantage of having a uniform design to work from while doing away with the negative impact of artistic egocentricity in the workforce.

It was a case of everyone pulling together for the common good, and the result was good in so many ways. But I'm not going to pretend that Wedgwood's was some kind of utopian venture, nor that all his workers had an equal financial or even emotional investment in the enterprise. I am simply looking at the benefit to the overall system of having those two advantages – a common goal and the close involvement of those leading or managing the system – as evidenced by their attention to detail and, more importantly, by their attention to the working practices and welfare of the community involved.

Compare the story of Wedgwood's innovations at Etruria with a story that came out of the USSR in the dog days of Communism. It made the 'you couldn't make it up' columns of British newspapers at the time.

Years of mind-numbing, unmonitored and unheeded work on the production lines of a far-flung shoe factory resulted in footwear that was even more perilous and unwearable than a pair of Louboutins, although probably a little cheaper. The outcome was as sad as it was surreal, and it came about because the poor benighted workers had been so relentlessly and repetitively doing tiny elements of the overall task of boot-making (no temperamental designers involved here) that the tedium led to a complete dissociation of self from the whole point of the factory's existence. The result being that for several weeks one shift spent their entire time happily attaching heels to the toe sections of the boots passing before their glazed eyes. And nobody noticed. Nobody noticed because everybody had become so alienated from the overall good that there was no clear purpose left, no clear goal. They found no significance in what they were doing or felt that they were of any significance in doing it. Who cared?

As I've suggested before, that way a kind of fragmenting and fragmented madness lies. The kaleidoscope people of Chapter 4 were fragmented and behaved in non-social (or at least not in pro-social) ways as a consequence of their fragmentation. (It could be argued that there's only a very fine line between Graham's actions in the episode that ended with him throwing away a new carpet and Soviet era workers mindlessly sticking heels on the toe end of boots.) On the whole, though, kaleidoscope people have fragmented through personal experiences which have left them individually unable to process significance in normal ways.

However, this chapter is about shared values and community behaviour, not individual actions, and the fragmentation the boot story demonstrates is a *group* experience. The whole Soviet group acted in a fragmented way because absolutely no one was rooting for significance. No one was joining the dots. No one was behaving in a pro-social way. There were no shared goals. And the consequence of this was a total breakdown in meaning and in any functional outcome. This was not a collection of kaleidoscope people at work; it was a whole kaleidoscope society not working.

Unlike those Soviet citizens, we can save ourselves from this kind of madness. In our mutantly driven search for meaning in life, we have opportunities to look beyond a politically, psychologically and emotionally impoverished state. And if society lets us down, we can still seek significance through the links we make with those relatively small groups mentioned earlier.

Our current popular perception is that the state is pretty unsatisfactory, even alienating (though fortunately not all-powerful). Mrs Sharples and all those betrayed and abandoned children show us that society has let us down. Nosey parkers are out of fashion, social workers out of compassion and Josiah Wedgwood isn't here to provide us with the design-for-living template that would make us all feel we shared a vision and were part of the plan.

We find it much more personally satisfying and comforting to make connections with people who do share our worldview, our financial or cultural interests, our hobbies, our politics, even our prejudices (no matter how narrow they might be) rather than with society as a whole. Our response is think small, turn in on ourselves and gain some sense of belonging with 'our kind of people'. The reward for bonding is some of that cuddle hormone, oxytocin, but let's remember that it doesn't have a wholly positive effect on our relationship with the rest of the world.

Bonding with small groups rather than large ones means that much more of the world falls into the category of out-group, for which we will feel very unbonded sensations and often end up bullying or neglecting. The vulnerable people who fail to make connections with any subgroups are then going to fall into most other people's out-groups and find themselves being almost universally dropped by the wayside of life. And that is a very powerful argument in favour of trying to rebuild a better version of the bigger society that someone famous once mentioned.

Redesign for living – what needs to change

It grieves me to say this, but to some extent we have to blame Shakespeare for the way things are at present. It was he who got us asking the question, 'To be, or not to be?' rather than, 'To do, or not to do?' It was his question that focused attention on the interior rather than the exterior life, the singular rather than the social, the experienced rather than the acted life. It was the beginning of a centuries long drift towards subjectivity, which these days has become more of a stampede. With the result that if we personally don't like something that is happening in our world, we now want to change everything about it. We believe in the supremacy of us and now, for why? Because we're worth it, goddammit!

The round table

We are no longer willing to put up with a less-than-perfect bigger society, with situations we haven't chosen and with people who aren't our kind. A curious and rather sad illustration of this trend involved the huge circular tables in the Pump Room at Bath – historically that most social of cities – at which social interactions between strangers had been enforced for a couple of hundred years. In recent times, though, it was thought more appropriate that these should be replaced by a greater number of smaller, more intimate and more exclusive tables which limited gatherings to four. There was a bit of an outcry by diehards at the time, but the inevitability of the final outcome was never really in doubt. Small and exclusive has become beautiful.

We no longer see greater value in those wider connections symbolised by the original Pump Room tables, in the naked exposure of ourselves to Other, except, of course, in cyberspace. In cyberspace people like to think of themselves as being globally connected, as linking up with the widest society possible. But how realistic is that perception?

According to research commissioned on behalf of healthcare provider, Benenden Health (2013), one in five people in Britain has not spoken to a stranger in six months, much preferring online communication. Of the two thousand participants in their research, 43% said they were more comfortable communicating online and a quarter said they relied on the web to reduce the need for face-to-face interaction. Many of them declared that small talk was unimportant, pointless or awkward. Clearly, these people did not feel that they owed any duty of social engagement for the good of maintaining the big society (presumably assuming at some deep level that their online community could and would provide for all their own present and future needs) and nor did they see any kind of problem in following their own inclinations and desires so unswervingly.

So it seems highly unlikely that they were making connections, even in cyberspace, with anyone following a totally different agenda from their own. In real life, even in today's world, we still have to make allowances for unexpected problems, put up with things (especially on public transport) and take on board other people's unpalatable opinions. But in cyberspace we can find a like-minded community, one that will offer very little challenge to our sense of self. Why engage with people on the train, or even watch how they're behaving, when you can insulate yourself completely behind your smartphone?

It's a bit at odds with Mr Bennet's comments towards the end of *Pride and Prejudice*, 'For what do we live, but to make sport for our neighbours, and laugh at them in our turn?' Although Mr Bennet has his faults in the domestic sphere, Jane Austen was clearly fond of him as a character. I can't help but feel that Jane Austen, who lived in a world which had no welfare system to speak of and who knew that people had to rely on interactions between neighbours for most social support, was using her novels to express a philosophy for the survival of the intelligent individual in a sometimes disagreeable, usually hyper-monitored, always socially alert and critical world.

She and people like her succeeded, not (like sensitive moderns) by isolating and refusing direct interaction, but by not taking society or themselves too seriously. They did it with and through humour. But humour, or at least the style of humour we call irony (Jane Austen's style of humour), requires a certain degree of detachment and the ability to look at life from the outside. In our self-absorbed world such attributes seem hard to find nowadays, but given them, it should be possible even for us to see the absurdity of humanity's pretensions. Which thought takes us back to the central thesis of this book, because if we are able to understand and accept the essential madness of thinking that there is any fundamental meaning to life, then we are put into the more powerful position of having both choices and control.

We can decide that it's all too depressing (like Kurtz, in Joseph Conrad's *Heart of Darkness*) or we can recognise that in order to carry on with life in any functionally meaningful way *we must make an active choice to share in the common delusion* – that is, the delusion that there actually might be meaning, shape and significance to be found in life; the delusion that now connects us as common members of this species. And then we must elect to participate in the delusion willingly for the sake of the smooth running of society. For the sake of the greater good. For the sake of surthrival itself – which is to say, ultimately, for our own sake. That bit of complexity is what Jane Austen managed instinctively both to understand and achieve – which to my mind is what makes her novels both so completely brilliant and so totally relevant today.

What we need to be aiming for is a population that can detach, look at itself and where it's going fairly objectively and then recognise the need for a conscious and willing commitment to a life that works for the good of all. Not just for the good of the individual – because even the individual life depends, in the end, on the wider world around it.

Research that supports the cause

Research 1

An unlikely ally of Jane Austen, in his belief in the necessity of social engagement, is Antonio Damasio of the University of Southern California. His research into social emotions, such as compassion and admiration, has led him to a position which is not a million miles (though maybe two hundred years) away from hers. He and his colleagues write:

If replicated, this finding could have important implications for the role of culture and education in the development and operation of social and moral systems; in order for emotions about the psychological situations of others to be induced and experienced, additional time may be needed for the introspective processing of culturally shaped social knowledge. *The rapidity and parallel processing of attention-requiring information, which hallmark the digital age, might reduce the frequency of full experience of such emotions, with potentially negative consequences.* (Immordino-Yang et al., 2009: 5; my italics)

Their findings imply two things which relate to my argument:

1. People who make their human connections over the internet, rather than by having slower, more complex, more multi-sensory and interactive experiences with others, may well risk losing some of their capacity to bring about and experience appropriate emotions about the psychological situations of others. In other words, they risk losing some aspects of human empathy (thus inducing a diminishing loss of interest and involvement with real others).
2. Therefore, they will be decreasingly interested in even the concept of a wider society and almost guaranteed to have no interest in joining in with conversations at big round tables.

So what is the actual finding? Essentially, Damasio and his team have been looking into how and where social emotions (those which lead to moral and community behaviours) 'happen' in the brain. They found not only that a number of expected brain regions, such as the extraordinary anterior cingulate, are involved in the experiencing of admiration (a non-pain-related social emotion) and compassion (a pain-related social emotion), but they also discovered that previously unsuspected areas of the brain were also involved in these same experiences. The new suspects were the posteromedial cortices which include the posterior cingulate cortex.[2] What these newly identified regions bring to the Pump Room's big round table of social engagement seems to be *self*-related consciousness processes, rather than the apparently more obvious *other*-related consciousness processes that might have been presumed.

These findings might, at first, seem counter-intuitive, but it appears that we need to have an internal model of our own self and how we experience experience before we can project understanding of the same onto others. As Damasio and his colleagues observe, 'simulation on one's own self is an important means to understand others' (Immordino-Yang et al., 2009: 2).

Given the observation that brain behaviour is about more than just the regions involved, it is nevertheless still important to have this information. A journey is about more than the places at which you

---

2   In 2007, P. Read Montague and his team at the Baylor Institute, Houston, identified this area as being involved, or rather *not* involved, in some of the deficits of high-functioning individuals with autism and Asperger's (see Chiu et al., 2008). They showed that these people could not recognise their own intentions, and so could not sensibly forward plan for them or infer other people's intentions.

stop, but without knowing what they are and how they are linked there is no journey at all. Therefore, it is very helpful to know which brain regions are involved in the processing of social emotions. But, as always, the overall picture is a bit more complicated. In this case there is an important distinction between the way that we respond to other people's *physical* pain and their *social and psychological* pain. The journey time between the regions involved is rather different. The path between the brain regions involved in the compassionate response to another's physical pain, being evolutionarily older and so more deeply established, leads us to a quicker and more instinctive state of empathy and sympathy than the one involved in the compassionate experience of another's social and psychological state.

This explains why we need to have more involvement with others and more direct and immediate exposure to them if we are to achieve levels of psychological and emotional connectedness equivalent to the physical sympathy for them that we more instinctively and immediately experience. Put simply, it is more instant and instinctive for us to try to save a stranger from falling under a bus than it is for us to try to save them from heartache or loneliness.

The conclusion that we must draw from Damasio's research is that it's no good cutting ourselves off from the rest of humanity by metaphorically choosing to sit at the small and exclusive Pump Room tables. That way lies, if not autism per se, then an autism-like state – one which will not only lead to a less willing engagement with others but also (chicken-and-egg) to a less *self-aware* state.[3]

---

3   I have personally experienced changes in behaviour when out and about which suggests that this cognitive shift may already be happening. An unboundaried aspect to physical behaviour shows up not only when people are actively texting or making phone calls as they walk. (Which is pretty much most of the time. According to a study by Stony Brook University in New York (Lamberg and Muratori, 2012), this has been shown to lead to a 61% increase in lateral deviation during walking, as well as a 13% increase in overall distance travelled! Surely proof of lessened consciousness.) As they're simply making their way from A to B, it also results in many more collisions than people used to have, as well as multiple near misses and jostling of nearby elbows, shoulders and so on. It's as if people have become clumsier in their navigations and negotiations for space, and in their ability to plot a course as they're walking – behaviours which suggest a reduced capacity to be fully self-aware and self-reflective; a reduced capacity to be aware of others and the impact that we're having on them; together with any recognition that such a loss might matter, or have consequences for all of us in the longer term. I find this worrying.

Research 2

Michael Bond, a freelance writer specialising in psychology and the behavioural sciences, adds weight to this concern when he makes the following assertion:

> The upshot is that my own self is not so much about me; it's as much about those around me and how we relate to one another – a notion that Damasio calls 'the social me'. This has profound implications. If a primary function of self-identity is to help us build relationships, then it follows that the nature of the self should depend on the social environment in which it develops. (Bond, 2013: 42)

Bond supports his contention by looking at studies carried out by Richard Nisbett at the University of Michigan. These studies (e.g. Nisbett, 2005) have shown that while Western oriented people look at experiences as individual items or effects more or less in isolation from the world in which they are happening, Chinese people (and East Asians in general) tend to look at things in rather more contextualised ways. The consequence of the differing ways in which these culturally distinct societies conceptualise and shape material, which will eventually be stored in memory, is that their populations' autobiographical memories tend to be laid down in different formats. Western memories are more likely to prioritise personal achievements – they are more subjective, more focused on the self – while East Asian and Chinese memories are more likely to focus on events of wider social or historical significance.

This finding quite strongly suggests that people from Eastern cultures will be more emotionally attuned to the idea of society itself than Western people are – or at least more than Westerners are today. Also, by implication, is the notion that if we as individuals are becoming more self-centred and unaware, then part of the reason for this development is that we are not expected (by society) to find the bigger context as interesting or important as ourselves.

Thus it seems that whichever way we look at it, we only have ourselves to blame for any deficits in care, compassion or social engagement, either as members of a society that is failing to expect our full commitment to it or as individuals who are failing to take the time to engage with other individuals and to share experiences with them. The more time we spend within our own space (mentally or geographically) and the less we attend to the outside social world, it appears that we will become less and less functional as members of the species formally known as Homo sapiens.

Research 3

If further proof is needed of the connection between social or cultural expectations and human brain development and subsequent behaviour, then we have to look no further than the local nursery gates. There we will find harassed mums and dads who are either vainly attempting to restrain their struggling, squawking tinies or hopelessly giving up on the attempt, while all around them voices mutter sympathetically about the 'terrible twos'. It's as though these parents have to endure some kind of innate human torment, a rite of passage as horrible, inevitable and natural as period pain or filling in a tax form. The bitter truth is that expectations of stages of personal development (and therefore tolerated behaviours) vary widely between cultures, even in matters which we might suppose to be biologically determined.

For example, in child development it was long accepted in countries such as the United States and Britain that because there is a phase in cognitive development when the growth of the 'understanding language' part of the brain outstrips that of the 'using language' part of the brain, then a child's ensuing frustration will inevitably work itself out in the semi-feral behaviour that is fondly called the terrible twos. However, psychologists Christine Mosier and Barbara Rogoff, who have worked with mothers and children from cultures which are differently tolerant of childish behaviours, have concluded that the problem is a culture-specific nightmare – one which is very much the outcome of the way some Western societies expect their children to behave (Mosier and Rogoff, 2003). Neither the phrase 'terrible twos' nor even the concept exists in many parts of the world.

In my own work with parents and children, I have also come across many mothers from a variety of places from sub-continental Asia, Africa and even from parts of Europe, who have been equally certain that a terrible twos phase isn't an inevitable part of childhood. Their explanation as to why their own children have behaved rather less problematically (or rather less horribly) than many Western children, has tended to mirror the findings of Mosier and Rogoff. It is to do with the amount of individual autonomy that their various societies have encouraged (or rather not encouraged) in their young.

After all, the more the individual is prized and prioritised in a society, the more any given individual will expect its own agenda to determine the way life as a whole works out, and the less interest it will show in the existence (and priorities) of others. Then, as subjective priorities vie for pre-eminence, even between parent and child, there will be increasing frustration all round. As adults are capable of exercising some control over their own behaviour, then hopefully their frustrations will be worked out in indirect ways. On the other hand, the frustrations of 2-year-olds will usually be worked out more directly in meltdowns and temper tantrums.

The picture is very different in societies which do not presume that childhood is about the growth of autonomy in readiness for a life lived according to principles of individuality and personal development. In these societies, childhood is either a gradual journey punctuated by various culturally significant rites of passage, from an almost wholly indulged special time when there are no expectations that the child can or should exercise control to a fully completed state of adulthood that has 'put away childish things' (which is what happens in Native American cultures, such as those studied by Mosier and Rogoff). Or it is a time of emotionally special but formally secondary status when the child learns that there are hierarchies and tiers in all areas of life and that no one individual being may leapfrog their way to the top without either damaging social structures or losing out on the acquisition of highly valued personal qualities, such as courtesy or diligence (which is more the case in Asian and 'traditional' European cultures).

These societies take it for granted that adults have more rights than children because they have more knowledge and wisdom, together with more experience of how things are and need to be. They also take it for granted that adults are not challengeable by children, and so they do not experience childish behaviour as challenging in quite the same way that many parents who have had to be helped by television 'super nannies' seem to have done.

What we loosely term 'more Western societies' no longer assume greater rights for the adult than for the child in the way they once did, and so, seeing all individuals as equal, may feel more challenged, both by a child's competing rights and by that child's behaviour when it experiences frustration of its 'rights'.

Now that we no longer expect a child to be primarily a social creature, one formed by the wider community, but instead see it as a work in progress on its way to fulfilling its own potential, we tend to assume that children already have it in them to develop all manner of attributes, given little more than the right amount of encouragement. But do they?

Fourth piece

In the coda to Chapter 6, I mentioned marshmallows in connection with Alice Miller and questions of self-restraint in childhood – something she definitely saw as an inevitable development in the maturing process. However, there is a seminal piece of research that suggests that things work rather differently. It all began with children and the allure of the marshmallow.

In the late 1960s, Walter Mischel, a professor of psychology at Stanford University, ran a series of studies which monitored a selection of 4-year-olds as they were offered the choice between eating a sweet treat (usually a marshmallow) immediately it was on offer and delaying eating it for ten minutes in order to gain an extra sweet. His purpose in setting up the experiment was to see how and when children gained the ability to delay gratification – that is, to exercise patience and self-control. Later, for various reasons, he went back to revisit his cohort and in doing so made a stupendous discovery (Mischel and Ayduk, 2004).

It appeared from his follow-up data that the ability to delay gratification, even at age 4, correlated exactly with that subject's later academic, financial and emotional success in life, as well as with their ongoing states of physical and psychological health. It seemed that whichever mental processes were involved in self-control were also the ones which promoted wellbeing across the board and which set up the self for survival. As Mischel suggested, we may not be able to control the world as such, but we are able to control how we think about it and about ourselves in relation to it.

Controlling thinking includes managing the way we think about 'hot' stimuli. Hot stimuli are those which make an immediate and sensory appeal to our appetites, leading to instantaneous rewards; the opposite, 'cool' stimuli, appeal to our higher, more rational selves. It's chips versus Chekhov, if you like; only for the kids it was marshmallows and Oreos that lit their fires. What Mischel found was that if we can cool the effect of hot stimuli by distracting ourselves and focusing our attention elsewhere, then not only are we killing temptation but we are also using a life skill that will stand us in good stead in all areas of life. This is an example of 'metacognition' – that is, knowing how to know or thinking how to think; it is an element of being aware of ourselves.

Part of this ongoing research project also looked at how metacognition develops in individual subjects. The findings here are fascinating as well. The younger babies involved who went on to develop the necessary skills for self-control were those who, from the beginning, showed enough interest in the outside world that they were able to distract themselves by watching what was happening around them whenever they had to cope with short separations from their mums. In other words, they found it an interesting distraction from any internal upset they felt. On the other hand, babies who were more clingy were less distractable. Unable to find anything to interest them beyond their own sensations, whenever they were separated from their mums they gave in to grief and howled. It's John Bowlby in another guise (see Chapter 3), and although more sophisticated investigations into the neural correlates of this skill (the brain systems involved) are still ongoing, it may come as no surprise that, together with the prefrontal cortex, both the anterior cingulate cortex and dopamine pathways seem to be part of the equation.

Angela Lee Duckworth, a psychologist working with Mischel's fundamental premise, has found that the ability to delay gratification is a far better predictor of academic success than IQ alone (Duckworth and Seligman, 2005). This ability appears to depend greatly on the development of an interest in the outside world from the earliest age (and on the ongoing development of the brain regions referred to in Chapter 3). So, doing as well as you possibly can academically not only involves wide-ranging curiosity and social connections but also confident and loving parental care from the start.

In other words, education, interest in the world beyond the self and 'good' love, which promotes both self-control and adventurousness, seem to be intertwined. Mischel himself says, 'This is where your parents are important' (see Lehrer, 2009), and goes on to advise parents that they should train children in waiting and in restraining their appetites (cooling their hot stimuli) and should also demonstrate the principles behind these skills in their own behaviour. What price Alice Miller now?

A healthy society needs a style of parenting that is most likely to produce outwardly oriented (and therefore more self-disciplined, capable and successful) people. These are the ones most likely to promote pro-social behaviours. The common enemy to all this, it seems, is the prioritisation of self over society. This is not only because of the detrimental effect of egocentric behaviour on the smooth running of all the systems that society has set up for the maintenance of those who are least able to care for themselves, but also because of the detrimental effect that egocentric behaviour ironically has on egocentric individuals themselves. According to research such as Mischel's they are likely to be less successful overall, less healthy and less intelligent than their more integrated peers.

It would appear that community is good for us. However, in the West, at present, we still have a series of more or less unchallenged beliefs in place which support the rather novel notion that the self must, and should be, prioritised for the good of the health and/or wellbeing of the individual, who is somehow understood to be separate and distinct from society.

A brief résumé

Let's return to the question which brought us to consider all of this: what complex social reasons might lead to a breakdown in culturally shared values and expectations of agreement with, and engagement in, community behaviour? We have looked at a number of factors which have a relationship to the breakdown in culturally shared values and so on, which is really more that of sibling than parent. That is to say, they run hand in hand with the breakdown rather than actually spawning it. The main ones are:

- *The professionalisation and specialisation of services.* This development has had the unintended consequence that ordinary people no longer feel that they have either the qualities or the right to understand or intervene in certain community matters. This has had an isolating and a dividing effect.
- *The loss of common goals.* Rather than feeling bonded to the wider community by means of shared goals, many people identify with and feel more closely bonded to subgroups.
- *Technology.* Especially technology which focuses concentration inwards, on self-rewards and on relationships formed in cyberspace (which are really only taking place inside the head and not in externalised multi-sensory ways). This is likely to have the effect of diminishing the connectedness necessary for both a full sense of self and a full appreciation of society.

- *Cultural expectations which encourage the prioritisation of self over society.*
  These have seen the evolution of less than pro-social
  behaviours, even in small children.

These factors have all had the tendency to *internalise* us. At the risk
of being repetitive, and because this is so important, I shall go over
the dangers of this again. Doing is about externalising life, being is
about internalising it (just ask Hamlet). We can see from the marshmallow studies, as well as from the work of Damasio (and the
pronoun studies mentioned in Chapter 6) that, ironically, focusing
on the world outside the self is generally much better for that self
than focusing in on it. Focusing in on it, talking endlessly about it,
about 'I, myself and me', correlates with depression, poorer health,
lower academic achievement and with a lower sense of significance
– however counter-intuitive that might seem.

This is all a rather circular process, but how can we possibly feel
really significant without a fully felt and experienced external world
to endorse the way we perceive ourselves? Without which feedback
the whole business is a bit like singing in outer space. However, if
the outside world loses confidence in its own foundations, it becomes
shaky, losing credibility as a sounding board, and failing to provide
either externalising feedback or support. And it's then that we fall
back on building our own defensible towers.

Right now our world seems to be losing that confidence in itself.

Chapter 8

New Values and New Shibboleths

New values and the loss of cultural confidence

Each generation has to find its own way, and to do so it has to reject the past. Quite simply, it's a job in which every generation must play its part. However, there's rejecting the past and then there's kicking it when it's down.

A significant cause of that loss of confidence mentioned at the end of the previous chapter – a precursor to the breakdown in culturally shared values – was the post-war generation's attack on the underpinning values of the world in which they grew up. These values had worked well enough in wartime, in largely industrialised conditions and in pre-welfare, tight-knit, often overcrowded and closely related societies. However, they seemed harsh and irrelevant to the generation raised in the improving conditions their parents had worked so hard to achieve. It was these better conditions, and perhaps the reluctance of many people to talk about their experiences of the Second World War, which prevented that next generation from fully recognising just what it had taken to survive the war and its grey and challenging aftermath. And so, with the carelessness of the entitlement that rising standards were bringing to many areas of life, together with a lack of understanding of the part played by self-denying practices in the production of those rising standards, a new generation wanted to kill the golden goose. Duty, patience, delaying gratification, centuries old traditions, hallowed family practices, putting others first, children being seen and not heard, deferring to elders – all were found wanting. Often this was with good reason but not necessarily with conscious thought-through good reason. It became a bit of an all-out knee-jerk rout.

Almost as reactively as those values went, another set of values came in. These were, in their way, as unthinkingly adhered to as the previous ones had been by earlier generations, but with less time-honoured practice behind them to endorse their efficacy. Given that these new values are commonly shared, it's ironic that they should have led to a breakdown in expectations of agreement with, and engagement in, community behaviour (to parrot Darwin, I'll add, 'I think'). However, if I'm right, then in order to redesign the way we live, these values will need to change too – or at least our unquestioning acceptance of their validity.

The new values – what have they ever done for us?

What follows (in no particular order) is a list of current values that may be open to question.

Feelings: our new religion

We're constantly told that feelings are important. But what on earth are they? How do we measure feelings, identify them and prove that they are genuinely being experienced as described? How do we know that one person's version of a feeling is the same as someone else's? We assume that feelings matter and we believe that prioritising the evidence they provide is desirable.

'How are you feeling?' someone asks after a bad event in another person's life. Many kinds of therapy would founder without the belief in the supremacy of feeling states over just about all other states of existence. But who questions what a feeling actually is? I tried this once – and almost got away with it. I tried suggesting to one of the foremost figures in addiction studies, a person who is also a leading light in a major rehab clinic and who shall remain nameless, that to prioritise feelings in treatment for addiction was something of an *ignis fatuus*, a misleading flame, as feelings only amounted to cultural interpretations placed on physiological sensations, or as I put it, 'sensations mediated by cultural expectations' (which is what Damasio is saying in Immordino-Yang et al., 2009). Being infinitely mutable, these interpretations are less easily worked with than the actual sensations themselves. He looked at me as if I was from outer space. He may have had a point: it *was* the alien anthropologist who spoke.

Feelings are not 'truths', and there are no provable, consistent or even necessarily desirable baselines that one can set for healthy feelings. There may be certain desirable or optimum ranges of neurotransmitter activity which will be experienced as physiological sensations, but that is rather different. It's akin to the difference between appetite and hunger, or assuming that feeling hard done by is much the same as feeling cold. As various indicators – from Elizabeth Loftus's eye-witness testimony studies to cognitive behavioural therapy – make evident, our feelings in response to events can be both misleading and easily manipulated. And yet they continue to be taken as almost fixed truths about a person's inner state. 'But tell me truthfully, what do you *really* feel …?'

This mantra hijacks truthfulness much of the time, and many people try to conjure up either non-existent or unknowable feelings just to satisfy other people's hunger for them. This can happen in relationships in which one partner fails to be expressive enough for the needs of the other, who is then convinced that they are in some way hiding something. This is because we have all had it so firmly impressed on us that sharing feelings is the only real way to show closeness to someone. Much better than, say, being there, carrying on offering reliable support, sharing activities, sharing parenting and any number of other demonstrable but not emotionally showy totems of togetherness.

Research carried out by Dr James McNulty, a social psychologist at Florida State University, supports this contention in a rather interesting way. He has found that 'gut reactions' – physically sensed responses – are truer indications of someone's attachment to a marriage partner than are the words they use about their supposed feelings (McNulty et al., 2013). This has nothing to do with them lying, even to themselves, but about their inability to detect the true state of their relationship, especially with regard to underlying doubts about their prospective partner. In a series of clever tests in which people were asked to respond physically to either positive or negative words briefly flashed on a screen in combination with photos of their beloved, Dr McNulty and his team showed that partners' physical responses were truer indicators of attachment than were consciously verbalised ones – which were often the result of wishful thinking. He made the following comment about the relative significance of physical versus consciously emotional responses:

> But these automatic, gut-level responses are less influenced by what people *want* to think … If they can sense their gut is

telling them there is a problem, then they might benefit from exploring that. (McNulty et al., 2013: 1119–1120)

He and his researchers concluded:

Although they may be largely unwilling or unable to verbalise them, people's automatic evaluations of their partners predict one of the most important outcomes of their lives – the trajectory of their marital satisfaction. (ibid.)

So, as far as Dr McNulty is concerned, emotional expectations (possibly culturally determined ones) can get in the way of accessing true *physiological* feelings. In fact, there is a wealth of evidence that there are some specific categories of people – in particular, those on the autistic spectrum – who find it very difficult to access sensations in what might be called a normal way. They also find it very difficult to cross-reference sensations, self-awareness and language. This means they find it literally impossible to put feelings into words. There is even a pathologising term for the condition, alexithymia, which means, 'no words for emotions'. It is not peculiar to autism as such, but it is usually considered to be co-morbid with a number of dysfunctional psychiatric states in general. So, with a nod to the exception that is Dr McNulty's (rather more interesting and useful) finding, it seems that feelings absolutely *must* be equated with good mental health in our touchy-feely world.

The consequences

In the various therapeutic, corrective and educational institutions I have visited or worked in, those inmates who have exhibited an inability to express feelings have often run the risk of being bullied. Their failure to deliver anger, sorrow, guilt or whatever has been demanded of them in appropriately expressed, emotionally resonant language has been seen as evidence that they are incapable of change. Because it now seems to be axiomatic that changes in behaviour will only come about as a consequence of changes in feeling states, what tends to happen in those situations is either the bullied individuals will react badly and aggressively because they are expected to produce something quite foreign to them and can't. They will then be unfairly punished, essentially for their failure to be someone other than who they are. The point (that they are incapable of change) will be proven. Or, if they are more compliant and generally clever, they will produce something that seems to fit the occasion, a script suitable for a similar situation, perhaps one they came across on TV or in a film. This will generally satisfy the governor/therapy team/parole board/examiners and a successful outcome will be claimed for the auditors.

However they work out, whether negatively or seemingly positively, the expectations and outcomes in these situations are both limiting and unhelpful. The problem of working with the narrow and inflexible expectations of others is not confined to pathological or sociological special cases. Essentially, we have no way of knowing how many other apparently normal people fudge their responses to questions about their feeling states, either for fear of letting others down or just because they are afraid of coming across as not quite right. While the outcome of ordinary people doing this may not contain as much potential danger as the scenario in which a fundamentally unreconstructed offender has managed, by learning an emotional script, to pass themselves off as conscience stricken, rehabilitated and ready for release, it may still result in frustrated expectations, lost dreams and heartache.

By prioritising a feeling agenda over other possible ways of relating and responding to one another and to life, we risk limiting our understanding of what human beings are and how they truly process experience. We also risk making society so uncompromisingly subjective and so inflexible about what is important that our chances of achieving the greatest good for the widest possible population will inevitably be compromised.

It sometimes seems that we're more than halfway down that road already. There are some situations in which actions and activities that are clearly in the interests of the many aren't allowed if the 'feelings' of the few are likely to be compromised. An A level literature class was prevented from studying Sylvia Plath's poem 'Daddy' because one Jewish student objected to the way Plath likened her relatively blameless father's behaviour to the sadistic oppression of the Nazis. Her emotionally charged departure from the class was considered to give her more rights over what was taught than the quieter appreciation of the complexity of Plath's work gave those who wished to carry on studying her poetry.

This is only one small case, but the principle that strong feeling states create both virtue and entitlement is taking hold. Just think how much advertising and marketing uses the word 'passion' to sell products: 'I'm passionate about my ... beef pies/radial tyres/work with the disabled' – you name it. Why precisely should your strong feeling state make what you do worthier, wiser or more compelling for me? I'm simply asking. Equally, the rights of the few can quite comfortably be ridden roughshod over if they have somehow failed in their duty to show the appropriate feeling responses. They clearly do not care as much as other people and so it matters less if their situation is given less consideration.

A poignant and quite worrying example of this misunderstanding of human behaviour concerned a young woman with an Asperger's diagnosis. During her adolescence she had shown a few 'inappropriate' behaviours. When she became pregnant, the local social work team became involved. Once the baby was born they decided to carry out an assessment of her ability to care for the child, focusing in particular on her ability to provide appropriate emotional support. As part of her early special needs education, this young woman had been taught the importance of making eye contact when communicating and the need to smile to put people at their ease. So, while she was being observed by the social workers (caring for a newborn baby – a tricky enough test for the best of us) she smiled determinedly. The social workers deemed this inappropriately frivolous behaviour. When, in time, they told her they would be taking her child away, she stared at them while continuing to smile; this they interpreted as hard evidence that she didn't care anyway. Later on, after the child had been adopted, I asked her what would have happened if she had stopped smiling. She said she would have burst out sobbing and she did not want to do that in front of them.

It is quite possible that by taking her baby into care the social workers were doing the right thing. I can't make that judgement. But she never laid a finger on her baby or exposed him to any direct physical threat. She simply failed to *demonstrate* the appropriate feelings. Presumably Baby P's mother made a better fist of doing that. As a fellow drugs worker used to put it, 'It's the crying baby who gets the milk.' It's often the unemotional ones or those whose emotions work in different ways who fail to cry loudly enough to get themselves heard.

It is no more fair or reasonable to prioritise people because they are just *so* sensitive than it is to overlook people's inner states because they are not at all demonstrative. This simplistic, dualistic way of defining and categorising humanity seems unlikely to achieve the cohesion and cooperation on the desired basis of shared values that we're looking for. In the same way that cultural expectations have placed limits on what we might expect in terms of child development, it seems that by placing either positive or pejorative meanings on what are basically physiological sensations, twentieth-century cultural expectations have also restricted the possible interpretations of actual sensations and made people less able to read their own physiological states ('Oh, you *must* be feeling so sad.' Really?), and thereby produced a stick with which to beat people. 'Feeling' people being so much more authentic, and emotionally sensitive and appropriate than 'unfeeling' people. Obviously.

We all sense things; we simply place differing interpretations on what we sense. But elevating feeling states to the position of eminence they now have and elevating feeling people to the role of Grand Inquisitor also risks raising subjectivity and the individual state way above the social and community state. Which is not at all what is wanted or needed if we wish to create more community behaviour.

Feeling good about ourselves, or self-esteem

The self-esteem agenda has become a straitjacket. No one shall be called 'Fatty', no child shall be told that their achievements aren't up there with the greats and no one shall be found wanting if there is any possible way of redeeming them through wishful thinking. Unfortunately, it seems that societies where a little more critical judgement is applied appear to be making more progress in a whole variety of arenas to do with education, readiness for work and even health and happiness. Do we risk losing out because we have a fear of hard work or because we have a fear of being made to look inadequate?

Rather than risk exposure to these sorts of judgements, and driven by the need to feel good about ourselves, it appears that many of us are turning to the internet for evidence that we really are 'liked' by large quantities of people. In days gone by, if you were rubbish at sport and weren't much better at making real people like you, you didn't get picked for the school team and had to try a bit harder on the sociability front. Now, even if you have absolutely nothing of substance to offer the world you can still gather a huge collection of Facebook friends. But if the necessity of building up self-esteem and remaining unchallenged in our supreme belief in ourselves results in virtual relationships rather than in connections with real people, then I think it's about time we thought twice about whether or not we are actually worth it. What price are we paying to keep our inner delusions intact?

Is the girl in the railway carriage who first puts on her make-up and then plops her feet up on the seat opposite so she can have a comfortably loud but horribly intimate chat on the phone really going to lose out substantially by being told that her behaviour is unacceptable? Yet her assumption – that she is a valuable being whose actions, if prompted by her current needs, should never be challenged – is one that is totally aligned to the principle that she must never feel the caustic effect of shame for fear that she will be damaged for the rest of her life.

Roy F. Baumeister, long-time researcher into self-esteem, makes a similar point when he describes studies into the building of self-esteem at Virginia Commonwealth University (Baumeister and Tierney, 2011). One finding was that while the students' self-esteem went up, their performances declined. The authors make the wryly understated observation, 'They just felt better about doing worse' (ibid.: 191). In the chapter entitled 'Raising Strong Children: Self-Esteem versus Self-Control', they outline many of the arguments against the efficacy of the self-esteem movement in producing more successful, honest or otherwise better citizens and sum up by observing:

> Too many students, parents, and educators are still seduced by the easy promises of self-esteem. Like the students in [Donald] Forsyth's class in Virginia, when the going gets tough, people with high self-esteem often decide they shouldn't bother. If other people can't appreciate how terrific they are, then it's the other people's problem. (ibid.: 193)

Such as those people who have to share a railway carriage with someone who couldn't be bothered to get up early enough to do their make-up and who can't begin to imagine that anyone might object to them behaving as if they are still in their bedroom. Or perhaps, more accurately, can't begin to imagine anyone. Period.

In its fundamental lack of recognition of Other, self-esteem, like its street cousin, 'respect', is really only too often an excuse for telling the rest of the world to back off and leave *me* to do what *I* want, unmolested by consideration of anything or anyone else. Behind the concept, though, there is really only one drive and that is for significance. If you need to beef up your belief in yourself it could be because your essential sense that you are significant is compromised. Or it may be that you fail to see enough meaning in the outside world to make up for this deficit – which is a variant on the first possibility. The bottom line is that early parenting has failed to engender a core sense of self, and however much you huff and puff and try to blow the rest of the world down, you can't genuinely inflate your own significance later on in life. Truly esteeming yourself can't be retrospective.

The only way to make up for the empty space is to credit accomplishments or actions with the significance that will make their achievement fulfilling in their own right. It is always going to feel more satisfying to bake a tasty cake or help out at a charity event than to be so important that you feel you can walk all over others. Probably best of all would be to bake a tasty cake *at* a charity event. Then, not only do you get the kudos of producing something everyone likes, you also get the added benefit of full immersion in the bigger cause.

Happiness

Other feeling-related new principles that might need to be challenged include happiness. It's no longer enough that we have the right to pursue happiness (as Thomas Jefferson decreed in the US Declaration of Independence in 1776). Now it seems we should consider it our right to be happy almost permanently. There are happiness classes at leading Berkshire public school, Wellington College; there is a movement called Action for Happiness; you can 'release the power of happiness in you' by enrolling on Robert Holden's eight-day happiness programme; you can read a book called *That Happiness Project* which details the author Gretchen Rubin's semi-religious year-long quest to achieve greater happiness in her life; and you can take a happiness test to see how happy you are (which is rather like taking a pregnancy test to see how pregnant you might be).

It's all up there with the chief constables who regularly intone, 'We don't want to stop people having a good time ...', as they excuse the amount of money they spend each and every Saturday night policing the aftermath of people 'having fun' and hosing down the streets of the towns and cells of the police stations the funsters have visited. (I've been in those cells and they didn't look or smell like a whole lot of fun to me. You wouldn't have wanted to enter them in open-toed sandals, either.) It's become a given that fun, happiness and having a good time are incontrovertible rights, and not only will they make the individual life more satisfactory but they will also add to society's health and wellbeing in general.

According to a number of contributors to a 2006 BBC programme, *The Happiness Formula*, which looked into the science of happiness, there is some evidence that happiness leads to longer life. Alas, that claim has been challenged. It's also been claimed that happiness leads to better health and resilience, although the rider 'we have not got proof' was added to those claims and no definite causal links were established. According to another happiness researcher, Daniel Kahneman, professor emeritus of psychology and public affairs at Princeton University, the 'Standard of living has increased dramatically and happiness has increased not at all' (quoted in Rudin, 2006), which is not exactly what you might expect to find if there really was a causal relationship between happiness and an overall improvement in wellbeing.

However, according to other happiness researchers, the matter is much more complicated than the question of whether or not a state of happiness can actively lead to wellbeing. Their research suggests there is a flip side to happiness, a darker aspect to it than any of the positive thinking gurus allow for – one which quite possibly leads to more negative outcomes in life.

June Grüber, assistant professor of psychology at Yale University, and a number of her colleagues, have also been researching happiness. Their conclusions still allow that happiness is, in general, a Good Thing and may promote overall wellbeing, but they have found that it is by no means an unalloyed good, being actively toxic on occasion. They believe it should always be seen as a trade-off.

The following are some of the problems that she and other commentators have found that too much happiness may lead to:

- *Riskier behaviour.* Having too optimistic a view of life and its possibilities and taking less time to process information leads to increased risk taking. Alcohol and drug use can rise among some very cheerful types (Gruber et al., 2011; citing Martin et al., 2002; Cyders and Smith, 2008).
- *Mania.* Being overexcited can seem positive and life enhancing but it may be only a whisker away from desperation. Young children who scream endlessly in playgrounds may seem to be having a really good time but they're often overstimulated and unable to process what they're experiencing. Although onlookers may encourage small children to 'enjoy themselves' in this way, they're not really helping them to experience fun. Hyper-stimulation is not a genuinely positive state (Gruber et al., 2011; citing American Psychiatric Association, 2000).

- *Demonstrating less gravitas.* People who are excessively happy come across as less weighty. Constant happiness can be irritating (perhaps only someone like Boris Johnson can get away with being seemingly up all the time). For others, the expression of occasional anger and low mood seems more plausible, more realistic and more sympathetic to the rest of us (Gruber et al., 2011; citing Van Kleef et al., 2006). In negotiations, expressions of anger lead to more concessions from others (another detail which doesn't quite tally with the other more positive happiness findings).
- *The paradoxical effect.* Pursuing happiness may lead to lessened happiness, as anything less than perfect happiness will be experienced as disappointing (Gruber et al., 2011). (As Bolingbroke says in Shakespeare's *Richard II*, 'the apprehension of the good, Gives but the greater feeling to the worse'. By which he means that once you believe in the possibility of achieving a perfect state, having to put up with anything less is going to leave you feeling pretty bad.)
- *Anti-social behaviour.* Too much satisfaction with one's own personal state can be very self-serving and lead to gloating and aggressiveness towards others who have less to brag about (Gruber et al., 2011; citing Baumeister et al., 1996).
- *Laziness.* The promise of more happiness is a spur but present perfection leaves you unwilling to make more effort. Why bother? Even thinking yourself into a state of perfection can be demotivating (Kappes and Oettingen, 2011) (you are already internally rewarding yourself with a rise in dopamine, so it's a case of job done, even though it really isn't).
- *Dangerous oblivion.* Cheerful people simply do not take as much notice of the world. As Sonja Lyubomirsky, a professor of psychology at the University of California, says, 'You don't want to be too happy if you are monitoring a nuclear power plant' (quoted in Cook, 2011). Relative misery is also relative reality.

Basically, it's the same old story: focusing on happiness is focusing on yourself which has the perverse effect of disconnecting yourself from other people. Result: less community and less happiness.

And now, for a pot pourri of other new values that offer dubious value if we want more fundamental community connectedness.

Letting it all hang out

'If it feels right, do it.' That sounds a bit hippy-dippy. Perhaps the worst of that era's excesses look pretty ditzy to most people now, but the principle that ignoring your inner promptings might in some way harm you still hangs on, as does the belief that it's not really anyone else's business. Which, of course, it is – if we are to be a wider community.

If your child wanders around the restaurant or lies screaming on the floor; if that young woman does her make-up on the train, eats her breakfast or talks loudly about her latest cervical smear; if I want to pee at the side of my car in the layby or eat with my mouth open as I walk down the street; if that bloke grows his hedge to ridiculous heights or plays head-banging music till dawn – all of these things should be everyone's business, if we share the same values and goals. The one overriding 'right' of the individual to 'do their own thing' should be seen for what it is: an assault, however unintended, on the overall good of the community.

Never forgetting that each of these behaviours exemplifies a rather desperate and sad pursuit of significance by those of us who have not found it in more healthy and straightforward ways. Fitting in, rather than having bits and pieces hanging out, is ultimately a better way to feel relatively significant.

The equality agenda

It might seem contradictory, given the previous section, but fitting in is not the same as being equal. And being equal is not the same as being the same. However, there is currently a somewhat distorted belief that being on an equal footing with others means being the same as others. This belief underpins the equality movement, which has morphed from wanting *equal rights* to wanting *identical rights and opportunities*. For all. Regardless of some quite fundamental differences between people – differences which even exist between identical twins and which some scientists now believe are down to what they call 'random epigenetic variability'.

Psychologist Eric Turkheimer, from the University of Virginia, used the research of Gerd Kempermann, from the Center for Regenerative Therapies, Dresden, Germany, to try to figure out how identical twins (same DNA) can end up with quite different personalities (Hamilton, 2013; see also Turkheimer et al., 2014).

Kempermann and his colleagues looked at forty genetically identical mice, raised in identical circumstances with all the same facilities to hand, and discovered that despite their identical background these mice developed in different ways (Freund et al., 2013). Some became much more adventurous than others. They also found that with behavioural change came changes in brain development: the hippocampi (involved in memory and navigation) of adventurous mice grew more new brain cells than the hippocampi of the others. Turkheimer et al. concluded that tiny early differences, most probably the consequences of chance or of random genetic events, become amplified as the feedback loop between behaviour and brain influenced personality change. This, they concluded, explained why one twin could end up wanting to be an adventurer while another might want to stay safely at home. None of this related to the opportunities which had been made available to them – not necessarily something the equality purists want to hear.

In the 1960s and 1970s there was a determination on the part of many psychologists and sociologists to prove that gender itself was a cultural construct and a great deal of money went into research to prove it. I was briefly involved in some of that research, together with a friend and our two very small children, one boy and one girl. We were recruited by my old university to take part in a day of experiments. These consisted of some cleverly constructed tests of our toddlers' pre-existing gender bias with regard to working roles, some tests of our own biases and working and household functions, and finally, and grandly, an immersive play experience for the children. They had absolute freedom within a wonderland of never-before-seen or even imagined American dream toys to select and play with whatever they most wanted.

Neither of us adults was remotely traditional in our views, lifestyles or even in our skills. My friend was a hippyish, non-TV-watching artist, musician and pacifist; I was as happy restoring houses, building walls and cleaning cars as ever I was doing housework. We both worked (hardly the norm for young mums then) and all our questionnaire responses reflected our essentially non-traditional ways. So what did our non-traditionally brought up toddlers rush helter-skelter to embrace within that play emporium? My friend's little boy found the one and only machine gun, which had been hidden at the back, and with it he wiped out the imaginary forces of the army of conscientious objectors who had prevented him from doing this for all of his life to date. And my daughter? She found the cutest, pinkest little ironing board and iron and with that she ironed away as if all the prickly feminist principles she had ever heard needed to be smoothed away for eternity. (Mind you, she has never ironed again from that day to this.)

I don't know what we proved or disproved to the researchers that day, but I was convinced that gender was *not* largely a cultural construct. Nothing I have discovered since through neuroscience has dispelled this belief. Neither do I believe that expectations of what we should be doing with our lives should be based on anything as simplistic as gender alone.

In February 2012, a study by the University of Michigan into the effects of Norway's introduction of quotas forcing large companies to have 40% female directors was reported in the *Sunday Times* under the heading '"Golden skirts" weaken business' (Gillespie, 2012). It appeared that the consequence of this apparently well-meaning attempt to force equality between the sexes had resulted in poorer overall performance in the companies involved and a drop in their share value. Hardly a result in line with the greater good of the people whose livelihoods depended on the businesses. Even now, as time has allowed these relatively inexperienced women to become accustomed to their new roles, the outcome is still hardly in line with a genuine equality agenda. What has happened is that a very small number of women have now specialised in the business of becoming directors – and are now directors of quite a number of different companies.

These examples were about gender equality, but the principle applies to many other equal rights matters such as making people special or forcing single issues to take priority over general welfare. These narrow ways of dealing with difficulties and challenges create as many problems as they solve. They always mitigate against the bigger picture and lead to yet more, if different, divisions and resentments. Make one group special, such as the selected women directors, and another group, the as yet unselected, will always feel hard done by. Expect that society will naturally produce something you don't want, such as stereotypical behaviour, and nature will find a way to surprise and confound.

Taken to the extreme, might a single-minded pursuit of equal rights actually lead to unintended and dangerous consequences? Say, for example, a technically brilliant and autistic student of medicine decides to become a GP. Arguably, under the guidelines being produced by the National Autistic Society and the Department for Work and Pensions, they would have such a right. (Of course, you could ask how anyone, prior to such categorisations, would have been aware of any potential problems.) But what if a diagnosis of autism implies that this person has reduced communication skills and that language will mean subtly different things to them than it will to others, including potential patients? Does a disability employment right supersede a service user's right to best practice, or vice versa? It may seem 'nasty' to introduce this scenario, it may seem unlikely, but it's not utterly implausible. (I know a couple of autistic GPs and I would not want to be put in the position of having to explain to them either my complex emotional state or symptoms which I found difficult to describe.) Perhaps we should actually be brave enough to have the debate.

Victims/survivors

Everyone's a victim now or a survivor of something or other. Princess Diana is probably the patron saint of both. Let's be honest: if you're still alive, you're a survivor – and that's it. But that's not what people mean when they use the term 'survivor'. They mean something more qualitative. Being a survivor implies you are superior, that you have been elevated by your experiences. You have been elevated by being a victim in the same way that Princess Diana was a victim or that Marilyn Monroe was a victim (of the studio system, or of powerful men, or of men in general).

I have sat in on innumerable groups and meetings in which survivors and victims have extolled their own and one another's virtues for having 'made it'. The same is true of addiction groups. They frequently express their sense of victimhood and courage in the face of the 'disease' of addiction. Three things strike me about this:

1. They are limiting their own identities to *being* someone (a victim/survivor) rather than *doing* something. Does this suggest that they were always passive and reactive rather than proactive? Is that a clue as to how they became a victim? And does perpetuating that form of identity allow them to make changes more in line with having greater involvement with a wider range of Other?
2. This is a form of special subgroup with a different mentality, and therefore focused on 'I, myself and me' – and we've already looked at the risks involved with this way of construing experience.
3. Confessional programmes on daytime TV and certain

newspapers encourage this way of looking at experience. They pass on a toxic inheritance to any young people who are exposed to it.

Two stories a few years ago came to epitomise what might be called the yin and yang of victimisation. One concerned a brainy school-girl who had gone missing from home because, according to her parents, she felt she was being bullied by classmates for her clever-ness and enthusiasm in class. Her mother (a special needs head teacher) said her daughter had to be the best at everything, but that this was intrinsic to her and had nothing to do with her upbringing. She added that her daughter was intense to the point that every-thing, good and bad, became a major life crisis to her. The mother then said of her daughter, 'She is sometimes quite contemptuous of others – it comes over as sneering' (Loudon, 1996). The daughter had also been bullied at her previous school so special efforts were being made to support her at her latest school. 'One of the things she has been learning is getting on with others but it is particularly hard for *some people*,' (my italics) said the mother. The other story concerned a boy who had a phobia of putting his head under water (Armstrong, 2006). As a consequence he couldn't swim, and was so teased by his mates that he decided to get over his fears and learn to do just that. He went on to become Britain's youngest serving life-guard and hoped to go on to teach swimming as a career.

The girl in the first story appeared to have organised her disap-pearance. I obviously hope all was well with her in the end, but I cannot see it, as the headlines did, as the sorry tale of 'the girl driven away by bullies'. If any behaviour was bullying, then it was her showing contempt for others and using emotional scare tactics. But what did her mother mean by the words, 'some people'? Some peo-ple as in those who just happen not to get along with others, all by themselves? So much of what she said appeared to distance herself from all responsibility for her child; just as she distanced her child from all responsibility for *her* behaviour in turn – and turned her into a victim rather than a perpetrator of action. In contrast, the young swimming hero was able to take a proactive rather than a reactive stance when he was bullied (where does teasing end and bullying begin?) by his mates and made his life better as a consequence. No doubt he will be a brilliant teacher because he knows learning to swim is not only about technique.

Genuine and life-changing bullying exists, and it's by no means always as a consequence of victim mentality. However, I doubt the wisdom of elevating the status of victims and survivors to almost heroic proportions. It's one thing to cope well with the 'bad' things life throws at you, but it's quite another to define yourself primarily by how you have reacted to them, and in so doing credit yourself with some kind of special attributes. This suggests a mind which fundamentally perceives itself as being of such little significance, as having so little to offer the world, that only things done *to* it, rather than *by* it, can make it seem in any way worthwhile.

Stress

This relates to the previous section in that stress and how we react to it has become a marker for how we place ourselves as individuals. Do we cope or do we collapse under duress?

Stress has come to be a very dirty word, responsible for ill health, substance abuse, inability to cope, financial collapse, poor relationships – you name it, stress is responsible. But what exactly is stress? Google it and you will find several million results which suggests a certain amount of uncertainty. Some sites tell you that it is the precursor to mental ill health and give advice on how to avoid it, while others talk about it being akin to a stimulus, a necessary element of being purposefully alive. If we refuse to face anything that might make our tummies wobble, even the teensiest bit, then we are not going to be much good to anyone else; we will be far too busy thinking about how we feel inside to put up with the demands that any outside factor would place on our time and attention. By trying to avoid every kind of stress, we will actually make the situation worse, because we will lose tone in our 'stress muscles'.

Many organisations are so keen to relieve us of stress that it's quite surprising that we seem to be suffering from so much of it. From automatic doors which save us having to push and pull, to satnavs which save us from having to work out routes and plan our journeys in advance, to online diaries and internet shopping, we are surrounded by innovations intended to save us from thinking very much at all.

By comparison with previous generations, who barely went fifty years without major all-encompassing wars (complete with ghastly injuries, annexation of farmland, poverty, mass rape and starvation), we have little reason to complain that we can't cope. And yet stress is not about the absolute difficulties we face, it's about the relative difficulties we face. We appraise situations for their potential threat to us, just as other animals do, only they perceive threats in the physical environment whereas we can be threatened by abstract matters such as our lifestyle, our self-esteem and our belief systems. If we feel that something dear to our sense of self, our *sense of significance*, is being attacked in any way then the automatic fight-or-flight system kicks in. We become tense, our heart rate goes up, we sweat, our breathing becomes shallow and the stress hormones adrenaline and cortisol are released. We are ready for extreme actions and reactions, waiting on the edge of a precipice of possibilities – and that is both wearying and all-absorbing. We have no attention or space for anyone or anything else. Our brains go into automatic mode, we have fewer sophisticated soft skills available, so we succumb to fear and anger and all the other primitive emotions that generations of evolution have not quite managed to eradicate.

We cannot yet immunise ourselves against the effects of stress, but what we can do is alter our perceptions of what we feel threatened by. Again, much of the current problem is down to perceiving ourselves as all important.

- *Stressful day at work?* Can it possibly be as bad as working down a mine or fighting invading hordes?
- *Stressful time with the children?* Well, who is in charge? Do you need to fill the day so full of child-centred activities or keep everything as germ free as in a TV advert?
- *Stressed at not doing as well as your peer group?* Stop comparing.
- *Can't fit it all in?* Who is asking you to? 'I'm *sooo* stressed out.' Why? Are you absolutely certain that stress has not, in fact, become the touchstone of how significant you are? That it hasn't almost taken on the status of success or achievement?

Let go. You're just not that important. If your input is absolutely and genuinely necessary, then make your efforts purposeful and targeted. Don't put as much effort into how you're feeling about them as into the actions themselves. In that way stress becomes useful. It is the precursor to actions that will make a difference. Taking action is the best way to relieve stress.

Toughen up

Sometimes we just need to toughen up a bit and learn how to manage difficulty. Although there are perhaps better ways to toughen up children than these I came across – in a prison and at a public school – which only goes to show that social status alone does not unstressed people make.

The first involved a young woman whose case history I was taking, prior to arranging a drug treatment regime. Like so many women in prison she had been in a whole series of abusive relationships with men and would hardly have known what 'coping alone' meant. However, like so many women in prison, she vehemently defended her parents against any possible accusation of mistreatment:

It's all down to me. Don't blame my dad – he only wanted the best for me, to protect me. He taught me how to defend myself – he taught me to get it in first, then he knew I'd be okay. He only hit with a stick to show me how to get in there first. I had to get in there first and then I'd be okay, I wouldn't get hurt.

Clearly, that hadn't worked. She had been in a permanent condition of defensiveness, was quite stressed out and had used drugs to dull sensations that made no sense to her. After all, why should she feel hopeless when her parents had loved her so much?

The second was possibly even more curious – allowing for the fact that here the parent had thought at some length about her approach to toughening up her child. She was an anxious kid and her mum didn't want her to live life on the edge. She wanted her to go for it and enjoy life to the full. The way forward seemed obvious to her. She had made it her business to be late for just about everything so that her daughter would, on the total immersion principle, learn how to deal with the stress that these situations brought on in her. Simples! She merely wanted to know if I thought she was doing the right thing because her daughter still seemed to get quite stressed out about school.

Toughening up has to be a bit more sophisticated than either of these two parents realised. It has to be based on developing a core sense of security, and it has to be followed by demystifying all the totems of significance that we have developed to make up for any early lack of that core sense of security. But it can be done.

Catch-all

I began this chapter by saying that, ironically, the new values which have replaced the more traditional values have, despite being culturally quite commonly shared, led to a breakdown in expectations of agreement with, and engagement in, community behaviour. And in order to redesign the way we live, we need to challenge our unquestioning acceptance of their validity.

I have already covered some new shibboleths – these almost unquestioned totems of modern thinking – and not wanting to set so great a challenge to thinking that brains switch off, I will deal with some more here at a rather faster pace. One reason for lumping them together is that they seem, even more so than the previous examples of new values, to share the disadvantage (for community purposes) of working actively against the upholding of what might be called universal standards – universal at least in relation to the large subgroup which is any wider cultural community.

Tolerance, judgement, prejudice, criticism, gossip. All v. v. bad? Well, no. They are neither all bad nor all bad in themselves. This is a baby and bathwater situation; by throwing out the idea that anyone has the right to monitor and pass comment on other people's behaviour, we have also to give up on the idea that there is a set of standards which we hold to be more valuable than others, and that this set of standards pulls us together into a community, which can then be relied on to back up and support any individual who is acting upon that set of standards.

The consequence of this has been that, in effect, anything goes if 'I, myself and me' will it so, regardless of whether or not the action/attitude/objective is in line with the overall smooth or beneficial functioning of society.

- **_Tolerance_**. It is often the most 'tolerant' of people who boast that they are only intolerant of intolerance itself, while actively condemning others for being 'so intolerant'. Irony, or a bad case of 'whatever I believe in must be so'?
- **_Judgement_**. 'Who am I to judge?' is so often the mantra of those who are unwilling to follow judgement with action. Does a particular lifestyle harm someone less able to fend for themselves? If so, we should all judge and then act. We all judge anyway, all the time. If we didn't, how would we know which TV programme to watch, where to go on holiday, whether our children were behaving in ways we thought safe

and/or appropriate or whether a neighbour's actions were merely eccentric or likely to set our house on fire? If we didn't, how come *The X Factor*, *Strictly Come Dancing*, *Big Brother* and all the rest of these interactive tests of people's 'accomplishments' and desirability are so extraordinarily successful?

Problems arise when what people really mean when talking about judgement is, 'Thou shalt not make different evaluations from mine.' When a person asks whether they are fit to judge, aren't they really saying, 'I judge, but what I'm judging is whether *you* have the right to determine things *I'm* not prepared to think too hard about'?

Fortunately I am not alone in believing the anti-judgement tendency has gone too far. Sir Michael Wilshaw, the Chief Inspector of Schools in England, head of Ofsted and a former head teacher in inner-city schools (and so with vast experience of problem families), told a Commons Education Select Committee which was looking into the state of children's services:

> These families need to know that they can't go on treating their children like this ... As a head teacher I used to tell parents that they were behaving badly and that they were bad parents. It didn't often go down extremely well but nevertheless that was my responsibility and it's a responsibility of social workers. ... but families have got a huge part to play and communities have got a huge part to play in supporting children. (quoted in *Guardian*, 2014)

It's a start.

● ***Prejudice.*** Prejudice is, of course, judgement's presumptuous kid brother, ever ready to leap in when least wanted and primed to act without thinking. But, actually, without an ability to prejudge (and act on that prejudgement), how would humankind ever have known that sabre-toothed tigers weren't going to be any more cuddly this time around than when they wolfed down your forebears, or that people goose-stepping in black shirts were unlikely to bode well? Prejudice is nature's way of saving us having to work things out from first principles all the time. It is something we should value as it takes much of the strain out of life. It is also something that many people with autism spectrum disorder cannot benefit from as they find it harder to cross-reference memory, context and generalising from the particular. They usually find life very stressful and overwhelming; having a short cut to decision making would be blissful for them.

- **Critical gossip**. Where would Jane Austen have been without critical gossip? And where would we be without her acid wit and brilliant observations on human behaviour? After all, gossip is the forerunner of Facebook. But gossip is far more responsible in that it can often be traced back to a source and even confounded. This is much harder when the whole world is doing the gossiping. Gossip was a corrective, a way of limiting behaviours at a time when there were many fewer social services and laws to govern how we could reasonably and acceptably behave. Gossip was also the jungle drum warning girls that such and such a man's intentions might not be entirely honourable, long before Google was available to disclose all.

By the wholesale rejection of all of the above, our current version of polite society has brought a raft of unintended consequences. If we don't judge, how can we assess risk? How many children have been left in abusive households because no one wanted to be the one to judge a parent's lifestyle as 'inappropriate', 'harmful' or just plain 'bad'? And, surely, there is no one so deluded that they are not prepared to discriminate between parents who torture, starve and kill their toddlers and those who don't?

If we tolerate everything as a 'lifestyle choice' or as a matter for the individual, yet never criticise or condemn, how do we help people prolong their lives by losing weight (and in so doing, prolong the life of the NHS)? Criticism can work. Many people lose weight because they've been called 'Fatty' once too often – it's all about promoting self-efficacy, a belief that change can happen and that the individual can be (at least partly) responsible for bringing it about.[1] This is where the individual comes into their own. They take

---

1   Self-efficacy is the term used by Stanford psychologist Albert Bandura in his 1977 paper, 'Self-Efficacy: Toward a Unifying Theory of Behavioural Change'. He later said that self-efficacy is 'the belief in one's capabilities to organise and execute the courses of action required to manage prospective situations' (p. 3), or the belief in one's own capacity to be the agent of one's own life – also called self-agency. People with a strong sense of self-agency view challenging problems as tasks to be mastered, develop deeper interest in the activities in which they participate, form a stronger sense of commitment to their interests and activities, and recover quickly from setbacks and disappointments. In contrast, people with a weak sense of self-agency avoid challenging tasks, believe that difficult tasks are beyond their capabilities, focus on personal failings and negative outcomes, and quickly lose confidence in their personal abilities.

personal responsibility for behaving in ways that support the whole, rather than relying on the whole to take up the slack when their personal choices cost society too much.

The balance between individual and community is upset when the individual asserts a right to as much freedom of choice in matters of behaviour and belief as the new values propose. However, there is another possibility. By accrediting so many people with victim status, agreeing to call them 'survivors', saying, almost axiomatically, that they may have been discriminated against whenever they fail to get a job or when they lose a job, declaring that they have been treated prejudicially if something fails to measure up to their ideals, prioritising someone's hurt feelings at being excluded over the running of an event, then society itself risks creating the conditions in which learned helplessness or weak self-agency flourishes. Individuals can become so infantilised that, like poor Mrs Sharples' sister, they fail to see that they, personally, could make a difference.

As with the over-specialising and over-professionalising of social responsibility, convincing people that they are on the receiving end of others' actions and behaviours, rather than being on the delivery end of their own, is most likely to result in a general inability to see themselves in context. They fail to perceive themselves as responsible parts of a whole that depends on each individual connection being good enough. As researchers into personal agency, Robin Vallacher and Daniel Wegner, put it, 'High levels of personal agency represent the tendency to understand one's actions in terms of its consequences and implications, whereas low levels of personal agency represents the tendency to see one's actions in terms of its details or mechanics' (Vallacher and Wegner, 1989: 1). In other words, responsible people connect their behaviour with the past, present and future, and understand its effect on the outside world; helpless ones see only an action in isolation of any impact it might have had, or might have, either on other people or on their own future.

So, back to the redesign idea. We need to take a step back from the internalising, subjective, individual agenda that has been promoted as much by society as by the individuals who drove its early incarnation (and who still urge its ethical advantages). We need to move forwards to a more community-orientated agenda if we wish to have a healthier (and, ironically, happier) society overall.

Sharing the delusion –
in the nicest possible way

At the beginning of Chapter 7, I recounted the contrasting brief histories of San Gimignano and Siena and compared their radically different approaches to questions of town planning and social inclusion. I then examined the relationship between shared values, common goals and personal responsibility and how this relationship can be made more or less functional with respect to engagement in community behaviour, according to how self-centred or selfless those shared values are.

My basic contention is that good societies can only work when values are in place which mitigate against the individual self and in favour of the better functioning of the wider community, when the nature of the common goal is clearly represented to all and held up for everyone to recognise, and also when the individual finds that life feels more significant when they commit their efforts to the greater good than when they commit them to the pursuit of personal goals such as happiness and self-esteem. When people do this, they feel more significant as a consequence.

Ultimately this is all about sharing a delusion, one that says we need meaning in our lives – something bigger than mere survival, something other than mere concrete necessity. This delusion is an outcome of that very early hyper-connectivity that left us feeling uncomfortable if we couldn't cross-reference a zillion different inputs and excitations and place some form of abstract interpretation on them. Calling this a delusion is not to say that it is therefore totally without function because, as inheritors of a fantasy, we are left with nothing if we do not keep it going (or we become kaleidoscope people, fragmented and alone). We need to connect – as widely as possible – in order for our brains and our communities to get the stimulation they need to thrive. And we need to have a common purpose in order for that stimulation to work in favour of order rather than entropy.

Of course, it's very easy for me to make these claims, but you might well be asking, where's the evidence? Where's the specialist research to prove the point you're trying to make? Well, fortunately for me, even though there has been relatively little formal research into community as opposed to individual resilience, the results of the work carried out by sociologist Robert J. Sampson, at the University of Chicago, are both in line with my presumptions and actually quite compelling.

Collective efficacy

One of the key areas of Sampson's research was an investigation into levels of crime in neighbouring areas of cities and the reasons why some areas seemed to suffer from greater levels of criminal activity (and especially violence) than others, even when social status and poverty levels appeared to be similar. I think it must be pretty much unarguable that good societies (in the sense that they work for the good of all) have low levels of crime and bad ones (which fail to work for the good of all) suffer from high levels. So this research is likely to provide evidence very much in line with what we're looking for.

In a paper titled 'Neighborhoods and Violent Crime', Sampson and his colleagues hypothesised that 'collective efficacy, defined as social cohesion among neighbors combined with their willingness to intervene on behalf of the common good, is linked to reduced violence' (Sampson et al., 1997: 918). They went on to propose that 'the *differential ability* of neighborhoods to realise the common values of residents and maintain effective social controls is *a major source of neighborhood variation* in violence' (ibid.: 918; my italics).

In other words, areas which have shared values and use them to impose controls are less violent than those which don't. They added that the control they meant was not formal, institutional control (i.e. 'specialist' professionalised control), but rather 'the capacity of a group to regulate its members according to desired principles – to realise collective, as opposed to forced, goals' (ibid.).

They then referred to matters like monitoring children's play, 'hanging around' by youths, kerb-crawling, drugs, adult spats and so on, suggesting that the processes of monitoring and intervening, in the certain knowledge that these processes were in line with shared values and would be communally endorsed and supported, were key to limiting opportunities for interpersonal crime. Stable but not necessarily tightly geographically boundaried communities were necessary for mutual trust and cohesion. They added:

> In sum, it is the linkage of mutual trust and the willingness to intervene for the common good that defines the neighborhood context of collective efficacy. Just as individuals vary in their capacity for efficacious action, so too do neighborhoods vary in their capacity to achieve common goals. (ibid.: 919)

They found that collective efficacy (which might otherwise be called 'community agency') worked to protect everyone from becoming victims – even those who might otherwise have offended. Sampson, in other research carried out in the Chicago area, also found that areas which lacked what he described as a 'resilient social infrastructure' were more vulnerable than others at times of disaster (e.g. hurricanes and other natural phenomena). And he went even further than that, suggesting that the more social engagement there was in an area and the more social altruism, the fewer properties were likely to be repossessed in the event of an economic meltdown:

> Qualities such as the shared willingness to intervene and civic engagement constitute a social resource that helps explain the well-being of communities – in good times and bad … Just as humans need social connections as well as physical resources to survive and thrive, so too do communities. (Sampson, 2013c)

Just as Sir Michael Wilshaw observed.

The Olympic torch – a light was lit

Here in Britain, nothing could have made it clearer that community spirit works wonders for morale and wellbeing than the success of the 2012 London Olympics. So far so supportive of Professor Sampson, but what about the much vaunted legacy of the Olympics? Has that stood us in ongoing good stead?

Well, sadly the sporting legacy does not seem to have been all that it might. However, the community aspect of the legacy is apparently doing rather better. According to a report in the *Daily Telegraph* (White, 2013), the Mayor of London's junior volunteering programme is going strong in London. In one inner-city primary school in Lambeth, a small early act of volunteering – the growing of little pot plants and then hand-delivering them to local elderly residents – has led to a positive cascade of benefits, or even a cascade of positive benefits. These have included children voluntarily sharpening pencils, picking up litter, helping with the lunch queue and even volunteering to be on the school council – something almost unheard of before. There has been an amazing increase in self-confidence among the pupils.

Veronica Wadley, the Team London coordinator who was involved in the volunteering project from the start, said, 'if you integrate volunteering into children's lives there is something more. Self-esteem, confidence, communication, teamwork, all improve. These are soft skills that ultimately lead to an improvement in educational results' (quoted in White, 2013). Volunteering, the ultimate in community engagement, is not only good for the community but, apparently, it is also good for the individual as well.

A light that keeps on burning

In another newspaper report in January 2013, we read of Margaret Miller, who, as a girl, was apparently thought not strong enough to become a nurse (McIntosh, 2013). And so in 1939 she became a committed volunteer for the Women's Voluntary Services (WVS) instead. Over seventy years later, and at the age of 102, Margaret was still volunteering, not only for the WRVS (the WVS became the Women's Royal Voluntary Service in 1966 and the Royal Voluntary Service in 2013) but also for a local stroke charity. Not only does Mrs Miller insist that she gets more out of volunteering than she puts in, but she also says it has filled a great deal of her life and 'brings a great feeling of satisfaction'.

Researchers into volunteering, James Nazroo and Katey Matthews, have suggested that there is strong evidence for 'the relationship between volunteering and well-being in later life', and that 'in the case of older people … an engagement in volunteering may be particularly important in providing a route, or opportunity, to remain engaged in socially meaningful and valued roles' (Nazroo and Matthews, 2012: 5, 8). In other words, volunteering will provide significance in life and allow a person to feel that they themselves are still of significance at that time of life when both might be in some doubt.

Cast into the darkness of the single self

If volunteering is the necessary spirit of community connectedness and personal wellbeing, then loneliness is the basis for isolation and ill health in all its many varieties. This has been understood for a very long time. It has been suggested that Shakespeare was the first person to use the term 'lonely' (although the word 'lone' existed before) in *Coriolanus*, which is about the corrupting effect of power. He understood better than anyone else that states of being also made for psychological states. For him, brain, body and behaviour were always intertwined.

In the character of another seeker of power, Richard III, he not only makes his physical deformity and difference a correlate of his psychological deformity and difference (not very politically correct these days, I realise, but it was over four hundred years ago), he also recognises that both will impact on a man's (or woman's) way of relating to life. And so, after a long night in which Richard ruminates on his own isolation and essential loneliness, he has him go into battle, where, according to Sir William Catesby:

The king enacts more wonders than a man,
Daring an opposite to every danger:
His horse is slain, and all on foot he fights,
Seeking for Richmond in the throat of death.

In other words, he acts in the riskiest way possible. His social exclusion has made him a gambler. Which is exactly what three researchers said was likely to happen to lonely people when they presented their findings to the annual meeting of the American Psychological Association in Hawaii in 2015. Rod Duclos, assistant professor of marketing at Hong Kong University of Science and Technology, professor Echo Wen Wan of the University of Hong Kong and Yuwei Jiang, assistant professor of marketing at Hong Kong Polytechnic University, wrote an article titled, 'Show Me the Honey! Effects of Social Exclusion on Financial Risk-Taking' (Duclos et al., 2013). The findings were so compelling that the authors suggested that no major financial decisions, such as getting a mortgage or taking out a pension plan, should ever be made shortly after any significant social upset, such as the break-up of a relationship.

Their experiments were carefully designed in such a way that it was clear to see that it was the sense of being excluded, per se, rather than the sadness or pain that might have gone hand in hand with exclusion that drove the risky behaviour. This included not only flighty fiscal gambits of the more mainstream kind but also betting on horses and gambling in casinos.

It is already well known that lonely people are suckers for signing up for things like credit cards and gym membership (it used to be bulky mail order catalogues) because doing this creates a vicarious sense of belonging, but they are much less likely to sign up to helping charities. In this way, loneliness becomes a form of vicious circle:

isolation leads to internalisation of gratification, lessened interest in connectedness and then, inevitably, to increased levels of isolation and so on and so on.

As we have seen from the arch-psychologist himself, Shakespeare, it is not only in the field of finances that lonely people take risks. It can also be in much more improbable places such as Bosworth Field. For lonely people, the correctives that are in place for better socialised people – correctives such as external observation, monitoring and critical (positive and negative) comment – are largely missing from life. Instead of following the normal routes, they take their directions for life from inside their own heads – as we already know, not the most reliable of beasts. And so, for the lonely, it can suddenly seem like a very good idea to dive into battle without care for the consequences, to smoke too much, to eat inappropriately and at inappropriate times, or to enter into relationships with the most inappropriate people on the planet. Never forgetting the acquisition of all those cats.

Not only do isolation and loneliness lead to poor physical, mental and financial health for the isolated and lonely themselves, but they also incur much greater costs for the wider community. This is because poor health, especially in old age (which is when most people are likely to become isolated and lonely), is one of the greatest costs that society has to bear. Loneliness is as bad for your health as smoking fifteen cigarettes a day, and although that might reduce the population a bit, in the meantime all those heart attacks and strokes (Cacioppo and Hawkley, 2014) are going to cost us dear. So, it's going to make sense all round to try to address loneliness and isolation and to do as much as possible to create that necessary sense of collective efficacy, which has less to do with specialists telling us all how things must be done and more to do with doing things together. That is, more to do with shared values and the belief that not only are we all in it together but also that collectively we do have the resources to improve life, whereas singly we can only make ourselves feel good in the short term.

Critical thinking

Events like the London Olympics and disasters like 9/11 or Hurricane Sandy can bring people together in collective acts that work for the common good. Although fewer things are achieved and fewer people devastated in these rare events than happens all the time in less overt ways, nevertheless, it seems that people collectively, as they do individually, need the added impetus, the stimulus for dopamine and therefore for motivation, that excitement brings. Although most of us would hate to think of ourselves in this way, we do by and large respond to dramatic change and challenge in positive and energised ways. As so many people who lived through the Second World War have said, it was the most alive they had ever felt.

I am not suggesting that we need to engineer a crisis in order to get the kind of engagement I've been talking about – crises can often be divisive. But we could take a punt on seeing the condition we're currently in *as* a crisis or at least as a critical juncture, a point from which we could take two quite different directions into the future. One would be, more or less, a continuation of the rather unfocused direction we're going in at the moment but with a few tweaks that acknowledge we're not entirely sure it's going to take us to where we want to be. The other would be in a radically different direction, one that involves us acting decisively and in the interests of a particular outcome, however temporarily unsettling or personally inconvenient that might occasionally be, rather than just following our own interests.

So, we could continue unthinkingly into a future that we don't truly want or don't feel we have actively chosen. Or, alternatively, we could think critically, believe in collective efficacy and instead of demanding, expecting or assuming that specialists and professionals should be making the future for us, we can set about sculpting it for ourselves – by means of every single little thing that we say and do.

Chapter 9

Significant Other

To misquote Dickens: it is the best of times, it is the worst of times. Today, most of us have everything that previous generations would have thought of as beyond luxurious and exciting. Possession of the meanest of family cars would have made Richard III invincible – and popular. But although modern Western societies have enough food, enough education, enough healthcare (not to mention enough cars), somehow it is never quite enough for us. We are never satisfied. Regardless of how many more of any of these commodities we demand, and often get, the need for yet more remains constant.

We seem to have lost the connection between effort and attainment (which is not necessarily our fault as too often we have had responsibility stripped from us). We expect external agencies to supply our needs: professionals, experts, governments, even other individuals. But this abdication of agency can leave us unable to see what we, individually, are contributing to the social malaise and in what everyday ways we are doing it.

The main message of this book is that one of the most compelling forces in human behaviour is the need to find significance. We've already looked at a number of outcomes and implications of this drive (the coda at the end of Chapter 10 tells an interesting and socially pertinent tale about the relationship between significance, crime, fear, the individual and the state). In this chapter, I want to look at how that overwhelming drive for significance may compromise even that which works in our own best interests by examining how the drive for significance, together with the consequences of damage caused to the sense of significance, can compromise our chance of achieving the desirable objective of collective efficacy.

What, though, are the totems of that significance for most of us? What are the signifiers – the things, events, processes, people – that might represent significance and become necessary to an individual's feeling that they, or the worlds they live in, have any meaning?

I will start by looking at one aspect of one of the greatest perceived providers of meaning in our lives – love.

(Romantic) love is the greatest thing

Rosa was a sadly damaged woman. Uneducated and brutalised in her early years, she was fundamentally inadequate and incapable of managing her life. She could not look after her two (apparently fatherless) kids, cook or clean, or even venture far from her house. She never dressed herself in anything other than the T-shirt and shorts or jumper and jeans of her teenage years. She seemed unable to recognise that, having benefited from social housing for much of her life, she owed some responsibility to both her landlord and the people around her. She neither cared for the property nor made the smallest attempt to control the behaviour of her many male visitors who were nearly always abusive, aggressive and domineering towards her long-suffering neighbours. When she was drinking she was as verbally abusive as her male friends. But once she had given it up she became silent and almost invisible – motormouth became motormouse.

In her mid-forties and with her children out of the (her?) way, Rosa settled down a bit and became an unlikely but wholly committed standard bearer for the virtues of life with a long-term partner. So much so that she even suggested to a single professional woman who was involved in her case that she, too, might get as lucky as Rosa and find herself as good a man as she had. She then enumerated and extolled his virtues as the professional woman struggled to keep her gagging reflex in check. Not only was Rosa's personal version of Mr Darcy no paragon of male beauty, he was no paragon of anything else either. He'd not been long out of prison. Having done time does not necessarily mean that a man is dishonest in all aspects of life, but in this Mr Darcy's case it rather suggested that his motives for finding a willing partner with accommodation were less than scrupulous. It was highly unlikely that he would have found himself quite as smitten with Rosa had her children still been living with her. But it never occurred to Rosa that, in his eyes, her status as available commodity (with housing benefits) would have been sorely compromised had he also been forced to take her status as mother (even as a fairly hopeless one) into consideration. Once he'd moved in with her she hardly ever saw her children again.

Rosa, although not having been in prison herself, was like most of the prisoners I have worked with, in that being without a partner, even for a short space of time, was almost unthinkable. She had no way of imagining herself as a separate and operative entity, no way of seeing herself as an independent but effective member of some wider social group. Like the prisoners, she could only see herself in relation to her partner; only when she was in a long-term relationship could she begin to see herself as a more fixed and permanent being herself.[1]

What was particularly interesting was the way she described both his wooing of her and his comments to her on the morning after their first loved-up night together. Rosa was completely bowled over by the fact that he had actually sought permission from her father before asking her out for a first date (remember, she had two grown children and was in her middle years at the time). She thought this was *so* respectful and romantic. Having followed this act of male gallantry by telling her that she looked a bit rough in the mornings, she found this yet another example of refreshingly respectful honesty, and *so* different, she said, from all the other blokes with whom she'd woken up.

Despite her fundamental sense that she was worthless, Rosa was so desperate to *matter*, to be of significance. In this respect she was like many prisoners, especially many female prisoners, in that she felt that being disposed of like some medieval chattel and receiving unflattering honesty was a measure of how much a man cared for her, rather than a measure of his Stone Age mentality.[2] She even saw his relationship with her as *the* special one in his life, so special that she was the one and only who could get him to do things her way ('Leave it to me, he'll do it for me', 'Let me talk to him, I know how to bring him round'). She couldn't, of course. It was her need to believe herself special that prompted such faith in her own abilities, but the reality didn't stack up in quite the same way. Ultimately, the behaviours (his) that she perceived as making her significant only served to emphasise how insignificant she felt deep inside. Why should anyone find it endearing to hear a man laugh at a woman's incompetence, saying, 'Well, she's only a fucking woman after all! What do you expect?' Yet Rosa did.

Time and again, women (the inability to respect oneself is not confined to women, but this form of significance deficit seems largely to affect women) go into relationships in which they only feel valued when they are being objectified. It is a curious variant on 'I,

---

1   No matter how unkempt, how drugged-up, how unlovely, how unappealing (sometimes with running sores and notifiable diseases) a prisoner might have been, they were rarely without a boyfriend or girlfriend.

2   Whereas men often take their anger and frustration out on others, and are inside for assault and so on, women are often imprisoned for arson – against their own property – having taken their feelings out on themselves.

myself and me' in which there is a sort of vacuum where self should be. The vacuum gets filled not by the voice proclaiming 'self' over and over again in as many forms as possible but by an external person filling the void with a self-shaped object of their imagining.

Erin Pizzey, founder of the first refuges for battered women, addressed a similar issue in *Prone to Violence* (Pizzey and Shapiro, 1982) in which she describes the complexity of women like Rosa's relationships with men. She observed that they frequently generated the conditions in which violence could flourish, largely because these were the (abusive) conditions they had grown up in and were therefore the only conditions they had learned to associate as representative of one person's significance for another. Only through abuse could they really see themselves as having any meaning. And, as (my) sequitur, only through the actions associated with responding to abuse could they see life itself as having any value or meaning. Everything else – be it education, children, work, art or anything that fails to mirror the high octane ding-dong of corrosive relationships – seems utterly without interest to them. This is why emotionally abusive soap operas go hand in hand with a society overly full of failed relationships.

For Rosa and people like her, the mutant human demand for significance is best met by a sexual partner. But though other significance needs might at first sight look very different from Rosa's, in fact we are *all* in search of significance, and when we don't find it, or have never found it, then, like Rosa, we extend our search into some very strange places – although not always quite as strange as her Stone Age Romeo.

The chemistry of love

A correlate of love, sexual or otherwise, is that strangely conflicted hormone, oxytocin. It's the hormone that is complex in its effects and, in the context of significant other, can become very complex indeed.

When Markus Heinrichs, the University of Freiburg's pioneering researcher into oxytocin, looked at the impact oxytocin had on human behaviour he noticed that this was significantly modified by both the individual and the circumstances involved (see Yong, 2012). He also discovered that oxytocin affects the way we perceive other people. This helps to explain why someone like Rosa can be so easily taken in by love. It could be said that love actually makes people blind – not just in terms of appearance; it affects all kinds of judge-ments. Heinrichs asked volunteers to take part in a game which required them to invest money in someone who was not guaranteed to be honest. Volunteers who had sniffed oxytocin beforehand invested more money with the dubious trustee than those who hadn't. His follow-up work showed that people in the grip of oxyto-cin become generally much more trusting of others, finding them also more attractive and approachable – given that they belonged in some way to their overall in-group. However, other researchers (e.g. Shamay-Tsoory et al., 2009; cited in Yong, 2012) have found that raised levels of oxytocin can lead to gloating on the part of winners in gambling situations and furious jealousy on the part of losers. These effects appear to depend not only on social context but also on the psychology and sophistication of the individuals involved.

Trusting the essentially untrustworthy, finding desirable the deeply unattractive and feeling intensely competitive and/or jealous are just aspects of the impact of oxytocin on individual physiology. It seems clear that the most needy people, as well as the least sophis-ticated, are going to be most at risk of falling foul of these effects. History is littered with examples of the great and the good falling off the wagon of rational sense in pursuit of the defining and moti-vating force of lurve. These historical/mythical megastars range from Cleopatra to Napoleon, from Dante to Bridget Jones (and was it really oxytocin that Puck gave to Titania in *A Midsummer Night's Dream*?). When it comes to being fools for love, someone as lowly as Rosa was never going to stand much of a chance.

Signifiers of significance

It's not only love that we over-credit with importance. There's a whole list of things we use as surrogates for significance – the totems, icons, symbols, objects or forces that we credit with mean-ing. Possessing or being involved with these things gives us the impression that our own individual selves, and existence itself, have both purpose and significance. Given that they are all really phan-toms of our brains, all that is left to decide is whether they are of equal value or whether some of them are actually less valuable than others.

Financial status

Personal wealth is an obvious candidate as a status symbol. Once we have enough to live on, anything above that simply becomes a means of measuring how important we are.

Work status

Most people identify themselves, both in terms of significance and success, by the work they do. Our relationship with work is often indicated by how we describe ourselves, whether enmeshed ('It's who I am') or pragmatic ('It's what I do'). For example, am I a teacher, or am I Fred Jones who either teaches or works as a teacher? Am I a politician, or am I Sally Jones who has a career in politics? Awareness of the needs of a greater whole – good; unquestioning over-identification with a special interest group – less good. If we over-identify the core self with a role or subgroup then we risk losing significance should that job end, if we leave the group or we are made redundant. Who are we then? It's long been acknowledged that when people with an enmeshed relationship with work are finally forced to stop working, they frequently not only lose all sense of meaning in life, but they also become more likely to develop medical problems and even die relatively young.

Individuals who work in highly structured organisations, such as the armed forces or religious establishments, often find, anecdotally at least, problems in adapting to civvy street when they leave these family-style structures. This seems to be particularly so for those who sign up for short terms (four years or less) in the forces. Whether a generic short-termism in thinking and in life is also indicative of a predisposition to problems, or whether formal and tightly structured organisations attract people with rather hazy boundaries who then often feel lost once outside the organisation again (in my years of teaching I found it was often the naughtiest, most damaged and unboundaried boys who were particularly anxious to get into the army), or whether the cause is something else altogether, it definitely appears that identifying yourself primarily by your work status can be a mixed blessing. You acquire significance vicariously but you may lose it intrinsically.

Special status

Special status is related to work status in a rather twisted way. For most people it is desirable to belong to a successful subgroup, either through work or culturally or socially. It brings not only kudos but also significance through acceptance. This is true even with subgroups that legitimate society outlaws. For example, inner-city gangs, heavily involved in violence and drug dealing, operate according to the same general principles – involving hierarchies, incentives and punishments – which also motivate and reward what we call civilised society. In fact, most civilised societies began in just these ways, only with feudal robber barons and the like running the show rather than urban gang leaders.

But there are some people so out of step with accepted social norms that they do not want to belong to, in the words of Groucho Marx, 'any club that will accept people like me as a member'. Usually abandoned, neglected or brutalised in childhood, they have felt their significance only through abrasive actions: through hurting rather than through soothing, through negative sensory experiences rather than through positive ones. These people are the naughty, wild, delinquent ones who tend to find status through not belonging. If successful in adulthood they are given to saying things like, 'Nobody tells *me* what to do,' and their anthem is 'My Way'. If unsuccessful, they tend to become prisoners with attitude. Their inner voice constantly intones, 'I know I exist because something harsh, cantankerous and roughly stimulating is batting backwards and forwards between myself and the outer world.' Not belonging gives them significance.

Association or membership status

These birds of a feather feel that they have taken on the shape of their organisation, giving them a form or a substance that they did not have before. Special interest groups, be they cyclists, eco-warriors, animal protection groups, urban knitters, chess players, guerrilla gardeners or NHS pressure groups, all help people to feel of value in themselves and that they are involved with principles of value. The specifics of the organisation's function may at times be less relevant than the fact of belonging and of committing to a cause. Some serial joiners move quite seamlessly from one impassioned cause to another as the sense of significance they get from belonging to a particular group begins to wane. However, there are cause-specific moments in history (wars, environmental causes, etc.) which bring people together in ways that generate the social cohesion that has been lacking in normal life, and which they look back on fondly (but usually only if they have won).

This form of silo mentality can be as harmful to the wider group as it is helpful for the individual. The dopamine and oxytocin rush that follows from focusing attention and the sense of belonging, making the individual feel 'right', also brings the downsides mentioned above. The feeling of reward that comes from being better, special and different from *them* is fed not by looking at the bigger picture or by connecting things and people as much as possible, but by creating (and even demonising) out-groups – even when the out-groups comprise much of the rest of society. Narrower forms of belonging may at times even prevent social cohesion. Currently, we appear to be suffering the effects of this as government policies designed to encourage the development of that hybrid beast, diversity, have largely failed to deliver on their implied promise of enhancing a sense of belonging within an all-inclusive society. People's behaviour is much more nuanced than most governments have the time and inclination to understand.

Codes of conduct

Codes of conduct, as well as manners, chivalry, ritual and ceremony, are all forms of shorthand which allocate specific and culturally agreed amounts of significance to people and events. 'What ceremony else?', Laertes cries in *Hamlet* when his sister Ophelia, suspected of committing suicide, is denied full burial ceremonial rites. This tells us to what extent early seventeenth-century society placed a value not only on someone's life but also on its own ability to value someone's life. The audience of the day would have understood better than we do the full meaning of Laertes' grief. This was not just for the direct and immediate loss of a sister but also for the loss of significance (although, as ever, Shakespeare is challenging all social norms by demanding religious and spiritual parity for the self-harming). Humans create ceremonies as their way of telling others that they are valued by *this* much. Although largely a human-specific behaviour, as it mostly relies on symbolic thought processes, there are many instances of animals performing what we term 'mating rituals'. Some, elephants in particular, seem to follow rituals around death in that they appear to mourn and even attempt to carry out simple burials by kicking leaves over bodies. So it seems that elephants (as well as flatfish) may have some primitive form of sense of self.

The humans who fail to appreciate ceremony and ritual are those least skilful at symbolic thinking – autistic people. They often seem to be at a complete loss to understand the sad behaviour of other people at funerals (even if they can feel sad about the physical loss of the person). And they are rarely comfortable when expected to be adaptive and flexible around codes of conduct which they treat as absolute and unchangeable rules (rather than as communications of meaning and intent), regardless of how much changing circumstances might affect matters. This is because autistic brains rely more on the comforting effect of the routine that often accompanies codes of conduct than they do on any abstract comfort that other people might find in the symbolic aspect of rituals or ceremonies.

The subtle difference between routine and ritual can easily be misunderstood, especially when people are having to deal with autism while only being familiar with the external, behavioural elements of the disorder rather than with the underlying neurology. It can sometimes appear to them as though autistic people find the 'knowability', the dependability, of ceremonies and codes of conduct authentically comforting in themselves. But routine, that pre-set agenda which offers reliability and demands little input, uses one part of the brain, whereas the symbolism which lies behind an authentic appreciation of ritual and ceremony (and which gets vividly realised in the mind of a devotee during ceremonials, requiring a significant expenditure of mental energy) uses a different part of the brain altogether.

For most people, ritual, ceremonies, chivalric codes and the rest really are signifiers of significance and are therefore straightforward and effective ways for making both individuals and events feel important and meaningful, especially if enough of society subscribes to the same ones. However, this is not so for autistic people. Showing them that they or their discoveries are significant by honouring them with awards ceremonies and so on is most likely to result in them wondering why people bother with such pointless stuff.

Pilgrimages

Each age seems to feel the need to look for meaning by going on some form of pilgrimage. For centuries, these ritualised journeys were wholly enmeshed with the old religions. However, by the twentieth century space travel had taken on some of the aspects of pilgrimage, representing Western humanity's need to connect the journey with the search for purpose and meaning. Now that space travel has largely failed to deliver on its implied promises it seems that we are once again turning to foot travel for the good of our souls (if not soles). According to Simon Reeve, presenter of the BBC Two programme *Pilgrimage*, in the last thirty years the number of people walking the ancient pilgrimage route of the Camino de Santiago in Spain, one of the most symbolic routes for signifying spiritual dedication, has increased a hundredfold. Even allowing for today's easier access, improved walking conditions and the like, that surely tells us something about people's need to search for meaning both through action and in place.

Arts

Creativity, artefacts, painting, writing, music and so on all provide individuals with the drug that most humans crave. When writers write, painters paint and musicians make music, what they are essentially doing is elevating themselves as individual responders, reactors, commentators and perceivers above the common herd; setting out their own opinion on the look, quality, behaviour of Other as being of greater than average significance, and thereby their own person, as parent of the whole enterprise, into something of significance too. If not actually stating that they are making more internal connections than most, they are at least implicitly suggesting that theirs is a way of knowing the world that is worthy of both externalisation and permanency.

Art and art forms fulfil a need not only for meaning and significance in the here and now, but for significance in the future. For some strange mutant reason, humankind alone appears to feel in some way diminished if all they leave to the future is more of their kind. Scratches, scrapes, squiggles and imprints on stone, paper, wax and now somewhere in a cloud, destined as much for future contemplation and enjoyment as for present, all seem to have the power to add value to current existence in ways that genuinely improve our physiological wellbeing and make us feel that both we and life make sense. Strange creatures, we humans.

Religion

With its churches, cathedrals and monasteries; its mosques, synagogues and temples; its imagery, incense and incantations, religion has been the repository into which was poured the creative and aesthetic energy of the medieval world. It was awe realised in stone and paint, the dream world realised in the concept of Jerusalem, a place in which you could invest your hopes, dreams and idealisations. It terrified and it improved. It gave focus and it gave purpose. It explained the inexplicable and it told you that if the explanations were less than explanatory – well, that was rather the point.

Religion covered everything that wasn't covered by anything else, and told you that significance, now and hereafter, was totally taken care of and you didn't need to worry your pretty little head about it ever again. So most people didn't, and no doubt had fewer crises of personal confidence as a consequence (or maybe that was the long hours and unrelenting physical work that left no time or energy for them). But even today, irony aside, religion, or rather a belief in it, does genuinely seem to offer resilience and protection against destructive habits. Although researchers into resilience in young people routinely identify personal autonomy as a protective factor, they have noted strong identification with a religious community as a protective factor as well, which seems slightly contradictory.[3] However, a religion which promotes personal responsibility and service to others may well be promoting a form of personal autonomy which will, in turn, help a young person feel in control of their life rather than dependent on others – and that is the key.

A study funded by the Swiss National Science Foundation (Gmel et al., 2013) found that adherence to a religious belief made young Swiss men less likely than atheists to smoke tobacco or use cannabis, ecstasy or cocaine. The study did not delve deeply into the reasons behind the difference, but one possibility I would suggest is that substance use, whether directly or indirectly, affects the dopamine systems in the brain. These are highly influential in significance terms, making or unmaking our sense that things matter. Dopamine levels also rise when we anticipate a reward (hence dopamine is

---

3 See http://www.encare.info/en-GB/riskyenvironments/resilience/factors/.

implicated in addictive cravings – see Appendix A), and what is heaven but the ultimate reward?

The work of Andrew Newberg, of Thomas Jefferson University, Philadelphia (Newberg and Waldman, 2010; see also Smith, 2014), among many other similar studies, shows us that dopamine levels are not only higher in believers but also that you can artificially tweak belief in non-believers if you artificially raise their dopamine levels. All of which goes to prove that not only can you get high on religion but also that religion fills a significant significance hole for many people. There are many other individuals, non-religious in terms of any belief, for whom the existence of the bricks and mortar of religion is still very important, and who would feel that something quintessential had gone from life if churches, cathedrals, temples, mosques, synagogues, cemeteries and all the rest were to disappear from the face of the earth.

Yearning

Yearning follows quite naturally from religion. Sentimentality, poignancy, bitter-sweet desire, nostalgia, melancholy, the Grail legend, Atlantis, folklore, folk music, Rachmaninov, cuddly toys for adults; all of these, together with a great many other hazy, inchoate stirrings of emotion, are the evidence of humankind's state of incompleteness. An incompleteness that is an inevitable outcome of our mutant need to connect up more and more, even as the connections themselves are creating an exponential expansion of the possible connections that might be made. In other words, we are condemned by our DNA to the endless, fruitless search. Only it's not really fruitless, because as Robert Louis Stevenson wrote in 'El Dorado', 'To travel hopefully is a better thing than to arrive.' The search, rather as Hamlet's question is more important than the answer, really is more important, in significance terms than the find.

Self-image

Although self-image might seem frivolous in comparison to weighty matters like religion and art, the way we see ourselves and how we are seen by others is probably responsible for more psychological distress in Westernised societies than all the other signifiers of significance put together. Although the gap appears to be closing, there is a definite gender bias in matters related to appearance. Women spend far more on cosmetics, hygiene products and fashion than men, and yet suffer many more crises of confidence than men about their appearance. These show up as eating disorders and body dysmorphic disorder (in which their perception of their body or of a single body part becomes completely distorted). According to the 2013 Girls' Attitudes survey, *Equality for Girls*, carried out by Girlguiding, 51% of girls aged 14–16 are already unhappy with their looks and 71% of girls aged 11–21 would like to lose weight. Three-quarters of that same age group of girls believe that boys expect them to look like the images of women and girls they see in the media. It is hardly surprising that so many of them feel they are falling some way short.

The experts are divided on the reasons for this. Has it got anything to do with the greater neuronal connectivity of women's brains compared with men's (which would allow for over-association and increased emotional responsiveness)? Or is it because of complex feedback systems within the brain which are less gender specific but still human specific? It's hard to imagine that cows or pigs care what they look like. This problematic area, our troubling capacity to be so self-absorbed about our appearance, appears to be yet another negative consequence of the human capacity to be self-aware. Even though some animals have passed the mirror test, indicating that they are physically self-aware (including bonobos, chimpanzees, orang-utans, elephants, dolphins and magpies),[4] the additional emotional/psychological element of caring about how we look and caring about how others look in comparison to us, and then making qualitative judgements about the desirability of certain traits over others, appears to be uniquely human (whatever anthropomorphic pet owners want to believe).

It is the caring about it that is the mark of the significance we ascribe to image. Not only does it matter to most of us how we appear to the rest of the world, but it also matters how we appear in our own mind's eye (How am I presenting myself, now, as I speak on the phone in an empty room?). Some people are so aware of the image they wish to project of themselves *to themselves* that they won't make a phone call without first putting on make-up. If personal presentation were only of importance because of the effect we are

---

4   Devised by Gordon Gallup Jr in 1970 to show whether an animal, marked with a coloured dot and placed in front of a mirror, could understand that the dot was on its own body, rather than on the image in the mirror. If it could it would attempt to remove it from its body.

having on the world outside, then why would women who wear full Islamic veils such as the niqab and the burka spend significant sums of money caring for their hair? And yet, according to Glenn Lyons, fellow of the Institute of Trichologists and clinical director at the prestigious Philip Kingsley Clinic, the quantity and condition of their hair causes many fully veiled women at least as much distress as it does women who have theirs on permanent public display (pers. comm.).

How we feel about ourselves, at a physical level, is largely determined by the messages we saw in our primary carers' eyes and heard from our primary carers' mouths. There is a lot of other stuff going on in our formulation of self-image as well, particularly in relation to all the representations of ultra-perfect human forms that we are subjected to 24/7, but if an infant is able to feel that he or she is just about the most important and desirable thing in the world to its parent, whatever its attractiveness in the eyes of the outside world, then that child will be much better able to live with the notion that while physical perfection may well be desirable, it certainly isn't the be all and end all of existence.

If more of us had had more of our significance needs met in early infancy, the cosmetics and fashion industries may well have ended up much smaller and the incidence of distressing conditions such as eating and body dysmorphic disorders would almost certainly be reduced. But even so, we can still all make a difference by reducing the focus on image and upping the focus on the more meritorious achievements of childhood and adolescence. If a child gets more 'oohs' and 'ahs' and congratulations for wearing a mini-me outfit or for touting a macho buzz cut than they do for reading well or caring for the welfare of their pet, then we can hardly be surprised if they suffer more from self-image problems as adults, can we?

This section is to an extent about satiety, about having *enough* emotional and sensory feedback from internal and external evaluative systems to stimulate the appropriate neurotransmitters, which will then make us feel motivated to want to keep on going. This is significance. And significance is necessarily a very personal thing. Although many totems or signifiers of significance will be universal, some will only be applicable for an individual or for a particular set of people, perhaps for cultural, gender or professional reasons – we can find significance in so many different matters. Significance adds a kind of shape and texture to life, and things we find significant become substantial, functioning like friends that accompany us on some part of our way through life. We must keep it in mind, though, that friends may not always be the best of guides.

The following list is neither a deep look at possible individual signifiers of significance (i.e. those friends), and nor is it a comprehensive one. It's here to help illustrate how the general system works and indicate the kinds of things that we, individually, may depend on to help us feel that life is worth living and that *we ourselves* are 'worth the whistle', as Goneril famously proclaims in *King Lear*. It is for each of us, once we are aware of the system, to decide if any particular signifier is more valid or beneficial than any other – given, as always, that the whole damn thing is a phantom of our hyper-connecting brains in the first place.

Politics

For many people politics is religion without the afterlife, a sanctified area that is not open to question. For others, politics is church without the God bit. In other words, politics provides them with a system of beliefs that amounts to a framework for living. Political involvement of any persuasion, at any level, confers a sense of internal significance through association with other like-minded people and through shared endeavour, and it confers external significance through the practical activities that promise a sense of achievement. The downside of belonging in such silo fashion is the potential for antagonism, envy, *Schadenfreude* and other equally unlovely feelings and related anti-Other behaviours (the oxytocin effect).

Food

People often assess their significance to others and offer themselves up for acceptance by means of food gathering, preparation and cooking (people over-reliant on this strategy are known as 'feeders'). They also compensate themselves by the same means if they feel under-appreciated or overlooked. These days, when food is readily available for most Westernised societies, it is no longer simply a necessity but more a hugely sophisticated bellwether for acceptability – dietary choices determining one's social standing as much as wealth or health.

Collecting

An unusual or valuable collection (from fine art or wines to bottle tops or old mobile phones) is a way of calculating both status and specialness, as in 'I have something that other people haven't'. Just browsing through a carefully amassed collection can be self-soothing in times of stress and can raise self-satisfaction and self-regard, even when the things collected have little practical or financial value.

Displays

Displays of dancing, singing, strength, endurance or even of Christmas lights or fireworks may all function as ways of achieving special status. This is especially so when individuals hyper-decorate their houses at Christmas, regardless of whether their spectacles are either attractive in themselves or acceptable to their neighbours. Using such displays for fundraising may also be a form of significance seeking.

Performing

To be centre stage is essential to many people's sense that they are worth hearing. They need the authority that both the platform and their endogenous (self-generated by the body) adrenaline-fuelled stimulation bring before they can either feel fully alive and authenticated or completely entitled to speak out or up.

Entrepreneurship and DIY

Running your own business or building/renovating your own house can bring a great sense of meaning/significance into a person's life. They are more self-determining, more in control and less at the mercy of others. This is especially true for people of a maverick or risk-taking personality and who need above average levels of stimulation.

Working long hours

Working long hours appeals to men and women who need to be necessary and who feel that being overworked and rushed off their feet carries more importance than being able to delegate, timetable and accommodate life's demands more fluidly. For them, a sense of their own significance is largely wrapped up in their performance rather than in their personality or acceptability for who they are.

Genealogy and tradition

As people find significance in knowing who their ancestors were, what they did and what they possessed – their inheritance, so traditional ways (e.g. craftsmanship) create a lineage of sorts too. A belief that these ways bring both a superior skill set and special status may help a person to feel that an extra significance attaches to themselves, to their work and to events carried out in traditional ways.

People pleasing and co-dependency

Some people appear to need to promote what they see as someone else's preferences over their own. However, it's more often that by always asking others to choose, rather than chipping in with their own preferences, they may, in fact, be placing a burden on others. These co-dependent people who seek significance through others' presumed approbation of their selflessness can often function perfectly contentedly if they happen to come across a life partner who is utterly demanding.

Munchausen/Munchausen by proxy

Patients exhibiting Munchausen syndrome (named after a fictional German baron who told tall tales) either make up or induce illnesses and injuries in themselves in order to get noticed and thus acquire some significance, so it can be seen as a form of attention seeking. The 'by proxy' version involves people (frequently mothers) who induce illness in others, usually their children, in order that they may acquire significance vicariously, as they have no expectation of being thought significant in their own right. Both forms are secretive. They can be very painful and even dangerous conditions for the one being harmed. However, the harm is not always obvious; on a small scale it can affect many people without anyone realising what is going on (over-fussing, over-diagnosing and over-medicating children can come into this category). Forms of Munchausen can manifest in many ways. For example, Jane, in the novel *Jane Eyre*, is an insignificant, overlooked and disempowered person who finally gains control over another – as well as kudos in the eyes of the world – by taking care of that other person's disability (which her own dark alter ego has brought about). This could be said to be the ultimate realisation of a Munchausen fantasy.

Self-harming and eating disorders

For imperfectly understood reasons, women appear to suffer from self-harm and eating disorders more than men. It could be because women focus more on internal feeling states. However, I worked with one male client whose arms, which at first sight I took to be heavily tattooed, were in fact railway tracks of stapled together skin, so there is no exclusive gender bias. Both conditions are associated with childhoods in which imperfect boundaries exist: some parent–child relationships are overly enmeshed, others vague to the point of hardly existing. The result is a person desperate to define the self, establish some form of autonomous control and/or create a much stronger sense of *existing* as a physical entity. They will often say things like, 'I needed to *feel* I existed,' 'Cutting was a great release' or 'I ate and ate until I finally felt I was all filled up inside. I couldn't take any more.' These all relate to an imbalance in neurotransmitter systems, and equally to a search for the physical consummation or fulfilment which will result in an appropriate sense of existing and being significant.

Secrets

Having a secret, knowing something no one else knows and having possession of a precious piece of intimacy are all about being special, being superior to those who are not in the know – in other words, being significant.

Guilt and self-loathing

Excessive focus on past misdeeds and many other forms of *apparent* psychic self-immolation are frequently instances of someone enhancing their own significance through an overemphasis on their own feelings. Taken to extremes this can even obliterate the suffering or harm done to others. A vicarious example of this concerns a badly behaved child who had damaged a valuable book belonging to an elderly family friend. His doting mother held the book up and, compounding any sense of grievance her host might reasonably have felt, said, 'Oh dear, it's quite torn. But you can tell he just feels so awful about it. You can see how badly he's taking it. Please don't make him feel any worse – he's almost in tears!'

'I just feel so bad about it.' Some people seem to thrive on feeling bad about stuff.

Anger

Anger can be a powerful stimulus to action and it can feel like a justification for all sorts of behaviour. 'Well, I just felt so very angry,' becomes a perfectly plausible explanation, one that's right up there with, 'I feel passionately about …', when used as a moral imperative. In fact, anger used as a fuel is really being used as a proxy for significance. If I have no right to do/feel/believe/deserve, whatever, because I am just not significant enough in myself, then *my strong emotions*, especially when they might imply threat of some kind, will act as my strongmen minders and do the persuading for me.

Desired principles

In the previous chapter I discussed the choices we could make about how we approach the future. Do we bumble listlessly into a future largely determined in ways nobody approved or approves of, or do we set about sculpting it differently for ourselves? Although the last few pages may not seem particularly relevant to that choice, it all connects up in the end – how could it possibly not!

Before we can achieve anything like true collective efficacy – 'the capacity of a group to regulate its members according to desired principles – to realise collective, as opposed to forced, goals' (Sampson et al., 1997: 918) – we must understand how we get to the point of sharing those 'desired principles' as this definitely seems the best bet for achieving the more attractive option. But before we can do that we have to understand, even if at only a fairly basic level, both what it is that motivates our current principles and what desirable principles may actually be.

My contention is that our principles – those we hold at an individual level – depend on our ideas about significance. If something is important to us, it is going to form part of our value system. Therefore, in order to understand how valid or valuable our values are, we must first understand what our signifiers of significance are and be able to recognise (as objectively as possible) their place on the social connectedness spectrum: are our current values pro or anti collective efficacy?

As essentially delusional and credulous creatures it is only too easy to tell and sell ourselves stories about who we are, what we believe in and how well-intentioned we are. The more aligned our self-images are with the *zeitgeist* (currently a rather sensibility-driven one), the more likely we are to believe our own perceptions of self. How else would one tragic woman (who was subsequently stabbed to death by her own adult son) have been able to advertise her services as a psychotherapist in the following way:

My approach is humanistic and non-judgemental. I believe there is a good reason for everything and that everything that we think, feel and do has meaning for us.

I have helped many people who have lost focus and struggled when facing challenges in their career or personal life. I am interested in people and how we have become who we are. I am interested in the patterns we have developed over time. (*The Times*, 17 December 2013)

At the very least there is a substantial mismatch between that poor woman's idea of how much she understood human brains and human motivation and the reality of her own nearest and presumably dearest's actual mental state. She is not alone. We are all capable of believing implausible things about ourselves and our intentions, provided that they fit and fulfil some inner emotional need, some essential motivating force. And that holds for things to do with social engagement.

The bottom line is that we need to know what motivates us (and this will be dependent on all those significance markers) before we can be sure that we are as pure of purpose as we like to believe. And it is only too easy to take an emotionally comforting route through life, especially when times get tough and challenging, or when others get tough and challenging, and then we persuade ourselves that, as Dickens famously concludes in *A Tale of Two Cities*, 'It is a far, far better thing that I do, than I have ever done,' when, perhaps, it is only a far, far better thing for that I do for *me* and the way *I feel* about myself.

In order to become fully engaged in collective efficacy – the best option for the greater good that we seem to have available to us – it is really important that we do at least recognise when we are focusing more on gratifying personal emotional significance needs than we are on delivering the pragmatic actions most in line with the overall good of the society to which we subscribe. Then we know we have a choice.

Of course, it can be argued that *all* the choices we are likely to make will, in some way, feed our emotional needs, because it could also be argued that survival itself is an emotional need. But we can become so nice in our arguments that we disappear up our own fundament. And that would never do. Let's at least try to be pragmatic.

Silo behaviour, individually and socially

If my need to gratify my desire for personal significance takes precedence over my perception of myself as a single (and very minute) component in a much larger social organisation, then my behaviour in any given situation is likely to be different (though maybe not overtly bizarrely so) than if I solely saw myself as an integral part of a much bigger whole.

Likewise, if one hand believes itself to be independent of other parts of the body, then its actions will not be synchronised with those of the rest of the body or be in line with its optimum organisation as a functional whole. Curiously, such scenarios do indeed get played out in some bodies.

In Chapter 4, I described a number of strange outcomes of loss of connectivity that occur when the brain's capacity to work as a functional unit is compromised for some reason. The typical outcome is an overall dysfunctional state in which it appears that almost no aspect of the system is working to any particular part's benefit.

One consequence of brain surgery for intractable cases of epilepsy is alien hand syndrome, and this provides a poignant illustration of what can happen when connections and cohesion break down. Normally, the brain's two hemispheres pass information between themselves via a connecting bridge known as the corpus callosum. This has the effect of synchronising activities and of inhibiting unwanted commands from either half of the brain. However, when certain forms of epilepsy get too bad, one way of controlling the frequent seizures is to cut the connection between the brain's hemispheres. Severing the corpus callosum is known as 'split brain surgery'. It affects the messaging between the two hemispheres, including the way instructions are sent to the limbs. According to some of the foremost researchers into this kind of surgery, Michael Gazzaniga and Roger Sperry, the outcome for a number of patients has been almost comical yet also totally disabling: they have acquired hands (it's often hands) that appear to have minds of their very own (*The Brain: A Secret History*, 2011, episode 3).

Sometimes a patient will find that they cannot even do up a shirt without the normally non-dominant hand trying to undo all the good work of the other one – undoing buttons as quickly as they are being done up, or light a cigarette without it being thrown away by the sinister (but in this case, good) guy, or pack items into a case without them being instantly unpacked again. These scenarios would provide comic material for a Charlie Chaplin film but they are devastatingly dysfunctional for anyone trying to live anything like a normal life.

It's not only the individual who can come a cropper. When one element of a complex system starts to act as if there are no imperatives but its own needs or desires, bigger bodies can also suffer fragmenting consequences. Within society, there are always conflicts of interests, every involved party adopting a position of greater importance than the others. Such situations are not easily resolved, especially when issues of significance are at stake.

In 2013 and 2014 large swathes of Somerset were under water for weeks, some parts for months. Somerset has always flooded, but it seems that the competing needs of farmers, house builders, householders, wildlife charities, local authorities (and the rest) not only made the resolution of the flooding that much harder but may also have contributed to its extent and duration in the first place. This was very much a case of topographical alien hand syndrome, one vested interest in the Somerset levels setting its stall above the others. Only by having a shared and overriding model that subsumes individual priorities, and a willingness to adapt to that model, will society reach any functional accommodation with nature over matters such as localised flooding.

Who's it all about, Alfie?

Perhaps we should learn to have greater emotional connection with the idea of a wider society and learn to love collective efficacy and the bigger picture (which includes other people). We should look beyond the gratification of our immediate significance-biased emotional needs and out towards the pragmatic needs of successful society.

Give this some thought. I, as an individual, will have all my deep needs for significance fired up, demanding their place in the sun; but, similarly, every other person will have their needs fired up demanding the same. From my point of view, it's all about me; from their point of view, well, they are under the erroneous impression that it's all about them. And don't other people make life difficult? Aren't they selfish and thoughtless? Not to mention mad, bad, dangerous to know and expensive for the rest of us to maintain? This all boils down to them believing that they, like God, should have everything made in their own image! As if.

And, given the stuff on brain function, isn't that all down to them having been damaged early in life and having what I'm calling a 'significance deficit'? They've ended up either feeling insignificant (easily achieved and deserved in *their* case) or failing to find anything of significance in their world (hardly to be wondered at, given their essential indolence, daftness, lack of enterprise or commitment), and in either case behaving in ways that are essentially all about them. Equally, they deny responsibility for anything they don't choose to be accountable for, especially if they can't see any immediate benefit to themselves in taking on responsibility.

Because if it's not all about me, but it may be all about them, how could there possibly be an argument in favour of my doing any single thing, anything at all, to try to make a difference? Aren't they (and their essentially wayward and irresponsible attitudes) always going to win out?

Well, finally …

Perhaps it is all about me – and about them. Perhaps it's all about *us* and what we do to each other when we fail to realise that. Then, instead of doing the collective efficacy thing and working with the bigger community need in mind, we try to ramp up levels of personal significance, and so, by not considering the *system* of human needs, we too often end up annihilating others and therefore cutting off our noses to spite our faces. Because when *I* annihilate *him*, though he may not then immediately annihilate *me*, I will have kick-started the 'what goes around comes around' process, and that won't be exhausted until everyone feels less important, less connected and altogether less part of the great and complex social dance of humanity.

Chapter 10

Do As You Would Be Done By

In this chapter we take a look at some examples of real-time real-world behaviours that may promote *me* and my interests but at the expense of others. The consequence is a general loss of connectedness and of collective efficacy.

What might *we* be doing to damage other people's fragile and precarious hold on their sense of significance? Might we, for example, be responsible for committing any of the following outrages on other people's sense that *they matter* in the grand scheme of things? Top of my list (which says something about my significance quotient) is one of the most outstanding and alarming developments to arise from the past fifty-year drift – okay, stampede – towards solipsism.

Failing to follow through on undertakings

This has become an absolute epidemic of unreliability. And I see unreliability as one of the worst possible offenders when it comes to annihilating people's sense of significance. Failing to follow through on undertakings, especially when there is absolutely no attempt to recognise the omission as a failing and then failing to apologise for the failure, is to suggest to the injured party that they do not merit courtesy, time, effort or any form of empathy at all.[1]

Following through on undertakings, or at least acknowledging the impossibility/unlikelihood of doing so, is not only to show respect to others (and therefore to their sense that they matter), it is also a marker of one's own ability to connect things up internally: verbal memory (the things that one has actually said), attention (in this case to others), focus (on the matter that has been brought up), self-knowledge (awareness of one's own probable behaviour),

---

1   If possible, things are even more damaging when the offender, on being reminded of a promise or undertaking, then acts as if a solecism, an offence, has been committed by the matter being brought up at all. In other words, it actually becomes *the other party's* fault that there is any discomfort.

forward planning, awareness of others' feelings (empathy), sense of one's own place or relative importance in the universe, sets of values, time considerations and constraints (was the undertaking going to be feasible in the first place?), commitments already in place, significance quotient (am I looking either to be satisfied by these means or to find these undertakings satisfactory in themselves?) and last, but by no means least, long-term goals. In other words, our reliability/unreliability quotient is actually one of the most complex and sophisticated markers of our own overall sophistication as thinkers and operators within the human sphere.

Abuse

Abuse of all kinds, from verbal and sexual to physical and emotional/psychological, is necessarily a denial of someone else's significance. Basically when one person abuses another, whether it's by chanting offensive things at football matches, raping, hitting or demeaning them, they negate them as a *person* and reassign them to the status of *object* – an object that can then be used to assert their own significance through the wielding of power. This is clearly such a starkly relevant topic that it probably hardly needs to have attention drawn to it.

Call centres

When they operate to set scripts and allocate tight time slots per caller, call centres are for many a source of deep loathing these days. They almost entirely overlook the needs and experiences of the caller in favour of a spurious efficiency; in other words, they render the caller totally insignificant. What can feel more disempowering than to be passed from one anonymous disembodied voice to another, having to repeat what has already been said, in the sure knowledge that the essence of what you are trying to communicate will be lost, and that what is going to be logged are patterns of words and phrases that might fit predetermined resolutions to standardised problems? You have become part of an algorithm. Great!

Being late

Everyone is late at times, but making a habit of being late shows a disregard for others and a blinkered immersion in one's own problems, either practical (work, childcare) or psychological ('I don't know why I always make myself late, I just wish I didn't'). For the person who is left lemon-like waiting for someone to turn up to an appointment or social engagement, the reason for the delay may or may not seem irrelevant, but either way the sensation they experience will be related to a loss of significance. It's pretty much a given that this is a matter of hierarchies of importance – being kept waiting is an indication of your status. After all, how many people would turn up late for an audience with the Queen?

Not responding to communications

In this world of incessant communications it would be impossible, not to say bonkers, even to try to reply or respond to all of them. In this context, by communications I mean those which are invited, expected, relevant in social or business terms and/or reasonable attempts by reasonable people to make contact over matters of significance. To fail to respond in some way to these communications, even if only by means of a nod, a holding email, text or call (why do I not even think of sending a quick note?) or a simple 'received yours – thanks' formula, is both to designificance the other and to demonstrate a failure to understand that Other is separate and different, and does not know what is in your mind and considerations. It is, in effect, autistic behaviour. While autistic behaviour is not, per se, the outcome of an indifference to others, it almost certainly is when being enacted by those not authentically on the spectrum.[2]

---

2   One very motivated Asperger's client wanted to engage better, both with his work colleagues and his wife. He was utterly delighted when he worked out that the way he was left feeling when a shop girl totally ignored his request for service was going to be very like the feeling others experienced during an interaction whenever he failed to give them any small token of feedback (even a 'hmm', a 'yes, well' or a nod). He was looking for help and was open to change, but it was still hard work for him to develop non-autistic responses. Why should anyone not authentically on the spectrum actively embrace behaviour that is problematic for those who are?

Failing to keep others in the loop

It's important to keep all lines of communication open in ongoing discussions and negotiations between individuals or organisations. Leaving one or more parties out will communicate to them that they are not worth the effort of contact – and this will not only leave them in no doubt as to their significance in the enterprise/solution/ whatever, but it is also likely to leave them feeling aggrieved, less likely to be cooperative and less prepared to compromise or feel satisfied with the outcome in any future negotiations.

Overlooking people in favour of others

Hamlet talks about this – 'the spurns that patient merit of th' unworthy takes' in the 'To be or not to be' speech (and no doubt hit a public chord even then[3]) – but matters do seem to have got worse with the introduction of modern technology which has allowed the needs of the disembodied voice to take precedence over the living breathing reality. There was an incident in a supermarket involving a till operator who refused to serve a customer while she continued with her mobile phone call (see Brown, 2013). In the furore that followed, the majority vote was in favour of the till operator. This shows that people do understand and sympathise with the need to be recognised. But even so, how many of us continue to take calls, read emails and use mobile devices in complete unawareness of those around us?

Betrayal

Betrayal, especially romantic betrayal, often hits us far harder than financial harms or even physical ones. This is because love is a

---

3   This section of the speech shows that some forms of human behaviour are endemic, as are human reactions. These are the very behaviours that lead Hamlet to feel he is being annihilated by the world around him; they are the words of one of the first known existentialists:

> For who would bear the whips and scorns of time,
> Th' oppressor's wrong, the proud man's contumely,
> The pangs of despised love, the law's delay,
> The insolence of office, and the spurns
> That patient merit of th' unworthy takes,

If anything links us to the past, surely this does.

powerful signifier of significance, affecting many neurotransmitter systems including oxytocin, dopamine, cortisol, adrenaline and serotonin. Betrayal is an annihilation not just of our bank accounts or flesh but of the very essence of who we are. It is the mother's eyes that reject, the breast milk that turns sour in the mouth, the loving arms that drop – in short, it is the repudiation of everything that made us come alive in the first place, it is the anti-life, the negation of our being. Betrayal says not only that we do not matter in the great scheme of things (something most of us need to learn and which, ironically, can actually be quite protective of self), but also that we *actively and specifically* do not matter, and that we have in some way been singled out for presuming that we ever did or might have done.

Reneging

A somewhat less emotionally intense form of betrayal is reneging on an agreement or any kind of debt. Reneging is not only saying, 'I and my financial, logistical, emotional, psychological or time constraints are more important than you and yours,' but also, 'The (maybe massively damaging) effect that my behaviour is going to have on you, your life/finances/family and so on are matters that my solipsistic brain just does not, and possibly cannot, compute.' In other words, this is either short-termism – an inability to see the bigger picture and the possible consequences of one's actions – or simply sociopathic behaviour.

Even delayed payment of invoices suggests that the late payer is unable or unwilling to take another perspective into account. Of course, that's a given with large organisations which are among the worst offenders vis à vis timely payments and among the least personally responsible or responsive of all. If the late payer is close to the person to whom they owe money, then their indifference will be experienced as undermining the other's sense of personal significance.

Prison

Being imprisoned is in some respects the ultimate practical form of loss of significance. Once incarcerated, a prisoner has as little day-to-day control over the detail of his or her life as has a child, and this brings on a sense of loss of agency. Part of the punishment that comes with a prison sentence is the knowledge that much of society imagines you as a lesser form of humanity. This makes you feel not so much *in*significant as *de*significant. It's as if coming to prison strips you of even the tiny remnant of significance that you might once have felt you had. This is the snake starting to eat its own tail; the victims of crime and the perpetrators of it become linked in a cycle of designif-icancing. A victim's sense of significance is always rocked by any form of criminal assault, as any crime is a violation of self. The criminal, in turn, has their independent humanity violated (though probably justifiably so) by their imprisonment, leaving them even less likely to care about anyone else; and so the merry game goes on.

Many prisoners have a sense of significance failure from the very start. They will have been brought up to be 'agency illiterate' (unaware of the basic principle that people can be in charge of their own lives) as a consequence of never having learned that they could be in control of their emotions – the very first things they have experienced. Instead, they will usually have been exposed to inces-sant displays of over-the-top emotion (on TV as well as in the home) and will rarely have learned to soothe themselves, being either shouted down when crying or pacified with dummies, drinks, sweets and crisps. Because they have never learned what is sometimes called 'emotional agency', they will have no template for agency as a general guiding principle of life. Not only does this leave them feeling less significant than people who are more in charge of them-selves, but it is also a primary reason for them ending up in prison.

This scenario becomes apparent when you go into most prisons. One of the first things to strike you is the sheer volume of noise. Shouting, screaming, swearing and incessant clanging, banging and crashing are the default soundscapes of many wings. Prisoners are emotionally volatile yet unable to understand that just because they feel something strongly, it doesn't mean they must follow through on that feeling. Many prisoners confuse noise and combativeness with significance. They don't realise that they are more likely to change their circumstances by making changes in themselves instead of trying to put their mark on life by making infantile and noisy demands on the environment.

If, long term, we want to make changes to the levels of crime we're experiencing, it's only by building a sense of significance (please note, that is *not* the same as self-esteem) in members of the prison popula-tion, rather than by diminishing it, that we will ever manage to change the behaviour of most inmates. Although it may sound count-er-intuitive and even soft to some, we need to concentrate on programmes which encourage them to develop a sense that they are significant and that they are integral and influential members of society as a whole, rather than the marginal, peripheral and shadow-less aliens that so many of them presume themselves to be. In this way they can learn that what they do does impact on far more things in many more ways than they currently realise. (Because most prisoners genuinely have no idea of the ramifications of their actions, they are also totally ill-equipped to evaluate them for themselves.)

Prisoners need to be given the behavioural tools – which they usually do not have – so that, in addition to being able to make more conscious choices about how they want their futures to look, they will also have the capacity to present themselves to the world in ways that are more in tune with realising those choices. Sometimes simply walking differently can make all the difference to how individuals feel about themselves, and thus to how the world responds to them. Let's at least give prisoners the means to be different.

The significance of driving

Driving a car is supposedly a source of greater pride than sexual prowess, sporting ability or financial acumen. You can accuse most people of being rotten at any of those and they will laugh it off quite happily, but criticise their behaviour behind the wheel and fireworks go off! So why on earth would I want to enter this explosive arena? Because it is in our driving behaviour that most of us happily, and daily, commit more unconsidered crimes against other people's sense of significance than in just about any other behavioural arena I can think of.

Driving betrays more about how our brains work than most of us would be comfortable knowing, were we aware of just how much we are giving away when we get behind the wheel. Someone's driving behaviour gives an indication of their personal areas of significance, their reliability in terms of their relationships with other road users and with any rules and guidelines devised for safe driving. We can make sense of someone's internal life by watching the way they drive. The following points offer some pointers for garnering better practical information about the attitudes and biases of a potential life partner or employee than many a psychometric assessment might tell us. For example, does their driving signify that they understand there is a world beyond themselves and their own needs, that there is a bigger picture (one which, incidentally, might also feature me/us and my/our concerns) in which they are only a bit part player? Or do their driving habits suggest that they are indifferent as to whether or not their behaviour leaves others (and one day maybe me or us) out in the cold and feeling totally insignificant?

Lights

There are many who fail to put their headlights on when driving in conditions which are less than absolutely dark but nevertheless potentially hazardous because of fog, spray, dull light and so on. Fundamentally, the world breaks down into those who put their lights on in order to be seen as well as to see, and those who only use them (and sometimes sparingly even then) in order merely to see. The first group breaks down into two subtypes: those who are rigorous in applying learned rules and those who have sufficient imaginative capacity to envision other perspectives. Both types evidence a capacity to be influenced by minds and needs other than their own and are in line with a non-solipsistic style of cognitive functioning – as well as being much safer drivers. The other category of drivers would leave you to pitch down the cellar stairs in the dark during a power cut as they hogged the torch.

Getting into the wrong lane/taking a wrong turn

When you make mistakes at the wheel such as getting into the wrong lane or taking a wrong turn, there are effectively two options available. The first is to take your medicine like a grown-up and inconvenience yourself by continuing with the course you have taken until you have the chance to turn around or otherwise take some rectifying action. The second is mentally to say, 'Yuk, I'm not swallowing that,' and to spit out the medicine into the face of the rest of the world. That way you inconvenience *them* as you partially pull back into your original lane at the lights, blocking the right filter as you do so; or stop dead on the roundabout, holding up everyone else until someone feels bullied into letting you back in; or do a U-turn where these are specifically disallowed for reasons of safety. Each of these says, '*I'm* the one who matters here. I couldn't care less about your concerns, and I'm absolutely not even going to think about the effect on overall traffic flow. I just don't do bigger pictures. They're for sissies.'[4]

Lane discipline

A few years ago a report by a driving organisation suggested that poor lane discipline was responsible for most of the hold-ups on motorways (see Barrett, 2014). This was clearly neither read nor heeded by most drivers, and certainly not by a female acquaintance of mine who once solemnly told me that she always drove in the middle lane on motorways as it was so much safer than going in and out all the time. Hmmm. The question that occurred to me was how would she ever know? Like most middle-lane hoggers she was blithely unaware of what was happening behind her. The kindest thing that can often be said about people who drift down the centre lane, while all around them people undertake, overtake or sit glaring on their tails, unable to pass, is that they have no idea of the chain of events they are setting off or of the danger they pose to others. They see no bigger picture and cannot imagine how they might look to the 'bigger society' helicopter overhead.

Use of mirrors

They fail to see the bigger picture because they don't use their mirrors. Solipsistic people are only theoretically aware of the world outside the self and have no need to check on its doings, needs and desires. They drive, oblivious, eyes fixed straight ahead. This behaviour is not solely confined to white van drivers but demonstrated just as frequently by the elderly and by those who fit no particular category. Check for yourself next time you're in the passenger seat.

Yellow lines and parking

I came across this reminder to parents (at a very expensive private school) not to park inconsiderately:

---

4   A similar situation arises with checkouts in supermarkets. Someone forgets an item or several items, 'bags' their place in the queue with their basket and happily goes off to do some more shopping.

Another plea to parents not to park on the zigzag lines during drop off and pick up time. We would also ask that you do not do U-turns outside the School as, apart from holding up traffic, this is a very dangerous manoeuvre and we are extremely concerned that a girl will be hurt.

These parents have had the wit to earn the money to send their daughters to a school that will honour their expectations for them. They want their daughters to acquire the skills and graces that such a school offers in its prospectus. They have had the foresight and imagination to envision their daughters' successful transition from said school to successful future (otherwise it would be a waste of their money). But, apparently, they also have the bone-headedness to think that this can all be supplied by *other people* modelling appropriate behaviours. So what are these delinquent parents actually modelling themselves?

- That they have little capacity to pre-plan and organise their lives efficiently.
- That as long as their own child's safety is covered no one else matters.
- That good manners and consideration for others aren't important.
- That in their solipsistic universe there is no bigger picture in which the overall functioning of society takes precedence over individual needs.
- That they can't see how their own children will, ultimately, be put at greater threat if this behaviour becomes common to other parents too.

Not that bad parking behaviour is limited to private school parents – it's common with all parents and school situations. Go out at 3 p.m. during term time and the chances are that you will find most blind bends within a hundred yards of any school sporting, not just double yellow lines, but as many cars as can fit onto them.

Even the best of parents, who otherwise want to instil manners, conscience and consideration in their offspring, have a blind spot about this behaviour. They fail to understand the mechanisms by which children learn self-reliance and resilience. These vital survival qualities are not the outcome of doing whatever is most immediate and convenient for your own personal needs, regardless of other people's needs, likely behaviour and the requirements of the wider social good. Their defence? They justify their actions using those universal get-out-of-jail cards, 'I just ...' and 'I was only ...' We know what you were really doing!

Local authorities and even governments are partly to blame for this kind of muddled double-think and for the constant low-level breaches of parking regulations everywhere. With one breath they tell us that double yellow lines are there for safety reasons and that to park on them is to imperil other road users, and then they give a special dispensation to drivers sporting disability badges and allow them to park there. Surely disabled drivers must be at even greater risk than more agile people as they either get out of cars or manoeuvre them into traffic at high-risk hot-spots. Why should it be considered appropriate by anyone, even a selected group such as the disabled, to pose an unusually high risk to themselves or to other road users? Are the areas of road bordered by double lines potentially dangerous, or are they not?

Have we reached a point where right has taken precedence over realpolitik for subgroups (cyclists also spring to mind)? Is this an outcome of silo thinking? If we believe in the concept of the greater good, then anything which works in favour of it must be understood by all elements of society as taking precedence over individual convenience. There must be consistency and as few special cases as possible because entitlement seems to lead to hazard. This means that councils need to be honest about their reasons for all forms of traffic management and to demonstrate that restrictions are for the benefit and safety of all. Otherwise, they will create both resentment and resistance (the outcome of people feeling they have been rendered either completely insignificant or relatively less significant than others). The way to avoid this is to find ways of reducing the sheer quantity of restrictions, which many people believe are more about revenue than about safety or efficiency, and then to enforce the remaining regulations consistently and rigorously. People resent unfairness. When they witness other people routinely flouting the regulations that they themselves abide by and 'getting away with it', the feelings they are left brooding over do nothing whatsoever to advance harmony in society.

In order to create greater harmony and safety on the roads, it would be better for everyone to think of themselves as 'road users' rather than as cyclists, motor bikers, car drivers, hauliers, runners, horse riders, pedestrians and so on, and thus encouraged to see themselves as subscribing to the unifying idea that 'we're all in this together'. How we think about road usage currently has the effect of discouraging people from realising that they may, at various times and various stages of life, be any of these things. The consequence is that we end up spoiling our own interests (and, worse, the interests of our children) in complex ways. Perhaps we should all have to sit a virtual test in which we take on each role in turn and walk/cycle/drive/ride a mile in others' shoes.

Moving on, I imagine that most people will agree with this last contender for the role of personal significance slaughterer.

Inconsiderate behaviour

That's other people's inconsiderate behaviour, never yours! It's the neighbours and all those others in public places such as city centres, parks or housing estates. Annoyance caused by neighbours is one of the greatest sources of distress that people experience in day-to-day life. *The Telegraph* tells us that as many as 95,000 householders move every year just to get away from their nuisance neighbours (Flanagan, 2014a). But, perhaps surprisingly, it is not the behaviour per se that is the main problem. Noise is quoted as being the commonest cause of annoyance, but we are well able to tolerate relatively high volumes of noise – when it suits us. We're okay with concerts or when we're making the noise ourselves. However, when one person's noise nirvana is another person's noise poison, noise becomes problematic. It's not just the level of noise but its intrusiveness and power to get under the skin that disrupts our lives; it represents an assault on the individual's ability to take control, as well as to matter enough to others. If we are unable to influence our environment (physical and human) our sense of significance is diminished.

Regardless of the details, whether rubbish, parking, dogs or noise, the overall message remains the same. When we're living in groups we have to put the interests of the smooth running of the total social enterprise above the individual desire either to follow too extreme or eccentric a path or to put two fingers up to the people around us.

This message applies to authorities as much as it does to individuals. Not that authorities actively choose to put two fingers up to the people they are supposed to be representing, but there are cases where the authority's interests become sufficiently compromised that they no longer seem ready or able to represent the interests of the wider social group with which they are meant to concern themselves.

The impact of designificancing the whole

What goes around comes around. If a person or group feels that they have been overlooked or deliberately adversely dealt with by those who are in a position to affect them, they then become disaffected and less committed to the overall cause. The end result is that they are more likely to behave in ways that keep the separate, different and essentially antagonistic ball rolling.

There is an analogy to be drawn here with cancer. This is now seen not so much as one unified disorder but as a series of diverse events. It begins with a single genetic variation and then diverges. As differences proliferate it becomes ever more harmful to the functioning of the whole. Instances of excessive individuality and diversity in human behaviour similarly proliferate and eventually overwhelm the integral nature of the whole, compromising the cohesion and viability of the social body.

Such activities cannot and do not promote the cause of the collective efficacy which so many students of social resilience believe is necessary for communities and the individual lives within them to flourish.

The Jane Austen solution

As the most socially alert of all great writers, Jane Austen's subtext is almost invariably one which promotes the practical, psychological and emotional supremacy of considerate, even self-denying, personal actions over the indulgence of immediate feelings and desires. A telling moment in *Emma*, and one which is game changing for the imperfect, deluded but nonetheless sympathetic heroine, takes place after she has made fun of an older, poorer, single woman, Miss Bates. She does this simply because she is bored by her, wants to amuse herself and seem witty.[5] The appropriately named hero of the book, Mr Knightley, tells her off for failing to understand that,

---

5   Many a commentator has criticised Austen for her seemingly cruel portrayal of the socially inept and unglamorous, but her real message is one of concern for their vulnerability in a world that hardly valued them at all. She realised how little personal power they had and how much their lives depended on the goodwill of others. 'Treat those who have less than you well,' she seems to be saying, 'and not only will they be dignified by your treatment of them, but you, and the whole of your society, will be judged more humanely in turn.' It was hard for her, given who she was and when she lived, to demand equality of pay, conditions and treatment for all; modern critics rather miss the point if they judge her on the basis of her failure to do so.

as the luckier one in life, she has a duty not only to spend time with the older woman and to take notice of her but also to treat her respectfully. He points out to Emma that the situation was once different, when the childish Emma was more than happy to know the older woman, and that, essentially, what goes around comes around – at any rate, with respect to courtesy and consideration. If in age or adversity we wish to be well treated …

For Jane Austen, the codes of conduct that guided correct behaviour also assured the protection of the feelings and ongoing social connectedness of the vulnerable and disadvantaged. Not for her the supremacy of individual inclinations and the indulgence of either heightened emotion or self-absorption. She believed that the individual could only be truly useful and self-respecting if they behaved both rationally and considerately, and did not generally place personal and therefore individual happiness above thought-fulness for others. In her works, the most obviously self-centred characters are nearly always figures of fun, sometimes subtly so, and those who behave with concern for others are always rewarded.

When the Jane Austen principle gets forgot

Homogeneity, the blending of things together, loses out to heteroge-neity, the diversification or dis-unification of things. We then end up with public behaviours that can quite frankly puzzle the minds of clear-thinking small children:

Mummy, mummy, if those men are supposed to be collect-ing rubbish, why do they leave so much broken glass and paper lying around?

Mummy, mummy, if you're not allowed to park here/go too fast here, why did that policeman not speak to that van driver/go after that red car?

Because, darling, none of them are unified or integrated in their thinking and functions. If the rubbish collectors happen to be collecting from bins, they are not necessarily bound to pick up litter from the road; nor are the police, if not actively on traffic duty, supposed to deal with traffic matters.

But why mummy? That sounds silly.

Too many questions, Freddie.

In the interests of collective efficacy we should all, as a matter of routine, be asking questions about such modern equivalents of the emperor's new clothes ourselves and not just leaving them for the next, hopefully clearer sighted, generation to wonder about.

Homogeneity, at least in the guise of social grouping, is more likely to be the norm in Latin cultures than in essentially Anglo-Saxon ones. In France, Italy and Spain you will still see mixed-age and mixed-class groups eating together in public, whereas in Britain and in large parts of the United States this is less common. However, due in large part to the introspective nature of the internet, habits throughout the world are changing. People cluster into specific categories and subgroups since it is so much easier to find like-minded people online than in a small village in the Loire Valley or out in the wilds of Catalonia. However, where families and cultures do still encourage greater levels of mixing between ages and classes, there is clear evidence that this homogeneity provides protection, especially for their young.

A study carried out at the Alicante Medical Centre, Spain, led by Dr Elena Compañ Poveda (Compañ et al., 2001) showed that teenagers from families who eat together have better mental health than those who eat separately. Whereas only 17% of the mentally healthy teenagers studied ate separately, 33% of the mentally troubled teenagers did, and these same teenagers were also more likely to miss family lunches and dinners at weekends. Dr Compañ Poveda said that sharing the experience of eating is a unifying ritual which promotes mental health. In addition to shared meal times, the healthier youngsters also shared in more family activities in general, such as parties, religious festivals, outings, holidays and simply talking, with many of these activities involving more extended family members too.[6]

In poorly integrated families – assuming that they are not simply indifferent or incompetent with respect to their child's welfare – parents often believe it shows greater consideration of their children's right to privacy if they appear not to be overly involved in what their children get up to (and with whom). Either that or they believe themselves to be rather less entitled than previous generations of parents were to interfere in their own children's lives. The consequence of both these ways of thinking is that they impose less on their children, as well as having fewer expectations of them with

---

6   The study was not a large one, but the researchers were careful to ensure that other factors likely to be involved in mental health, such as family income and education, were roughly equivalent. They seemed satisfied that the significant factor influencing the mental health status of these teenagers was engagement in family life.

respect to involvement in the household. In this way the youngsters lose (or never develop) any real sense that they have stakeholder status in that household.

There is a vast distinction between significance and entitlement. Acknowledging others' significance is not the same as making them entitled. In fact, entitlement can diminish them as stakeholders, as agents in their own lives – after all, the entitled do not necessarily choose to be placed in that position and do not necessarily merit or even want the advantages that entitlement brings. This is especially true in the case of children. Children can easily be given special status, but this can prevent them from seeing themselves as integral and practically valued members of family systems – without which they may lose rather than gain self-respect for what they are able to offer to the world. If they grow up valuing themselves only because they are in a specially entitled relationship to others, and therefore not knowing what they have to offer, once that situation changes, as it inevitably will, they are much more likely to flounder than children who have learned to see themselves as functional and significant members of a bigger group. If we want children to feel significant, we should not force a sense of entitlement on to them. Instead, we should encourage them to feel that they have something useful to contribute to the overall running of the household to which they belong.

While their intentions may be laudable, overly 'permissive' parents also misunderstand how the human mind works (probably because of the influence of people like Alice Miller on the thinking of the past couple of generations of child experts). Not only do we, as a species, frequently have very little idea of what we are actually feeling deep down, but given that teenage brains are poor at self-awareness and self-monitoring, whatever young people think they want (and often demand quite vocally from their parents) isn't necessarily the same as what they really want. When teenagers demand space and try to exile themselves from family events or from human contact in general, they don't necessarily understand what they're doing and what its impact will be on their own state of happiness (not that sabre-toothed tigers would get such an admission out of any of them).

What teenagers want, just like the rest of us, is to be significant. In reality, given the solipsistic nature of the teenage brain, a teenager is unlikely to be best placed to give another teenager the healthy rational attention and support that they really could use. They are much more likely (even though completely without malice aforethought) to be using one another for complex emotional needs of their own – even, for example, at times when they believe themselves to be in love and totally dedicated to the Other. This is one reason why teenagers who spend disproportionate amounts of time hanging out with each other, rather than in more mixed groups, can still feel lonely and misunderstood.

On the other hand, adults, and especially parents, have (or certainly should have) attention and concern to spare for others. Although teenagers may not always enjoy being regularly monitored, like Wedgwood's workers at Etruria, they do gain an enormous sense of significance from knowing that they're important enough to their parents that those parents still want to observe, care about, contain and protect them, however deeply the awareness of the benefit to them may be buried.[7]

Teenagers also gain enormously from being connected up to the wider community whether they realise it or not. As a group, they're rather like Patsy in that episode of *Absolutely Fabulous* (1992: season 1, episode 3) where she finds herself stuck in a tiny farmhouse in the middle of France. She's out of her comfort zone, bored out of her brain and totally antagonistic to the one available leisure activity – desperately uncool table tennis – until discovering that it's not half so bad with some white powder up her nose. But then, ignominiously, she discovers that she's been duped – the white powder was only talc after all. Her horror on realising she must *genuinely* have enjoyed herself while playing table tennis is, in the words of another

---

7   When my daughter was 15 she and a friend skipped school on the last day of term, thinking they would not be noticed. The school was aware enough and concerned enough that not only did they register the absences but they also rang both sets of parents to inform them. What follows is her recollection of that day:

When we decided to skive school, we were so worried about being caught out we hid in an old disused house for most of the afternoon. Eventually we plucked up courage to go into town, but as we were getting there we bumped into my parents, who had been alerted by the head teacher. They frogmarched me back up to school, where I was made to apologise to both parents and head teacher. This was completely mortifying and I was quite resentful that (a) my friend wasn't made to suffer the same humiliation, (b) I couldn't believe school would take an absence from the final assembly of term so seriously … my true belief was that a state school wouldn't do anything so ridiculous (and therefore I wished I went to state school), and (c) I could get away with nothing where I lived!

Now, with hindsight, as an adult with two children of my own, I can see logically that a school that takes both standards and the safety of its pupils so seriously is to be commended. I can also see that my parents were showing that they cared about me and my education in doing what they did (still a tiny bit of resentment, though, especially about being caught after doing nothing more exciting than hide away in a disused building!).

renowned sitcom, 'a televisual feast'. We can laugh at Patsy, but it's probably not such a good idea to actually laugh at teenagers should they ever inadvertently find themselves enjoying involvement in some uncool activity (something perhaps involving older people, a bit of manual labour or just general hard core niceness). However, it remains an extremely good idea to expect them to take part.

When young people are left to their own devices, with no apparent controls imposed on them from outside their own inherently solipsistic communities, the outcome can sometimes be tragic. A 2015 World Health Organization study found that depression is the top cause of illness for the world's teens. Although depression is cited as the top global cause of illness and disability for adolescents, suicide is the third biggest cause of death. Witness the sad cases of the suicides of a number of beautiful young people all of whom have persuaded themselves they were either ugly or worthless. They appear to have been influenced by peer group postings on Tumblr and other social media sites. An obvious factor in their impulsive acts of self-destruction is the lack of the more rational perspective and corrective a more mixed community might have supplied.

There is a horrible correlation here with William Golding's *Lord of the Flies*. The credo so beloved by the 1960s counter-culture – one that Alice Miller and writers like her seemed to subscribe to – was faulty in conception. In reality, refusing to interfere with the natural unfettered inclinations of the young of the species is not a recipe for freedom, creativity and instinctively self-limiting behaviour. Rather, it is a recipe for an unboundaried, inchoate and often tragic search for significance. If adults refuse to take notice or place restrictions and impose penalties, then young people experience a loss of sense of self, whether or not they recognise their feelings for what they really are. They feel *un*significant. Having no rooted sense that they matter for what and who they are, it's only too easy for them to slip into nihilism, negativism, pitilessness, depression and suicidal ideation.

Belonging matters. It really does. But although that is a huge part of the message of this book, it is not in itself an ultimate or unalloyed good. If we belong to too small a community the result can be bad: we may end up over-associating with and therefore normalising fundamentally unhealthy or anti-social behaviours (as in the virtual world of Tumblr, in cult-like organisations or in gangs). Fuelled by oxytocin we may end up creating despised out-groups and getting our high from feelings of *Schadenfreude*, envy or disgust. We may fail to understand the bigger picture and act only in the interests of 'us, here and now'. These are real and ever-present dangers. They are especially toxic when they lurk in the sweet disguise of significance. When an act or belief tends towards making me, or life itself, seem more meaningful (by generating more dopamine in my system) then it *must* be the right course for me – because it just feels so damned right!

Ha, ha – got you!

Another effect of dopamine, which specifically although not exclusively impacts on the left hemisphere's preferred activities, is to create its own sense of achievement and satisfaction. The left hemisphere, because it craves rational explanations for things, likes to be right. When it connects things up in satisfying ways it produces a shot of dopamine. This gives us the sense of achieving a goal; it feels so fulfilling. To put that into a day-to-day context, it pleases itself and doesn't necessarily feel any need to cross-reference with the external world.[8] It's a case of the left is always right and the right is always left trailing.

Dopamine makes the world a much more meaningful place; without it we would, like Parkinson's sufferers, feel demotivated and stuck. Nevertheless, we should treat its messages with some caution. Consider it not exactly as a snake-oil salesman but at least as a reasonably well-intended salesperson who gets paid on commission. It has a vested interest in keeping us on board.

Where does this fit?

This chapter explains how some human specific tendencies might be undermining our ability to make the most helpful choices in life – helpful, that is, if our overall aim is to subscribe to the collective efficacy principle – which has been shown to be the best way of achieving the social resilience that makes life better all round for the greatest number of people.

I have examined how both our drive for personal significance and our facility for *de*significancing others tend to compromise

---

8   This dopamine effect is one of the reasons that people with bipolar disorder, when on a high, are so self-assured about the credibility of their more outlandish schemes and can be so certain of their arguments and the positions they adopt. The same applies with some forms of schizophrenia. Excess dopamine enhances any inherent tendency to delusional thinking.

collective efficacy. This is largely because these aspects of humanity tend to mitigate against the genuine likelihood of us sharing desired principles – where these desired principles are the engine of collective efficacy.

The dopamine connection reconnects us with the founding principle that we are all, always, at the mercy of delusions, and that the only way we can make any sense of this old nonsense is if we, so far as is possible, share the delusion that certain specifics matter. The greater the number who can manage this, the higher the probability that more of us will gain.

So let's shake off unhelpful individualistic delusions about ourselves and significance, recognise the harm we might be doing to others' sense of significance, especially in our own barely conscious day-to-day behaviours, and then, in the light of our new found freedom to be more objective and pragmatic, look at the question of what should be informing and influencing our selection of desired principles. These desired principles will, according to the research by Robert J. Sampson, operate in the interests of the greater good and, almost inevitably, still be much more in line with our own more individualistic local and family interests. It's just that in the past few decades we have failed to see the connection. Finally, we will consider what collectively efficacious things we need to be getting on with.

As there's been quite a bit of negativity to date, let's look to a brighter future and start to do the things and behave in ways that will actually make a difference. But, first, another coda.

Coda: Who is the real prisoner?

Working with prisoners can be a very enlightening experience, and I wouldn't have missed my time in prison for anything. Although I had always thought that it might make for an interesting experience I still came away from my work in drugs and alcohol services and in education with a wealth and breadth of knowledge that I never anticipated. In particular, there was one unlikely outcome that I truly could not have predicted, and it was one which brought the most satisfaction to me personally. I was lucky, though, because the opportunity I had, through working in prison, to repair damage done and regain a sense of personal significance after being on the receiving end of a violating criminal act is one that is simply not available to most people.

It all began on a sunny summer's day, when three of us, me, a friend who was helping and my dog, were taking a break from painting and decorating and were enjoying that most English of summer pleasures, a cup of tea in the garden. My garden was relatively big but wrapped around two sides of the house, meaning that you could still see the main entrance from just about anywhere you were sitting. The driveway, which was long but straight, had been laid to gravel so, overall, the chances were relatively small of anyone being able to approach the house either unseen or unheard. Certainly they would have had to have been a real risk-taker to have tried it.

While in the garden, we probably got up a few times to throw balls for the dog and maybe even to inspect a few plants. At any moment, either one of us, or even the dog, might have turned in the direction of the front door or we might even have had to run inside to pick up a ringing phone. But we didn't. The deed that took place during those few minutes was very foolhardy, very desperate or very, very skilful.

Eventually I did go inside to make more tea. It was then I noticed a window slightly open at the front of the house. I knew I hadn't opened it and briefly wondered why my friend had felt free to open a downstairs window without bothering to mention it. Then I noticed my handbag was not quite where I remembered having left it, neither was my charging mobile (in fact, it and charger were nowhere to be seen at all). And then I went cold. I ran upstairs – gone were the rings that had been taken off and left on the dressing table while I was decorating. I usually wore them all the time – they were my mother's old cut-diamond solitaire engagement ring and an emerald ring of my own that had huge emotional resonance. Gone, too, when I looked in the drawers (never leave jewellery in the dressing table) were all the pieces of jewellery that I, my mother and my grandmother had ever owned, including all three wedding rings. Gone, among these pieces, was the simple gold-plated Victorian locket containing the one and only extant photograph of my grandmother as a young woman – the photo that was one day going to prove to my daughter and her cousin just how strong a family resemblance there was between all three of them. Gone, obviously, my new mobile phone; gone, too, some gold trinkets I'd bought as gifts – but none of those things mattered.

Only those who have been burgled will know the sluggish realisation and slow burn of suspicions that creep in. How long had someone been watching me and my house? What else had they taken? Virtually every drawer in the house had been carefully ransacked. This was no novice operator; everything had been thoughtfully choreographed and skilfully carried out. It had been pre-planned, but what had they spotted that they hadn't been able to take? What was still left worth taking? Would they come back for it? Had anyone I knew inadvertently (or worse still, advertently) let on about anything, anything at all? And that great Holmesian question: why hadn't the dog barked? Had it been someone he knew? These and a thousand other thoughts and questions raced through my mind at the time or insinuated themselves into it over the next days and weeks.

I lived alone; would the person responsible come back? Were they always just across the road, watching the comings and goings from the house? If they could just walk in when I was there, could I ever be safe inside it again? Equally, could I ever safely leave it again? What would have happened if I'd encountered them, mid-burglary? Would I ever feel free to return to my own home in the dark?

And then, could I ever assuage the guilt of losing the precious and hard-won totems of previous generations' emergence from absolute hardship? The golden links between the women of the family, their loves and their daughters?

The police, I have to say, were relatively swift and relatively efficient – largely, I suspect, because mine was one of a string of local burglaries; they seemed to have an idea of the burglar's identity. I remain to be convinced that they would have been quite so assiduous in nabbing 'my' burglar if his successful prosecution wasn't likely to have impacted so significantly on the force's crime statistics.

I am truthfully very pleased that they did their job efficiently, but my gripe, then (this was about thirteen years ago) and now, was they did not do it in a way that made me, the victim, feel like a significant factor in the overall operation of justice. Oh, yes, they sent me an information pack about their ongoing and successful domestic burglary operation, and no doubt they asked me if I wanted counselling. But they would have done as much for me had I reported seeing a crime taking place in the street, which from an emotional standpoint is a different beast altogether.

In due course the detective in charge of the case informed me that they had apprehended the burglar and that he was pleading guilty. Great, I thought, I want to see the whites of his eyes. I want to *know* him, as he has known me. When, I naively asked, was the trial date? It turned out that I had no right to know. As he had pleaded guilty the matter, effectively, no longer concerned me at all. Baffled and outraged by such an indication of judicial indifference, I asked who was he? What was his name? Who was it that had done this thing to me? It turned out that I had no right to that information either. He had pleaded guilty. Job done.

I turned on the tears, I turned on the charm, I turned on the emotional blackmail. This man (I was allowed to know it had been a man) had been through everything I valued; he had been through my knicker drawer for heaven's sake, and yet I had no right to even know so much as his *name*?! Maybe I appealed to the detective's heart, maybe to his fear of female tantrums, who knows, but he did, grudgingly and with many protestations that this was a *very* particular favour he was doing me, give me a name.

I had to be satisfied by what he told me although, deep down, I never truly believed him, imagining that he had just made up a plausible sounding name to keep me quiet. Rather less deep down, I was pretty put out that I obviously represented such a sideshow to the police, just another seemingly quite tiresome element of this great game they called crime.

Time went by. Not being a particularly nervous or paranoid person, I wasn't incapacitated by what had happened. Even before the burglar was arrested, and after only a couple of nights on my own in the house, I began to feel relatively confident that there wasn't going to be a repeat visit by anyone, and I began the process of reacquainting myself with 'normal'. However, as a single woman, living on my own, I did become much more alert to all manner of threats than I had been before. I was, if I'm being absolutely truthful, living in a fairly permanent condition of low-level fear. And that fear was mostly of the unknown, the unknowable and, as the saying goes, fear itself – that dark shape in the night, that slight whisper behind the wind, that small twisting lurch of the guts that accompanies any little loss of control over events.

Loss of control. That, fundamentally, is what fear is all about. What could be more effective in creating a sense of loss of control than when either the self or the self's protective environment is violated? Then all your touchstones of normality disappear. Your internal emotional barometer and your amygdala/cortisol/adrenaline systems go wild. You are left stranded in a state of heightened alert. It is, to say the least, an unrestful condition to be in.

But, like I said, I got lucky.

About four years after the burglary, I decided to study for a diploma in addiction therapy. I was offered the chance to do the work placement element of the course in the drug and alcohol service of a prison, rather than in the more usual private rehab facility. I jumped at the chance. It was fascinating work and once the diploma was finished I continued working in the drug and alcohol services of a number of prisons for real. A year or so later, while working in a Category B (near the top of the security scale) prison in the West Country, I noticed a name on the list of prisoners awaiting induction. This is the process whereby new (and, as in his case, revolving door) prisoners are introduced to the various procedures and elements of any given prison's regime, including the courses and help available to them, such as drugs and alcohol services. It was a name that rang a bell. Perhaps this was the very man who had invaded both my knicker drawer and my life a few years back.

At this point the story becomes a little ethically compromised. Although I was unaware of any restrictions that would specifically prevent me working with him, I suspected that it might not be exactly considered best practice if I were to become his dedicated drugs worker – should our earlier connection ever become known.

Reader, I worked with him all the same. My no doubt compromised thinking told me that there were already many things happening in prisons which did not align themselves too nicely with best practice, and that if my intentions were at least honourable, and I did not use the opportunity to gain any objectively measurable benefit from it for myself, then I should be able to square working with him with my conscience. I did hope to get an immeasurable benefit out of it for myself; but then, many a prison worker is there for reasons that wouldn't stand the most rigorous test of emotional and psychological neutrality or objectivity.

When I finally faced my convict (shades of Dickens here), the unknowable dark force of my imaginings turned out to be only too human in the flesh. Grey faced, visibly weak and in constant pain, he was not old but so shot with drugs that his vitality could now only be rekindled with more of the same poison that was destroying him. He was so racked with muscle and joint pains that he looked the least likely person in the world to have access to the athleticism and sheer physical prowess that burgling my house must have called for. But I quickly discovered that this was the strange gift that heroin brought him – an inability to feel pain for long enough to be physically able to commit crimes that would enable him to buy the wherewithal to restart the circle.

I had a few unspoken rules for our meetings:

- He would never know about our historical connection.
- I wouldn't try to find out anything about what had happened to my jewellery (not that I imagined he would remember anyway).
- I had to discover whether he had committed any criminal acts before becoming dependent on drugs.
- If he hadn't – if his criminal behaviour was the outcome of his drug habit – then I would do everything I possibly could to help him get over the habit.
- Even more importantly, having discovered that he had children whom he wished to protect from drug-taking and from a life like his, I would do everything I possibly could to engineer post-release support for him and his whole family.

Don't get the wrong idea. He was neither a particularly likeable character, nor a man with whom I naturally bonded. Nothing like that. This is not some heart-warming Hollywood-style tale of redemption. He was an angry man, one who had about the average amount of self-knowledge and self-pity for a criminal – which is to say, very little of the first and quite a lot of the latter. And, of course, he expected the external world to fix him. However, he also appeared to be genuinely disgusted with himself for what he had done, and carried on doing, to his family. This feeling for his family was his soft underbelly. That, alongside being about to hit middle age (the commonest reason for criminals to give up crime) and thus becoming quite simply bored and fed up with the whole business, left him about ready for change.

I will probably never know what the final outcome for him turned out to be, whether or not he is off drugs and away from crime. But I mentally doff my cap to him all the same, thank him and wish him well. *He* was *my* redemption.

In recent times, restorative justice has become flavour of the month. In principle it appears to be a good idea. It has been judged to be working with respect to helping both victim and offender to come to terms with the nature of the crime and their parts in it. The idea behind restorative justice is that in order to feel more empowered the victims of crime should have more say in some aspects of sentencing and, if wished and under certain circumstances, should be able to engage in actual face-to-face interviews with the offender. The offender then has some facing up to do, both to the nature of their crime and to the effect it has had on victim and/or community. Overall, restorative justice should work to integrate the concept of crime (as an abstract, legalistic construct) with the reality of the crime (as a gratuitous targeted action against a sensate individual or group).

However, although restorative justice is quite ground-breaking, at least for modern times, my encounter with my criminal was even more effective than restorative justice. Not only did I achieve closure personally, but I was able to rebuild a sense of my own significance. One of the first things to be stolen from me, when Burglar X walked into my house uninvited, was my sense of my own significance. I and my right to control entry to my home were of no matter to him, no matter at all. His drug-fuelled needs simply superseded any rights I might previously have thought I had.

Then, my sense that I (as the person most intimately involved in this whole sad burglary business of property, loss and fear – the one most affected all round) should be entitled to have access to any, and indeed all, information relating to what had happened was completely trounced by the anonymising institutional systems that had been clearly put in place for the benefit of process but certainly not for the benefit of me. Again, I, as 'me, myself', seemed to have been completely stripped of significance.

In all stages relating to the burglary – even after conviction and even while in prison, so far as I was concerned – Burglar X had had the upper hand. This was because he had seen me. He knew me, where I lived. He knew my dog, my house, the contents of my cupboards. He knew my knicker drawer. But I knew nothing of him as a person. For me, he was just the unknowable force that had impacted so disruptively into my possessions, my emotions, my life. But with one brilliant stroke of luck, the tables were turned, the boot was on the other foot, and the worm, too, was able to turn. Even better, the worm was able to choose *in what particular way* it wanted to turn. The choice this worm made was based on the belief that I would be able to gain more power over him if I did him good!

From *Inspector Morse* (e.g. the 'The Day of the Devil' episode from 1993) to the recent Swedish/Danish cop drama, *The Bridge*, screenwriters have played with the idea of aggrieved victims insinuating themselves into prisons and getting inside the minds of prisoners, so that they may, personally, determine how the offender should experience their punishment. For these victims, it's not enough simply to know that the offender is in prison and so incapable of further crimes. The important thing is to have a kind of power over them and over their peace of mind, similar to that they once had over you, their victim.

So it was, to an extent, when I worked with my offender. He became just that – mine. Mine to manipulate, but in my case, unlike the fictional cases, also mine to improve. Where he had known my address, I discovered his address. Where he had known with whom I did or did not live, I discovered his marital status – even talked to his wife. Where he had monitored my movements, I could monitor and even influence his. Where he had rummaged through my knicker drawer, I rummaged through his intimate past, discovering all his dirty laundry.

I could do all those things, and then choose not to use them offensively as some simple-minded primitive reaction to his original behaviour. To have done so would have been to turn myself into him. Much more powerfully, I could reconfigure things and prove my power, and therefore significance to myself, by casting the chain of events differently. By refusing to play his old game and by making a new game all of my own, one that he went along with by choice, I could reclaim my identity and my sense of my own significance.

I gained a form of perverse pleasure out of doing him good. I don't mean to claim any righteousness over this at all. Right, maybe, inasmuch as what I did worked in his interests and in society's too, but righteousness, no. I gained in too many other ways to need or want the cherry-topping of righteousness. Since that time I have never had any knee-jerk unreasoned fear of just about anything. I do still have reasoned fears (sabre-toothed tigers, Saturday nights in country towns, that sort of thing), but no longer do I fear Fear itself.

The reason behind this new found freedom is that when I was working with my prisoner, *I* was determining what was happening – how much information I could discover from him, how much emotional scouring I wanted to put him through, how much effort I was prepared to put into arranging his pre-release meetings and post-release support systems. Where restorative justice programmes fall down by comparison is that the victims involved in them do not have this privileged control over the circumstances of their relationship with offenders; they are still, effectively, at the mercy of other people who make decisions on their behalf, and permit or do not permit their entry into prisons and access to prisoners. Certainly, no way will they ever have access to any personal information about the offender which the authorities deem not pertinent.

The cordon sanitaire that gets erected between victim and offender once the crime has been handed over to the professionals is the product of the same mindset that outsources so many other social obligations to agencies and experts. These range from local traffic management to care of the vulnerable and elderly. It's yet another example of our increasing dislocation from the management of our own affairs and from any sense that we have, or should have, a significant stake in the running of things that impact most heavily on us – things like justice and, specifically, the treatment and management of those who have offended against the things we hold most dear. We have become mere factors in the complex construct named 'justice'. In the process justice itself has become dehumanised. Our fundamental need to regain some sense of power over our own lives, or to impact personally on those who have impacted so severely on us, barely merits more than a theoretical nod from the policy makers.

I was given an amazing opportunity to discover how potent it could be to play the part of protagonist in my own drama, and how therapeutic it was to stage manage this morality tale of my own devising. Although it might seem to have been a vastly individualist and self-indulgent way of dealing with things, and thus at odds with my main theme of operating for the greater good, I truly believe that it is far more in line with the interests of collective efficacy that individuals should feel proactively involved in processes, once those processes have been collectively determined as being for the good of all. Punishment for crimes is a collectively agreed social process – quite rightly so – but the enactment of punishment has become so detached from the great majority of us that we have lost any sense of it actually being a collective process. The consequence is that it has, in practice, largely ceased to work, either for the satisfaction of victims or for the improvement of criminals. At present both sides, in the main, feel aggrieved by the way the system operates.

For much of the time, in fact, the work being done in prisons is not actually carried out by highly specialised professionals. Uncomfortable reality can be only too easily hidden behind that cordon sanitaire; there are many more ad hoc arrangements in prisons than people outside might care to believe. Much nominally specialist work is carried out not so much by genuinely accredited specialists but rather by self-selected silo groups such as addiction charities. I have worked alongside people who are still so much in the grip of their own addictive thinking that they have no problem with cannabis use, either for themselves or for the prisoners, as it's not considered to be a hard drug. Their business, at least as they see it, is solely to get the prisoners off hard gear.

We need to rethink the relationship between crime, the state and the individual in ways that would also address questions of significance and fear. I'm not suggesting that every affected individual should have an automatic right to go into prisons to work with 'their' prisoner, as I was privileged to do. But we should recognise that a relationship between offender and victim does exist, one that has been forced onto and works against the victim. In the interests of genuine justice, that victim should have the opportunity (if wished) to reconfigure that relationship. This could be easily and relatively cheaply achieved by giving each victim the right to have face-to-face, or even face-to-voice (for those victims who wished to retain their right to anonymity), electronic engagement with their offender – when and for as long as the victim wishes, within the overarching requirements of security and prison regimens.

Crime is anti-society, but we should never forget that it is also anti the individual within society.

Chapter 11

Principles in Practice

I've already talked a lot about prisons and prisoners, the relationship between crime, significance and fear, and how the way that reclaiming a sense of one's own significance, through regaining a measure of control over the relationship with an offender, can be hugely therapeutic for the victims of crime. This chapter is about what should be informing and influencing our selection of 'desired principles'. To that end, I'm going to switch the focus away from the victim and towards the prisoner, and look at the way prisoners tend to see their relationship – with life itself rather than the victim.

We need case studies to understand complex human behaviour. This chapter is largely about how people make ethical decisions. The reason for focusing on prisoners, apart from the fact that I've worked with quite a lot of them, is that this provides clarity about 'principles in practice' in a practical sense.

Prisoners make surprisingly good case studies because, first, they are physically available in relatively large numbers and easy to monitor (university students are the preferred subjects in many US studies, although they diverge more from 'normal' than your average prisoner!). Second, prisoners tend to be more than usually present – attentive, in the moment (assuming they're not still actively high and bouncing off walls) – as they are subject to fewer of the distractions, especially the electronic ones, that prevent many people from engaging fully with any individual, interview or exercise.

Third, prisoners, surprisingly, are unusually emotionally available in ways that most people in the outside world are quite simply not. This is especially apparent if you're working, as I was, on highly emotive material and in confined spaces. Under these circumstances prisoners tend to jettison their usual high vis emotional protection, their hard man (or woman) carapace. I've lost track of the number of prisoners who have looked at me, partly in sadness, partly with defiance, and said, 'I've never said this to anyone before …' and then gone on to tell me things that, in the outside world, they would have died sooner than acknowledge. And I experienced this with all classes, all cultures, all colours, all creeds.

So, not only are many prisoners far more transparent than most people can afford, or are prepared, to be, but as they are also men and women who have inevitably cocked up in some fairly significant way they tend to embody a far more interesting array of the unwanted characteristics (such as moral equivocation) that have emerged as by-products of our mutated DNA than just about any other group of people (with the possible exception of our political classes). In prisons you find a wealth of fascinating material.

Prisoners find themselves at crossroads in their lives, especially when nearing the ends of sentences, and are in the position of having to make significant choices about the direction they want their lives to take. Very few adults find themselves having to make such conscious, wide-ranging and far-reaching choices around restructuring their lives, and especially around restructuring what might be thought of as their ethical lives. So prisoners can afford us a rare opportunity to observe the deliberations and workings of the human mind under comprehensively challenging circumstances. They find themselves having to haul out and line up for inspection all the ingredients from the larder of life: core values, lived experience, cultural norms, educational attainment, family expectations, peer pressure, hopes and desires, medical and psychological problems, and a thousand other concerns, and then they have to make a selection from this scattergun smorgasbord for the menu they would hope to create. This whole process provides the interested observer with a uniquely helpful master class in thinking for coping.

The way in which prisoners mentally construct their picture of the world – how it works, what is important within it, how they relate to it – is not only very likely to define the manner in which that prisoner will cope on release, it is also, very helpfully, likely to offer the student of resilience a definitive blueprint of how the relationship between ethical values and resilience works, throwing light on the practical, emotional and psychological difficulties which we must all face from time to time.

In summary, prisoners provide us with a body of people who are more open than average, more easily monitored and they embody and model the difficulties and drives behind complex attitudes, states and behaviour. What's not to find fascinating and useful? What they have to tell us (explicitly or implicitly) about what influences and motivates their thinking and their behaviour can be useful in highlighting the complexities of how even the most seemingly valid principles may actually operate in practice – particularly given a distorted sense of significance somewhere in the equation.

The two stories I'm going to tell might appear misleadingly simple, but there is a level of complexity that emerges.

My first story is about a young male prisoner who had absconded some time before I met him, recaptured after a full year on the run and returned to the prison I was working in. Obviously he was not best pleased at this turn of events, and even seemed rather outraged that by being brought back to prison he was likely to end up costing the taxpayer far more than if he had been left to his own liberated devices. He had his principles, and as he said, 'I've paid my way the whole time I've been out there. I've been working, I've not relied on the dole like a load of these scumbags do.' (There may well be honour among thieves, but there isn't always too much respect.)

Leaving aside the fact that he had not actually been paying taxes while he was doing his bit for the economy, there was also the matter of where he had been living for that year and at whose expense. As I was not prepared to take him at his own estimation of his fiscal resourcefulness and probity, I pressed him on these points. He'd been living with his girlfriend, he replied, not scabbing off anyone else. I pressed him again. Did she own the place he'd been staying at? No, it was rented. Did she have a job, was she earning? No. How was the place being paid for? Slight silence. It was being funded by her welfare. He had never joined the dots.

On the opposite side of the personal accountability divide was the young man who had finally come to realise just how much of his short life he had already wasted in prison. Even though he had been on the receiving end of plenty of advice in the past, he only woke up to the reality of his situation when he was given an ultimatum by his girlfriend, along the lines of, 'Get yourself sorted, or I'm off.' Unlike Prisoner 1's girlfriend she was a hard worker herself and was not prepared to put up with her boyfriend's messed up lifestyle any longer. Once he finally picked up on the message that what he was doing was absolutely not in line with the love he said he felt for her and their child, he started the process of making his behaviour agree with his aspirations.

When I last saw him he had absolutely no doubts at all about what would now make him happy, about what would make him feel that he had left all that shit behind and was finally someone with a future rather than a past. This future was aligned with his aspirations, it would allow him to hold his head up, be normal and finally *do* rather than just simply *imagine* the right thing by his family. The thing that he had no doubt about whatsoever, the thing that would prove his good intent, the totem of being a properly paid (or paying) up member of the human race, was a mortgage. That millstone which most of us simply can't wait to get rid of! He said, 'Do you know what I want? I want to be like normal people. I want a job and I want a mortgage.' I could have cried.

It seems to me that the really significant difference in the attitudes of the two men was not so much the outcome of a fundamental difference in aspirations for the self – after all, they both wanted to be able to think of themselves as autonomous, self-reliant and in their own way responsible (Prisoner 1 actually had some half worked-out idea that he could, and should, be costing the country less than he had in the past) – but was more the outcome of a different system of delusions. Prisoner 1 was operating according to the highly subjective delusion that he, personally, was best able to determine what would achieve the outcomes he wanted (despite having no evidence to substantiate his own effectiveness at decision making). Prisoner 2 was readier to buy into a delusion that is routinely shared by most people in this particular society. This commonly held delusion says that property ownership marks you out as responsible, financially astute, farsighted, orderly and in possession of a whole host of similarly desirable attributes that other societies, in other times, would never have credited you with simply because you were prepared to take on financial risk. However, as a shared delusion, it is not only a marker of this society's standards, it also denotes a desirable principle which will operate in the interests of the greater good. This is that we should have both an interest in and responsibility for the financial, physical and procedural structures within which we live. By fixing on an objective that is so strongly aligned with society's shared principles, Prisoner 2 was always going to have a better chance on release into that society than Prisoner 1, with his idiosyncratic and fragmented approach to aligning society, principles and practice.

Ultimately, it's all about sharing the delusion and about acting in ways that are aligned with the principles relating to that delusion. The more we act in accordance with those principles, the more comfortable people will be around us. By acting that way we are embodying and enacting our concurrence with their preferred idea – that they are not thinking like victims of random mental processes, but are, in fact, connecting things up according to some natural order. This in turn means they are not, therefore, inchoate and meaningless accidents of nature after all. By supporting the desired principles of a particular society we are, in effect, protecting people from the dangers that are inherent in the contemplation of the over-connectivity of the human brain. We are saying, 'It's okay, it does all make sense. This is what the sense looks like. And the more of us who see it that way, the better it will be for all of us.'

Prisoner 2 had had enough of life lived on the wild side and finally made the decision to come on board and see the sense that most of society saw. However, Prisoner 1 still has a way to go; he may or may not decide to join the party. Most young men grow out of crime eventually, but only when he can better understand the relationship between principles and practice will he be in the best place to do so. It's not enough to see yourself as principled and fiscally responsible on your own terms. In order to be joined in that particular delusion by the multitude, you would have to set up your own religion or political party. In the world we live in, if you want to *be* principled, as well as *feel* principled, you have to align your behaviour as closely as possible to that which is commonly agreed to be most in line with achieving the desired principles of the wider society.

And those are?

To date, many of us have been thinking a bit like Prisoner 1, in that we've had the right aspirations behind our principles but have been about as good as he was at joining up the dots. We haven't been able, or perhaps prepared, to recognise when principles aren't well aligned with aspirations, nor, more significantly, where principles are on a different trajectory from practice. We haven't been as clear sighted and firm with ourselves as Prisoner 2 finally was, and as we must become if we genuinely want to achieve what we tell ourselves we want.

As a society we say we want lots of lovely and desirable things. We want to be free and we want to have the right to express ourselves, but we also want to be protected from hearing things we don't like. We want to have autonomy and the right to make our own decisions about how we live our lives, and yet we want the right to seek compensation for unexpected or unwanted outcomes. We want our children to grow up happy, fulfilled and free, and yet we want to micro-manage their time and their safety. We want to enjoy the wealth of goods, goodies and experiences that life has to offer, and yet we want to minimise the risks associated with enjoying them. We want to embrace diversity (in human activities), and yet we want to put controls in place to limit it in the wildlife population. We want to spread information about every minute detail of our activities via social networking sites and want all government activities to be open and transparent, and yet we want the right to opt out of allowing our medical data to be freely transferred between doctors and hospitals. And so on. Supply your own suggestions here. We all have our own *bêtes noires* but most of us can see that there is a bit of a mismatch between some of our aspirations and some of our principles, and that's before we even get on to practice.

At a time when apparently even our best educated kids' mathematical achievements are lagging behind those of the offspring of cleaners in China (Organisation for Economic Co-operation and Development, 2013) and when, according to a report in *The Times* (18 February 2014), more than half of parents won't let their children play rugby or hockey for fear of injury, thus exposing them to the greater risks of both obesity and dementia in later life ('Physical exercise is as important in staving off dementia as keeping your mind active, scientists have said', also from *The Times*, 18 February – Devlin, 2014), it looks as though it is more important than ever to look at the relationship between our aspirations, Sampson's desired principles (see Chapter 10) and our actual practices. We currently appear to be suffering from what can only be described as 'muddle think'.

We can no longer afford the indulgence of thinking and behaving like Prisoner 1, who felt rather aggrieved that his own inner intentions were not being recognised for the outstandingly superior ones that he, personally, understood them to be. He treated this outrage against him as being at least as significant as the practical reality of being back in prison again – where he was least likely to achieve the independent life he craved. If we want to achieve better outcomes than the headlines in Chapter 1 then we must acknowledge that some ideas/behaviours are more realistically likely to achieve what we want than others (and may even be, soft be it spoken, *ethically* better). And then we must, like Prisoner 2, knuckle down to the necessary yet dutiful and unexciting activities that will get us to where we want to be.

We must create a Holy Alliance between what we say we want, what we hold up as principles and standards that we should subscribe to and last, but very much not least, what we ourselves do in practice and what we will tolerate in the practice of others. It's no good doing all the right things ourselves, if all the time, maybe for reasons of moral equivocation, we allow others to be acting against what we believe and unpicking what we do. This is key to Sampson's findings on how resilient communities work. Once mutually desired principles were established, individuals had to be prepared to monitor, evaluate and control the unaligned behaviour of others.

It's not, in the end, a kindness to let the inappropriate behaviour of others go unjudged and uncontrolled; it actually works against us all. So many things, from non-directive psychological therapies, to non-judgemental stances by social workers, to acceptance of culturally determined linguistic norms in schools, have pitted practice against aspirations. The outcome has been a fragmentation of society and a loss of any belief that we might belong to a supportive and sustaining whole. We have also been left with any number of unintentional but tragic harms which have been suffered by vulnerable subgroups in the name of non-judgemental practice. Subgroups such as:

- Those mental health clients who may have spent miserable years wading through the mire of their psychological confusion with numbers of non-directive therapists, while any actual neurological conditions they may have had, such as Asperger's, have gone totally unnoticed and undiagnosed.
- The abused and injured children who have been inappropriately handed back into the 'care' of their drug using, alcoholic or mentally ill parents, just so that they may have the chance to bond properly with them, as a family.
- The legions of educationally disadvantaged inner-city children who have never been expected or encouraged to learn to communicate in ways that might be socially and academically relevant, or remotely in line with any aspirations they may have, so that their cultural heritage will be preserved.

As a society we have been guilty of tolerating inappropriate practice, in effect of saying that Prisoner 1's solutions to his problems are every bit as valid as Prisoner 2's, and he has every right to pursue them. But then we have been equally guilty of wanting to punish him when the inevitable outcome of his idiosyncratic beliefs has been an increased cost to society and a break-out of anti-social behaviour. We have also failed Prisoner 2 by not making quite enough of his achievements. Those going straight on release have never had as much support and encouragement as they should. Ditto, most people who go very quietly about their committed, pro-social and beneficial lives.

If we have been guilty of getting aspirations, principles and practice confused, but would like to get them more aligned, it's time to go back to Robert J. Sampson, and consider the question of what *should* be informing and influencing our selection of desired principles.

We need to consider our overarching aspirations as well as which principles for living we would need to have if we are to believe in the possibility of surthrival – that is, a condition in which we could do more than merely survive but could actually thrive too.

Here are my absolutes, without which I do not believe a truly healthful society, with human wellbeing at its heart, can exist.

Bottom line aspirations

- The best possible physical health for all – everything else stems from that.
- The best possible mental health for all – although dependent on the above, this needs extra consideration and input.
- A sense of belonging to a wider whole.
- And, of course, significance, both subjective and objective – believing that we, individually, matter; also that there is a point, a meaning, to the life we are living.

And your point is?

Life itself is not a delusion – unless a very grand cosmic one – but the concept of meaning *is* a delusion, the result of that mutated extra connectivity in our brain. It is a delusion that, like the prehistoric squirrel's acorn in the film *Ice Age*, is destined to frustrate us endlessly, because no matter how many threads we connect up and no matter how many patterns we impose on sensation and experience, there will always be more possibilities out there. This is because it is in the very nature of this process that meanings develop exponentially. To give another filmic analogy, think gremlins with water – the more they are touched by it, the more they proliferate. Far better that we should recognise that meaning, per se, is something of a nonsense and that the search for meaning is ultimately fruitless. However …

If we recognise the probability that this is the way things work then other helpful things follow. If we can accept the illusory nature of meaning, as well as recognise how our own significance agenda works and the part it plays in our particular schema for life,[1] then we will be in a much better position to overlook all personal, social and cultural considerations as we attempt the business of creating a set of *objectively* (well, objectively, as far as this is possible given the above) desirable principles which are aligned with our aspirations.

It is too glib simply to say that 'there is no meaning', especially as I've said that significance or meaning in life is essential to wellbeing. It's also too dangerous to say that all meaning is equal, which would be another way of interpreting what I've said (and too close to some of the relativist theories which I believe have already caused so much damage). So what I'm after here is to get to a position in which it should be possible to put together a set of desired principles, a system of living, that will work in the best interests of the aspirations of surthrival – that is, in the best interests of the greatest number of people. And although this is hardly an original idea, it still remains the one that is most likely to produce the healthiest outcome for any one of us, individually.

So, if meaning is a mutable rather than a fixed concept, we should be able to decide on the meaning that is best suited to our needs, and then, in the interests of wellbeing, stick with it *wholeheartedly*. Some might call that cynical or artificial, but I would say, in turn, that such critics were operating according to a personal and emotional agenda, rather than one in line with the greater good. Ergo, let's pragmatically agree a set of norms, a set of principles, which are best aligned to our aspirations and I think we will have most things covered.[2] All that will remain after that will be to make sure practice follows principles (as we've already seen, hardly the easiest thing to achieve).

Simples.

Surthrival's bottom line desired principles

● We should not confuse personal desires with personal good. (Note that authentic personal good, being dependent on the greater good, doesn't always or necessarily feel good at the personal level.)

---

1   A schema is a way of representing and ordering life internally – it also functions as a 'filter', allowing and disallowing new information and ideas, according to whether or not they make a fit with the schema.
2   Inevitably this is not a once and for all/wherever situation, as each generation and society will have different aspirations – this is about best practice.

- We should feel and be responsible for, and responsible to, those around us and not act for ourselves alone.
- We should understand that genuine significance depends as much on making a difference as on feeling important.
- Although we belong to the world, the world doesn't belong to us, and so we have a responsibility to do what works best for the world, including taking care of our own health (physical and mental) and the health of others (physical and mental).
- We should aim to do fewer things because we are worth it (that's just a delusion) and more things that are likely to benefit rather than harm future generations.

Keeping our eyes on the ball

We need to keep these aspirations in mind because it's so darned easy to confuse principles with politics (of every kind, national, local, ideological, office) and practice with protocols. By holding the end game or goal in mind throughout, it's going to be easier to determine if we're genuinely set on winning or merely intent on keeping the play in our own little corner.

Remembering that the overall ambition/goal is to achieve health, mental wellbeing, satisfaction and a sense of belonging, and that the above principles/game plan are mostly there to produce the best mindset for achieving that goal, what then about the practice itself? What do we actually do? And what about the play itself, the way we kick and dribble our way to the goal? Can we keep our day-to-day practices genuinely aligned with both the aspirations we have for life and the desired principles which are most likely to support those aspirations?

Chapter 12

The Practice

Everything stems from good physical health

The Roman poet Juvenal's phrase, *mens sana in corpore sano* – a healthy mind in a healthy body – has stood many generations in good stead. However, quite possibly through its associations, first with nine-teenth-century ideas around the survival of the fittest and eugenics and then with twentieth-century notions of racial purity and national socialism, physical wellbeing went out of fashion after the Second World War. Mass adoption of cool and emancipated behaviours – such as smoking and driving, fashions for skinny androgeny in the 1960s and heroin chic in the 1990s and then the wholesale selling off of school playing fields – led to successive gen-erations of young people who either didn't want or didn't get the chance to take part in team or individual sports. Although things are changing – sport has recently become much cooler again – the dam-age has been done, and, sadly, the playing fields won't suddenly divest themselves of all those boxy housing estates.

But let's be resilient rather than gloomy, because even without the benefit of a glass-fronted cupboard full of silver cups in our living room, there's still a huge amount we can do for our own health and, just as importantly, for the health of others.

Put down those cigarettes

When I first tried to persuade employers and clients in the world of addiction that good physical health was key to things like recovery and mental wellbeing I was looked upon, quite frankly, as some kind of extremist zealot. Suggesting that cigarette smoking was bad for physical and mental health was seen as fastidious and tyrannical. When I was delivering training to an NHS quit smoking service and asked how many attendees had been smokers themselves, many hands went up, as expected. But when I asked how many people were still smokers, several hands rather alarmingly wobbled upwards! Here was a definite mismatch, and I saw it as part of the problem.

How can you possibly give credible advice to people wanting to stop smoking when you still smell of fags yourself?

I found similar incongruences in the drug and alcohol services in prisons and in some of the most prestigious rehabs in the country – over half the people working in these places smoked. They not only saw nothing wrong with this but they also saw quitting as something positively to be discouraged. 'You can't expect people to give up all their comforts at once,' I was admonished more times than I can remember. Which, if nothing else, goes to show that even people who should be better informed have little understanding not only of the link between mental and physical health but also of the complex effects on our physiology of the things we put into our bodies. For example, smoking cigarettes depletes the oxygen necessary for breathing and for the muscles. Therefore, smokers' muscles tire more easily than non-smokers' and recover from exertion more slowly. When we see smokers huffing and puffing their way upstairs it's not just because their lungs don't work too well, nothing else about their bodies works too well either. Therefore, by quitting they have the prospect of setting up a virtuous circle; not only will they breathe more easily but they will also find it easier and quicker to recover from exertion. So the whole business of taking exercise becomes more rewarding and pleasurable as well as better for their physical health.

The other physical benefits from not smoking include decreased risks in all of these areas: cancer, heart disease, stroke, brittle bones, macular degeneration (eye health), teeth, fertility and children's health. The last benefit not only includes harms which children might have suffered from direct inhalation of others' smoke – for example, sudden infant death syndrome and premature thickening of the arteries, which can leave them at greater risk of health problems in later life – but also, courtesy of epigenetic factors, harms they might have suffered seemingly indirectly. It now appears that grandmothers' smoking habits can impact on a grandchild's chance of developing asthma. So we may have to give something up in order to get something better – not only for me but also for them. Either way, we get the personal benefit of doing the right thing. (In the next chapter I examine the impact that smoking has on mental health.)

Nothing can beat the fabulous sensation of being in tune with the universe that comes with being in peak physical condition. This doesn't mean being in peak Olympic condition as that is hardly a natural state. Peak condition is all about being as physically fit as is appropriate and achievable for one's gender, size and age. And that's something we can all aspire to. So …

Take up aerobic exercise

Aerobic exercise is one of *the* most important things we can undertake for the good of our health.

Long before Seb Coe decided to make it the title of his autobiography, I started a book called 'Running My Life' about my (successful) attempts to train for the London Marathon. Having finished the race, I then ran out of steam and never finished the book. Or perhaps it would be better to say, I ran out of running, because the frequently pejorative phrases used about running are utterly misleading. What I actually did was to cut down on my running. Running is good, running is natural, running is really all positive. It's when we don't run that things don't run so well.

Why do we say, 'I ran out of ideas'? That's nonsense. The truth is we're far more likely to run *into* ideas. I'm not alone in having discovered the power of running as a stimulus to creative thinking. We've long had fantastical notions of mad creative geniuses necking absinthe and lying around on chaises longues all day, but the truth is that dopamine, the neurotransmitter for creativity, is best produced by activity. And many of those old romantic images are pure tosh. People in the past simply had to take vast amounts of aerobic exercise if they wanted to get from A to B; it was in the nature of travel. Shakespeare and Dickens, who had two of the most creative brains in the history of humankind, walked thousands of miles in their lives. So did, unlikely though it might seem, that historical dope head, Samuel Taylor Coleridge. The laudanum may not have been particularly beneficial for his brain, but it was offset by the strolls he undertook between places as far apart as Devon, London and the Lake District. Even the decorous Jane Austen described herself in a letter to a friend as a 'desperate walker' – meaning a very determined and dedicated one. So the moral is, if you want to be successfully creative, don't hang around waiting for inspiration to come knocking on your door, put on a pair of trainers and walk or run your way towards it.

Not only will aerobic activity such as running help our bodies and brains to function better,[1] it also will help anyone to *know* their body or brain better – and thus to know themselves better. It is a brilliant way of discovering your capacity and your limitations, your best incentives and your most pernicious disincentives, your levels of

---

1   I refer to running rather than other aerobic activities as I've been doing it for decades. All aerobic activities will have similar effects.

tolerance and intolerance. And it will teach you to monitor your physical self and learn to integrate the perceptions from your body and your mind like nothing else.

'Running My Life' may be a punning and metaphorical title for a book, but it is also a pretty successful strategy for wellbeing. Perhaps we should move on from the negativity of phrases like 'running away from trouble', 'running into difficulty', 'running up debt', 'running people down' and so on, and start to dream up more verbal associations depicting running as the vital, healthy, wonderful and truly stimulating part of natural activity that it really is. (And it's almost free.)

Other more static sports, such as weight training, are also physically beneficial but in a different way from more aerobic activities. Working out with weights has been shown to improve the way bodies age, helping to maintain muscle mass and bone density, and thus the strength, stability and long-term functioning of the human body. But seeing exercise purely in terms of its contribution to bodybuilding has a downside. Good physical health is more than simple motor function and infrastructure maintenance; it is also dependent on the internal systems which help us to feel at ease in our own bodies, and this is where straightforward development of physique can fail to deliver.

Whereas aerobic activity raises both dopamine levels and serotonin levels (serotonin is often called the 'feel good' or 'happiness' neurotransmitter, although it has more nuanced effects than those terms suggest), it appears that weight training mostly affects our dopamine receptors. This has the effect of increasing a person's sense of purpose and achievement, but without the additional impact of increased oxygen it adds little to their sense of overall wellbeing.

In prisons I often challenged the unquestioned acceptance by both prisoners and staff that going to the gym was a totally unalloyed benefit for the prisoners. Not only did they frequently become virtually addicted to the ritual of bodybuilding because of all that dopamine-mediated intensity of purpose and achievement (especially bearing in mind their lack of alternative sources of pleasure), but they frequently also had access to steroids which, in conjunction with the virtually all-male atmosphere of a male prison, led to even greater than average levels of testosterone-fuelled competitive anger. This 'roid rage' is very unpleasant to see. The difference between competitive team games or aerobic workouts and the aggression of roid rage is the difference between a child energised and motivated by running free in wide open green spaces and one who is running around wildly and erratically fuelled by sugar and chemical additives.

So nothing in excess. Weight training within limits and aerobic activities – such as running, cycling, dancing, spinning, exercise classes – also within limits, although here the limits can be much more generously set. The reason for limiting even the best kind of physical activity is that if we don't put any limits on exercise, not only will joints, tendons and muscles suffer as they are unlikely to get sufficient rest and repair time between bouts of activity, but we may also be producing too much dopamine. An excess of dopamine, even when it's endogenous, is still addictive and can distort thinking and behaviour. People whose dopamine processing systems are set to erratic – the people we call 'addicts' – can move relatively seamlessly from being lazy feckless drunks to becoming hyper-motivated extreme coffee drinkers, sweet munchers and runners. Not for nothing do we call that euphoric feeling that comes after a few miles of street pounding the 'runners' high'. People who have self-control problems can experience them with exercise just as easily as they can with wine, sugar, heroin, cigarettes or gambling. However, notwithstanding the potential for abuse, the benefits of exercise most definitely outweigh the downsides and I would never argue otherwise.

Exercise is a must for heart rate, blood sugar levels, cholesterol levels, weight control, muscle mass, thinking clearly, being creative and generally being a better person all round.

If we want our children to develop into better all-round people – becoming independent, responsible and organised as well as healthy – we should definitely be encouraging and supporting them to take much more exercise than they are generally doing at present. Previous generations of schoolchildren had no option but to make their own way to and from school; this provided an inescapable opportunity for exercise, especially if you had to run away from the bullies. But now, for all sorts of complex reasons, including the bullies, parents find it easier to take their little darlings to school by car. So, not only are they setting them a bad example by parking on all those double yellow lines, they are also modelling how not to care for their bodies and how not to be resilient. They are actively demonstrating that taking the easy option, the one less personally and physically demanding, is greatly preferable to taking one that requires planning, time commitment and more intensive personal physical effort.

A study by the Policy Studies Institute at Westminster University (Shaw et al., 2013) has shown that whereas 86% of English primary schoolchildren made their way to school independently in the 1970s, only 25% do so now. The English experience compared unfavourably with the German one. German primary-age children are encouraged to travel independently by foot, bike or bus years before their English counterparts do. Not only does this impact on their physical health but also on their acquisition of life skills and cognitive development, which is dependent on the creation of a healthy balance between brain and body activity. Few parents consciously set out to make life harder for their children, and yet preventing them from acquiring (or at least making it hard for them to acquire) good habits like exercise and physical self-care can hardly be said to be caring behaviour. It's going to be much harder for those same children to adopt the necessary life-enriching, even life-saving, habits later on.

Mayer Hillman, senior fellow emeritus at the Policy Studies Institute, who has been involved in the Westminster University study from the beginning, says:

It is highly regrettable that so little attention has been paid to the damage caused by this erosion of children's freedoms and decline in their *quality of life*. Far more effort needs to be invested in reversing the process that has had such an unfortunate outcome. (Policy Studies Institute, 2013; my italics)

We know that exercise, especially in green open spaces, is good for both mental and physical health at any age and is particularly necessary for the developing child. Why is it not considered criminal when a parent, on whom a child is largely dependent, fails to provide their child with such a fundamental requirement of life as exercise?

Choose a rational diet

Talking about diet is a minefield of conflicting information and interests, so I am only going to touch on diet in relation to brain function. Given what I have already stated, it should go without saying that you need a diet that takes best care of your health. This includes considering eating behaviour as well as the actual foodstuffs consumed. For example, there is evidence that concentrating on eating, as opposed to eating while texting or watching TV, helps control calorie intake because you're not eating robotically in a kind of trance. A study from the University of Liverpool found that eating while watching TV not only led to a 10% increase in calories consumed at the time, but also to an even greater increase of up to 25% more calories consumed later on that same day (Innes, 2013)! So how and when you eat may be just as relevant to the matter of controlling diet as the actual quantities consumed.

And, of course, what we eat is hugely (as it were) important. As Garfield, the cartoon cat, famously observed, 'Avoid fruits and nuts: after all, you are what you eat.' Unlike Garfield, I do not pretend to be a nutritionist. There are numerous authorities who can give much more detailed information about the benefits of various food groups, vitamins and so on. It is vital to health that these things are well understood and that the best principles (if they can ever be fully established) are followed. However, there are some specific aspects of diet which appear to be particularly relevant to brain behaviour.

Sugar and the brain

Evidence shows that brains require sugar in order to concentrate effectively and to apply the mental control that we call willpower (see Baumeister and Tierney, 2011). However, an increasingly powerful argument based on research undertaken at UCLA (Agrawal et al., 2016) claims that sugar – and especially the fructose that is found in so many foods as well as in juices – is damaging modern brains (particularly their learning and memory functions) in a quite alarming way. Therefore, anyone wanting optimal conditions for their brain should look to their general sugar consumption and drink water rather than juices.

Fish oils, omega-3 and the brain

The same UCLA study (Agrawal et al., 2016) found that other, more beneficial, substances could also affect brain functioning. One category, omega-3 fatty acids, could actually help to offset the harms caused by modern diets which are high in fructose. Fish oils, high in omega-3 fatty acids, have long been believed to be good for the brain. Cod liver oil was routinely given to children throughout the

1940s and 1950s when, anecdotally, children were better learners than today. Some trials in young offender institutions, part funded by the Wellcome Trust, have appeared to show that anti-social behaviour has been significantly reduced when cocktails of vitamins and minerals, including omega-3 supplements, have been given to the inmates. Professor John Stein, brother of restauranteur Rick, is involved in these trials and is a great advocate of the overall benefits to brain health of appropriate quantities of omega-3, even being convinced that it can be helpful in cases of dyslexia. Some of the evidence available on the benefits of fish oil is anecdotal and open to question, but taking it in supplement form can do no harm and will be beneficial to joint health anyway.

Tryptophans

Tryptophans are essential amino acids, meaning that our bodies need them for healthful functioning, but as they are not produced by the body they have to be ingested. Tryptophan is a precursor to the so-called feel-good neurotransmitter serotonin, so it can be deduced that insufficient tryptophan intake may be related to depressive symptoms. There is some evidence for this. Professor David Nutt was involved in a study which showed that patients previously successfully treated with anti-depressants became depressed again when totally deprived of tryptophan (Bell et al., 2001). Although the same effect was not found with patients who had not been treated with anti-depressants, it was clear that there was a link between the serotonin-boosting – and therefore mood-enhancing – effects of anti-depressants and of tryptophan. As tryptophan helps people to relax, stay calm and sleep, then clearly it is likely to have benefits for physical health overall. The optimum way to introduce it into the diet is still uncertain, but to be in with a chance include foods rich in tryptophan, such as yogurt, milk, cheese, poultry, eggs and bananas in your daily regime.

Weight

Finally, it's worth pointing out the advantages to the human body of keeping weight under control. In addition to the obvious benefits for the heart, joints, internal organs, blood pressure and cholesterol levels, there is another blindingly obvious one that has only recently come to light – maybe people just didn't want to see the connection – and this is the extraordinary benefit to our brains of keeping our weight down.

A study of 1,352 middle-aged people carried out by Professor Charles DeCarli of the University of California at Davis (Debette et al., 2011) found that smoking, diabetes and excess weight could all cause the human brain to shrink, and that obese participants in the study were more likely than non-obese ones to be in the top 25% for people who showed the fastest rate of decline in both planning and decision-making ability.

If that isn't reason enough for anyone to either want to lose weight or never put it on in the first place, then maybe a sense of responsibility to future generations will be. For significantly over-weight people this responsibility extends beyond reducing future healthcare costs to an already overstretched NHS to protecting their own grandchildren from diabetes and obesity. Given evidence from a number of research projects, it is now believed that the diet an adult human follows can bring on changes in all cells of the body, including both sperm and egg cells (see Wanjek, 2012). These changes can, in turn, be passed down through following generations (this is epigenetics at work), meaning that a person's grandchildren may be born with a predisposition to develop obesity, even when they are not directly responsible for significant overeating them-selves. Who would wish to carry the can for that potential outcome? Not being prepared to look after one's own health for the good of others is pretty much the same as being prepared to actively harm them.

Sleep

There was a time when the idea of a completely 24/7 society seemed attractive to many people, including those responsible for licensing hours. These days, the notion of a 24/7 society looks rather naive and old fashioned. We now understand much more about the absolute health benefits of sleep and of getting it at the times that nature dictated. We have also come to realise that the idea that children should be free to decide their own sleep requirements and set their own bedtimes is unlikely to be of benefit to them. That was not a good health-promoting idea.

Children need sleep and they need good sleeping patterns to be established early on if they are to sustain the practice of what is now known as good sleep hygiene – incorporating the environmental and behavioural factors which promote and maintain good healthful sleep. Child psychologist and media guru on childcare, Professor Tanya Byron, says that many childhood behavioural problems, such as hyperactivity and slow development, can be blamed on parents' failure to teach their children good sleep behaviour (see Furness, 2013). She also blames much of their consumption of high-sugar and high-fat foods on their need to boost energy levels which have been depleted by tiredness. She complains that parents permit children to stay up late, snack through the night and wander around falling asleep wherever they want, including in parents' beds. She suggests that the consequences of this wayward parenting can be very damaging for the young and result in poor concentration and performance at school, depression and even self-harm.

Tanya Byron cites, as do many other experts, the negative effects on sleep hygiene of technology – smartphones, tablets, computers and TVs in the bedroom. Not only do they introduce stimulation into the one place where calm and complete focus on sleep are important, the bedroom, but they're also awash with lights, especially the blue LED variety. All light is known to suppress the pineal gland's production of melatonin – the hormone that controls our sleep–wake cycles – and blue short-wave light is the most melatonin suppressive of all. The consequence of exposure to this light is not only disturbed sleep, but also impairment of the immune system, obesity and raised risk of both heart disease and cancer.

Is 24/7 access to the latest bit of gossip worth that sort of risk? Night workers have learned about the risk to their health of following a topsy-turvy lifestyle, and as adults we do have some choice in this, but should we be exposing our children to the same kinds of risk when they don't have any authentic choice? Because, even at the teenage stage of development, brains are still too immature to be capable of making proper risk assessments. Children cannot foresee or evaluate the consequences of risky behaviour, especially to themselves, if it produces gratification and pleasure. (This should be evident to anyone who has ever had dealings with teenagers.) Although young teenagers would cry 'unjust' or 'not fair' were it suggested to them, they should be considered too young to make sensible choices about future prospects for their health. In other words, it really is up to parents and those adults who genuinely care about their wellbeing to set guidelines around bedtimes, sleep times and sleeping conditions, however painful or tedious the ensuing battles might be. The more people who make a stand, the easier it will be for all. There is power in numbers, and we do owe this amount of care to the future.[2]

---

2   To further support this plea, a recent study (Horst et al., 2011) also promotes the benefits of sleep, specifically as a reinforcer of learning. Dr Jessica Horst, at the University of Sussex, studied 48 3-year-old children, half of whom took a nap after having had a story read to them and half of whom didn't. They were read either the same stories or three different stories, but were exposed to the same number of unfamiliar words. They were then tested on these words two and a half hours later, twenty-four hours later and a week later. Those who had been read the same story and then enjoyed a nap performed significantly better at the word task than those who had not slept.
   However, when children had been read three different stories before either having a nap or not, the variation was even more extreme, with the 'nappers' performing a whole 33% better than those who had not slept. In subsequent tests it was discovered that the wakeful children never caught up with the nappers in word recall. This strongly appears to demonstrate that as learning tasks increase in difficulty (the new words from multiple stories scenario), so sleep becomes ever more beneficial. The more we want to progress, the more we need sleep.
   Dr Horst suggests that we should be very concerned that children appear to be getting less and less sleep, and says that lack of sleep is related to poorer vocabulary scores, childhood obesity and tantrums. She also says that classroom naps can be very beneficial for young children and suggests that they be incorporated into the timetable to benefit key academic areas such as word learning and arithmetic.

Chapter 13

Mental Health

The practice of good mental health is a prerequisite for our species to do more than simply survive – it's essential for us to thrive, too.

The practice of good mental health

There is a huge amount of overlap between physical and mental health, and much of what I have said about physical wellbeing will have had implications for cognitive wellbeing; the brain is a physical entity subject to many of the same influences as the rest of the body. Good mental health is to a large extent dependent on good physical health, but not entirely so. Some people have genetic predispositions to mental problems, and no matter how careful they are about their physical health, they are going to be more vulnerable to life stressors. There are also cases where people's excessive, obsessive commitment to physical fitness becomes, in itself, a mental health problem. It's a form of addiction which can in the long run, ironically, result in more physical harm than good. The *mens sana in corpore sano* principle applies for possibly 95% of the time but occasionally the relationship may cease to be causal.

Then there is the perennial question of what mental health actually is. For example, do developmental disorders qualify as mental disorders? Well, according to DSM-5, the latest of the American Psychiatric Association's *Diagnostic and Statistical Manual of Mental Disorders* and the closest thing there is to an international bible for mental health, the answer is largely yes. Autism spectrum disorder (though no longer Asperger's per se), ADHD and specific learning disorder (but no longer dyslexia) are all included in it.

However, not all countries subscribe to the US way of defining mental health matters, and there is continuing debate about this whole area, not to mention quite a lot of confusion. For example, one commonly used term, 'psychopathy', which most people would assume describes a specific mental disorder, does not actually appear in any psychiatric manual, despite frequent appearances in newspapers. And what do we mean by a 'personality disorder'? Is it something a person is born with, or simply a convenient way of describing a series of symptoms that go hand in hand with trauma, bad parenting or even undiagnosed brain damage?

Can a condition such as autism spectrum disorder be treated? Is it amenable to being moderated in its effects by differing styles of upbringing and education, or by medication? If not, what is the real point in making a diagnosis? If it can't be changed, it could be seen as an evolutionary difference, so we should not be seeking to impose on society the belief that it is wrong and needs treating. And is ADHD, as many people contend, *merely* the outcome of prenatal stress, bad diet, bad parenting, lack of behavioural boundaries and so on, or is it an actual mental health problem?

There are so many factors to bear in mind when considering what goes on in the brain that often the only agreement among experts is that it does all indeed happen inside the skull, so that is where they focus their research. However, even that assumption is now being questioned. Given that I am not an expert and would not attempt any conclusive definitions around brain-related matters, I think it might be simplest to use the common and generic term 'mental health' (although I would prefer the term 'brain health'), but use it to cover all the above mentioned areas, without siloing them into developmental, psychiatric, psychological or any of the other narrow definitions of disorder (or order, for that matter).

Mental health issues have always been at the mercy of sociological and political fashions, so it can be hard to know where those end and where professional interests begin. After all, where would your mental health-related career go if mental health problems were all finally resolved?

Too cynical? I'm sure most practitioners have a genuine concern for their patients/clients, but there are vested interests out there, especially among the theorists. Many of them may have little concern with the actual mental health of the individuals who are, or are likely to become, care service users (funding of services springs to mind). And then there may well be unintended and negative consequences of political or cultural positionings. For example, in the mid-twentieth century there was a huge shift in the understanding of the aetiology of certain types of mental health problems. This was brought about by women's groups vociferously objecting to any blame for mental health problems being attributed to mothers' poor parenting. They demonised researchers such as John Bowlby and made it difficult for anyone to take a critical look at generational cause and effect. In some quarters the legacy of this no-blame culture persists to this day, regardless of the recent research which says parenting is critical to child development. Whenever a case of child neglect or abuse is reported in the media, there is usually some interested party who will pop up and say, 'We can't just blame the parents' or 'X's mum had so much to contend with – she was doing her best' (why is it always the friendly but patronising 'mum' and rarely the more neutral 'mother'?). One of the worst knee-jerk responses of all is, 'No parent wants to fail their child. They want to do the right thing, but they simply don't have the right resources.'

I find such repudiation of parental responsibility patronising, pusillanimous, deeply disingenuous and possibly dangerous. It is also extremely offensive to those parents who are in similar circumstances to the ones being fingered but who do a much better job. And it fails to either model or reward behaviours that will not only make the world a better place but also save legions of children from mental and physical abuses of all kinds.

The evidence is fast becoming irrefutable that parents of both genders are to a great extent responsible for the quality of their children's cognitive and mental functioning. Most people are quite happy to take the credit for being good parents, so why not let it be a two-way street?

What do we want?

Surely, as a society, we want the best for our children and for their children. If that means causing offence here and there, or trampling on a few dearly held ideologies, does that really matter compared to condemning any single child to a lifetime's mental distress? Every time I hear that meaningless mantra, 'No one sets out to be a bad parent,' I want to throw something. It's like saying, 'No one sets out to be a burglar,' and then suggesting that we shouldn't punish them just because they've unwittingly found themselves inside someone else's house, idly picking up bits and pieces of silver. In both cases there were choices.

But if conscious choice wasn't involved in the decisions some people make about either having or rearing children, then society as a whole simply has to be readier to make conscious judgements. Why is an adult's right to have children so often seen as an absolute given? Can it genuinely be acceptable to bring a child into the world solely for the purpose of serving this contemporary right? We need to become more honest about people's capabilities and make judgements about whether it's right for them to do harm to others just because they're able to procreate.

We must move on from using children as political, social and emotional footballs. A child is not a commodity; to say that someone has the right to have a child when they have no demonstrable skills or understanding of the basics of childcare is tantamount to slavery, both of the person and the mind. Their child has no equivalent right to refuse to be born. A child brought up in particular adverse circumstances is almost certainly predestined to have both cognitive and psychological difficulties in later life. This is an uncomfortable reality that some people just don't want to hear or believe, preferring (rather like Charles Dickens) to live in a delusional paradise in which, given just a few tweaks and amendments to any negative inputs, all human animals have the innate capacity to grow brains that are almost indistinguishable from nice, sensible middle-class ones.

I can already hear the shouts of denial and the claims that what is really enriching in life is the diversity of human behaviour and mental difference, and that one cannot and should not impose a limit or a hierarchy on acceptable brain states. However, I beg to disagree. I believe that most people who advocate acceptance and tolerance of all mental conditions, who reject the possibility that one state is more desirable or fundamentally healthy than another, have simply not spent much time with the many tortured souls who wish (and go on wishing – I'm not talking about limited periods of mental breakdown here) that they had never been born. Who can really believe they have the right to insist others should go through a lifetime's misery just so they may feel superior in their own generosity of spirit?

To encounter a person whose experience of existing inside their own fucked-up brain is so desperately awful that they spend their days bashing their forehead against the nearest hard surface or smashing their arms into doors, even when their wrists are already encased in plaster from the last breaks, is to question any worldview that said their junkie mother was a fit person to give birth. And it is to question any view that says this person, having had sex imposed on them while in a fit of compliant drunkenness or drug-induced catalepsy, is likely to be able to generate a healthy new brain inside them – one with more potential than theirs for a future not utterly devoid of happiness or any kind of enrichment. It is far more likely that any life they conceived would from conception be experienced as a kind of mental, psychological, neurological, cognitive, physical and emotional 'Little Ease'.[1]

If we are going to talk about rights (just another of those delusions we humans are so fond of) then surely the right a child should have is to be born with a brain free from the shackles of someone else's drinking, heroin use or nicotine use. Otherwise they become the slaves of their parent's behaviour – denied the freedom to develop as they might otherwise have done. To say that is not the same as saying that we must educate our young in certain ways or inculcate ideologies or engage in any other such social/political undertaking; it is to say that, so far as it is humanly possible, a baby should be born with the neurological potential to make its own choices about its cognitive life.

Obviously people can't always help that their child is born with a cognitive disability. But when they can, and they choose to act against its interests, then, in the name of both individual personal mental health and social accountability, we should all care. It is an almost universally accepted human right that no person should be born into physical slavery and yet to this day we have done very little to control for cognitive slavery. Why have we been both so mired in double standards and so slow to act? We are just beginning to realise that we really do have some responsibility for other people's physical wellbeing (having, for a generation or so, rather pooh-poohed the Victorians for their occasional zealotry over such matters). Perhaps the time has come for us also to start to take some responsibility for what goes on inside the skull – both our own and other people's.

Enough of this lengthy diatribe. How do we go about it? That is to say, how do we take more responsibility for the psychological and cognitive wellbeing of the population? Or, in my preferred terms, how do we go about taking more responsibility for the brain health of the population? How do we begin to integrate such a consideration into the daily doings of our lives?

For a start, now we know more about the science of how we are put together, we should be brave enough to publicly question whether it is acceptable that in the name of freedom, feminism or fertility, some lives are so circumscribed from the beginning and often so full of pain that they are almost entirely without what we would call quality or meaning. I think that's the very least an alien anthropologist would think we should do.

---

1   A cramped torture chamber in which prisoners were left, often for very long periods, unable to sit, stand or lie properly.

If it turns out that the majority of people are against limiting a woman's right to have a child, whatever her physical, neurological, psychological or emotional condition, we should still be prepared to intervene during the course of any pregnancy, not just offering advice non-judgementally, but making it perfectly clear (via media messages, doctors' surgeries, social workers, politicians and through all public voices) that harming babies, before as well as after birth, is wrong, and that there will be penalties as well as encouragement over matters like alcohol consumption, smoking and, of course, drug use.[2] The birth of a damaged baby is not a private matter; even if we are prepared to overlook any considerations of the baby's own wellbeing and right to health, we still all have to carry the costs, socially as well as financially. Therefore, we should all have a right to set clear expectations for maternal behaviour. And who knows, as social pressure can be very effective, perhaps more vocal involvement on the part of the wider community could result in fewer risky pregnancies in the first place.

And once the child is here?

In a perfect world, all of the material in Chapter 3 would be taken to heart and the book would stop here. However …

Even given lots of positive intentions and the best start in life, things can still sometimes go a bit awry inside a person's head and often no one really knows why. Until recently we have not properly understood much about how the brain works. In fact, many people seem to have been in the grip of a fondly held belief that the brain just sort of, well, exists, and that once it has emerged into the world from its more-or-less-appropriate prenatal environment and has been more-or-less-appropriately programmed into its role as a kind of human engine thing, then very little, other than actual structural damage, is likely to impact on the way it continues to perform that role. But gradually we have begun to discover more about how the brain is affected by our behaviour and by the way others behave towards us.

Now it appears that our brains are continually subject to all kinds of performance-altering influences. Although a potentially

---

2   A law criminalising the harms caused to unborn babies by maternal drug addiction is currently being considered by lawmakers in Tennessee in the United States – see http://data.rhrealitycheck.org/law/tennessee-pregnancy-criminalization-law-sb-1391/. The first but not the last?

alarming prospect, this is actually good news because it means that there are things which we can all do in our daily lives which will impact positively on our own, and on other people's, mental health. We *can* make a difference.

A no-brainer

For example, technology has had an enormous impact on our brains in recent years. We have learned from some of the experiences we are having with it that brains are lazy. Early man (woman and child) had to take bearings from the world around them and base judgements on sensory information and past experience. But now we have automation.

The increasing tendency to automate such things as car lights and direction finding (satnavs) can both turn us in on ourselves – no need to take soundings from the world outside – and shrink parts of the brain that are important for learning, memory and identity. These are all necessary for good mental health which depends to a large extent on the interplay between our brains, bodies and the environment.

Evidence from a study at Manchester Metropolitan University (see Aviva, 2006) showed that satnavs require more, not less, mental effort. This is because having been told what to do, we then have to remember what it is we have to do, even as we're trying to do it, rather than simply working it out sequentially according to circumstances. Perhaps unsurprisingly, another study by the Transport Research Laboratory (Rudd, 2011) found that using a satnav slowed reaction times by 52% while alcohol only slowed them by 36%.

Relying on satnavs leaves us with insufficient capacity to pick up cues from the environment. We are unable to make sensible judgements because we cannot rationalise that information and integrate it with historical and contextual knowledge. In addition, that loss of capacity is being passed on to our motor systems, so that our bodies as well as our brains slow down – and that's without the excuse of psychoactive influences. So, clearly for the good of the whole brain–body interface, we need to rely less on technology, not more, as we seem to be doing! It's also a good idea to occasionally work things out from the world by navigating according to what we can see around us and to remembered routes and information inside our heads.

What is good mental health?

The fundamental question of what constitutes good mental health still remains to be addressed. It would be glib to suggest, 'Well, these things are all relative, and a lot depends on the cultural context,' so I won't do that. Instead, I shall stick my neck out (not for the first time) and attempt not a definition but a sort of checklist of healthy mental attributes, and that's as far as I shall go. A lot depends on the DNA we've inherited, our mother's and father's ages/health (mental and physical)/lifestyle/intelligence,[3] the circumstances of our conception, our prenatal environment, our post-natal environment/care/stimulation/diet and so on.

If enough of that is in our favour, we end up as winners in the lottery of life and should then be able to bring to it the following healthy mental attributes (in no particular order):

- Integrated sense of self − authenticity
- Consistency
- Confidence
- Self-discipline
- Outwards focus − well connected to the world
- Strong sense of perspective
- Sense of subjective agency (belief in responsibility for what one says, does, thinks and brings about)
- Openness to people, ideas and emotions
- Curiosity
- Ability to let go

I have not included Significance because that, like love or many of the other things you might consider missing from my list, is really a perception or emotional positioning − the consequence of healthy mental attributes and not an attribute in itself.

If, thanks to an adequate number of positive factors in our pre-natal and early lives, we have these healthy mental attributes in place then we will be resilient in the face of challenges and disasters.

---

3   Some recent research (Frans et al., 2013), found that older (45+) fathers produced more mutated sperm, which resulted in a greatly increased risk of autism ($\times$ 3), bipolar disorder ($\times$ 25), schizophrenia ($\times$ 2), ADHD, suicide attempts, substance use problems and low educational attainment. Other research, from Vienna University (see Knapton, 2014), found that older fathers were more likely than younger ones to produce children who were rated as facially unattractive for much the same reason − sperm producing cells appear to lose their ability to copy DNA faithfully over time; this negative effect keeps on growing as the years go by.

Resilience is key to good mental health. It means that we are able to avoid the temptation to give in to appetites or to collapse under stress. It means we can fail at something and pick ourselves up, dust ourselves down and start all over again. Resilience means having the strength to carry others with us, as well as keep going ourselves, when the going gets tough.

The best way to become resilient in the first place is to be loved for ourselves and not for anything we might represent, such as the vicarious fulfilment of a parent's ambitions, being a doll to dress up or a resentment figure to pick on. It's not an all-or-nothing scenario; there are people who have developed their own resilience from very unpromising starts in life. Maybe those little tell-tale signs of inner vulnerability will always show through, but these people can function and perform almost indistinguishably from the luckier ones. It's really all about wanting something badly enough and having the motivation to do whatever it takes. To an extent, we *can* dictate our mental health, and we can most certainly help others to optimise theirs.

Now that we have some understanding of what good mental health might be, let's look at the brain–body interface and at the ways technology, life events and human behaviour might impact it. Even querying the process would have irritated the ancients, as they always assumed that we were never more than a blend of things which they called humours, and that everything corporeal, including 'personality' and 'character', was totally dependent on the balance between our humours and our inner and outer lives.

While I don't think science is driving our understanding of human functioning back towards the humours, I do think scientific thinking is more biased towards words like *blending, balancing, interplay, interdependence* and *connectivity* than it has been for many years. In some ways, science is far less reductive than it was when it actually had less information to go on. Maybe a case of the more you know, the more you realise you don't know.

I shall now take a brief look at some of the factors which have recently been shown to influence that brain–body balancing act which really does seem to be essential to our physical and our mental health. I shall start with exercise, which I have already said is essential for more than just good physical health.

Noggin

The brilliantly named Noggin is more than just a small Viking marauder from 1950s children's TV, it is also a protein encoded by the NOG gene. One of its functions is to promote the growth of neurons in the brain, particularly in the hippocampus, which is involved in learning and memory. It does this indirectly in the following way. New neurons grow from neural stem cells which divide and produce 'babies' in a process called neurogenesis. But another protein, bone morphogenetic protein (BMP), reduces the rate at which this happens. What noggin appears to do is counter the effect of BMP. So, it follows that the more noggin we can produce, the more new brain cells will have the chance to sprout, particularly in the hippocampus.

So how do we increase the amount of noggin in the brain? By exercising our bodies! Research carried out, admittedly on mice, at Northwestern University, in Chicago, showed that, within a week, mice that exercised hard reduced BMP-related brain activity by 50% – meaning that these mice would soon become mouse geniuses (Gobeske et al., 2009). The scientists predicted that the same effect would apply to human brains and suggested there would be no upper limit to this form of exercise-related benefit for the brain. So, win-win: better bodies make for better brains.

And, of course, the benefit extends to mental health as well as to intellectual potential. Depressed brains show signs of hippocampal shrinkage, probably as a result of heightened levels of cortisol (the anxiety hormone) which is known to have an adverse impact on the hippocampus. By promoting hippocampal growth, exercise is not only going to produce better memory – which in itself will have something of an anti-depressant effect – but it will also promote a better and more motivated mood state.

Further, noggin is going to have a beneficial effect on the ageing brain, helping to keep us functioning well for as long as possible and helping to stave off conditions such as dementia. A recent study of almost 3,000 people, carried out by researchers at the University of Minnesota (Zhu et al., 2014), found that those who had the most physical endurance at the age of 25 performed best at cognitive tests twenty years later. And as poor performance at these mid-life tests is strongly correlated with dementia in later life, it very much looks as if there is no escaping the association between physical stamina and cognitive stamina. Therefore, exercise just has to be one of the most essential elements of any body–brain wellbeing programme.

Botox

Botox might seem an unlikely candidate for impacting on mental health (perhaps psychological wellbeing, but mental health?) until you understand what it actually is and what it is capable of doing.

Botox is a neurotoxin, a poison that targets the nervous system, disturbing the signalling between neurons. It is so toxic that it has been estimated that one gram of it could wipe out a million people! But in tiny doses it will stop signals going to certain muscles, effectively paralysing them. This, perhaps counter-intuitively, leaves them less stiff; the muscles relax and the skin around them becomes smoother. You might think that using botulinum toxin to smooth out faces for purely cosmetic reasons would account for the mental health benefits – after all, who wouldn't feel happier to look a bit younger? However, the unexpected anti-depressant effect which many users have experienced seems to have more to do with the complex interplay between our internal feelings and our corporeal selves than with vanity. This is supported by the fact that this relationship seems to work both ways. Although a grumpy-looking person may bring their frown lines on themselves by virtue of continually complaining, over time their emotions become enslaved by their facial muscles and they end up unable to experience happy feelings even when they think they should.

Thanks to Botox, it appears they no longer need to be in a perpetually enslaved state. The evidence shows that changing the way the facial muscles work can have as much effect on a person's emotional state as their emotional state may have once had on their muscles. It's the consequence of the internal feedback system working away within us; our bodies are as capable of telling our brains what to think and feel as our brains are capable of telling our bodies how to behave.

The Botox effect does not necessarily depend on how we actually end up looking. According to one dermatologist, even though a number of people who had Botox injections thought the end result left them looking less attractive than before, they nevertheless felt happier (see Britten, 2013). Clearly the Botox effect is not a psychological one (whatever that might mean) but a demonstrably physical one. Evidence from brain scans shows that when facial muscles have been treated with Botox there is a dampening down of activity in the amygdala (part of that emotionally angry/gloomy primitive limbic system). It looks as if there must be some direct link between the physiological and the emotional. When we put on a happy face

– even if we're faking it – we recruit different neural circuits and thereby change the emotional sensations we're experiencing.

This good news has led some experts to think that we should be able to treat depression and other negative emotional states in this way. But few things in life are totally uncomplicated and there is a potential downside to this. Some people have found that once Botox has ironed out their expression lines, their emotions, more generally, have felt less authentic, less connected to the self. And some have also found it impossible to produce tears even when they felt sad. So while we may feel happier when our faces look happier, it seems we may also lose some part of the person we have become. This research is relatively new, so it may prove possible to target the very specific muscles which express particular emotions. Botox can then tweak them to order without affecting others around them.

Embodied memory

Further evidence of the symbiotic relationship between the physical and the emotional self comes from some new research in Sweden. This suggests that memory, too, is a more embodied affair than has previously been thought, and this has consequences for the understanding of mental health. It seems that in order for us to be able to store new autobiographical or episodic memories (memories of events in our own lives) we need to feel that we are in our own bodies.

A study carried out by Loretxu Bergouignan and colleagues at the Karolinska Institutet (Bergouignan et al., 2014) involved 84 students who were subjected to a series of eccentrically memorable interrogations carried out by an actor. In some of the interrogations they were in their own 'normal' first person bodies; in others, using virtual-reality goggles and earphones, they were made to feel that they were outside their bodies – at the other end of the room, in fact – and therefore dissociated from their own bodies. A week after these interrogations, the students were either directly asked for their recall of and feelings about what had taken place or they had their brains imaged by fMRI (functional magnetic resonance imaging) scanners as they were trying to remember the same events.

Their out-of-body experiences were remembered much less well than their in-body experiences, even though the students responded equally well to the questions and *felt* that they had experienced the same level of emotion in each case. It was the scans that gave the game away: they showed that in the out-of-body scenarios the left posterior hippocampus (involved in learning and memory) was simply inactive, unlike when the students remembered the embodied experiences. However, their frontal lobes were beavering away, indicating that they were making a conscious effort to retrieve memories, although the memories themselves were less clear. The researchers concluded that 'efficient hippocampus based episodic memory encoding requires a first-person perspective of the natural spatial relationship between the body and the world' (ibid.: 4421), and that without this embodied first-person perspective memories simply will not be laid down.[4]

As a number of mental health disorders involve poor or patchy memory retrieval and a sense of dissociation from the body, it seems likely that this research could direct scientists towards a better understanding of the mechanisms involved in such disorders, which include debilitating conditions like post-traumatic stress disorder and depression.

My take on this is that, as the hippocampus has a role in both spatial awareness and navigation as well as memory, episodic memories are highly likely to be encoded and consolidated by means of the virtual journeys we see ourselves taking through the spaces of the mind. The self, which the first-person perspective helps to create a sense of, is like a little mini-me homunculus navigating in a self-referential way through all the elements of the story – temporal, spatial and emotional – all the while laying its 'self spoor' to help it keep track of its journey. It's that journey, complete with its time, space and feeling elements, which it later revisits when it's called on to produce what we call a memory. This analogy goes a long way towards explaining how we are able to retrieve all sorts of apparently lost information by navigating through personal mind maps or mind palaces (as envisaged in Mark Gatiss and Steven Moffat's *Sherlock*).

The corollary is that the less sense there is of an embodied 'I', the less remembered life there will be. All the evidence points to the need for us to have a deep awareness and knowledge of our own bodies, plus a strong sense of inhabiting our bodies in order to feel that we have lived our own distinct lives. This feeling is vital to

---

4   This study was also looking into the role of the posterior cingulate cortex and concluded that both hippocampus and PCC had important roles to play in body ownership and self-location, with the PCC integrating neural representations of self-location and body ownership from a number of key areas of the brain.

mental wellbeing. Without it we become disengaged, deracinated (rootless) and lose any proper sense of identity.

So, noggin, Botox and mind palaces all seem to play a part in the ever-evolving story of how mental wellbeing is created or maintained. This is in addition to the givens of genetics and early nurturing, not to mention the new things we are introducing which might be impacting on our cognitive and mental wellbeing. We need, for example, to understand much more about how new technologies are affecting our autonomy of perception (using or losing our personal awareness of the outside world) and our reaction times in relation to incoming data.

And then there are the substances which we introduce into our bodies and thus into the story of our mental health: nicotine, alcohol and other drugs.

Smoking

We have known for a long time that smoking is just about the worst thing you can do for your physical health. However, it has been something of a given that those with mental health problems nevertheless get a great deal of comfort and therefore benefit from smoking. Wherever I have come across people with problems like addiction, depression or anxiety, I have also come across therapists and institutions supporting and even encouraging the use of tobacco – as a suppressant of symptoms if not actually as a treatment for them. Rather than viewing smoking as a co-factor in addiction, the rehab world has tended to see it as a crutch for the souls of those who are both unable and not expected to cope. However, there is now support for my quest to have rehabs and other treatment facilities (especially those in prisons) treat smoking as a substance problem that must be dealt with alongside others, rather than as a chemical special case that can be dealt with softly-softly, if at all.

A wide ranging review of evidence from a number of observational studies of smoking has been carried out by doctoral researcher, Gemma Taylor, together with others, at the University of Birmingham (Taylor et al., 2014). They conclude that, although there has always been an association between smoking and poor mental health – one in which it has historically been believed that the smoking element has functioned to alleviate the symptoms and stresses of the mental health problem – the actual relationship is more likely to have been iatrogenic. That is to say, the treatment (the smoking) is likely to have been, at least partially, causing or exacerbating the mental health problem.

The study goes on to suggest that, perhaps due in part to the reluctance of both the mental health patients themselves and health professionals to risk any adverse consequences of quitting smoking, these patients are going to have a life expectancy eight years shorter than they would have if they gave up smoking. Something of a double-whammy for them, you might say.

However, the intention of the review was, in fact, to establish whether the effect of quitting smoking is likely to benefit mental health in the population as a whole, and not only in what might be called the established mental health population. The criteria looked at as indicative of general mental health status were: anxiety, depression, psychological quality of life, positive affect and stress – a pretty comprehensive list in terms of indicating mental wellbeing. The conclusions arrived at by the review were:

> Smoking cessation is associated with reduced depression, anxiety, and stress and improved mood and quality of life compared with continuing to smoke. The effect size seems as large for those with psychiatric disorders as those without. The effect sizes are equal or larger than those of antidepressant treatment for mood and anxiety disorders. (ibid.: 1151)

In other words, it suggests we are wasting resources of every kind if we continue to pump people full of anti-depressants when they are still smoking. It will be of far greater benefit to them to help them give up the weed.

The bottom line can be stated boldly: smoking is bad for health in every respect. If we are interested in creating and maintaining good mental health we should aim to be intolerant of tolerance, at least with nicotine. This intolerance should apply to e-cigarettes as well as to traditional ones. Whether or not they are chemically harmful (and that remains to be seen – why be an at-risk guinea pig, especially when an early study from Boston University has suggested they may be causing gene mutations in lung cells? – see Park et al., 2014), they are almost certainly psychologically harmful, normalising dependency and encouraging short-term gratification.[5]

---

5   See my book, *Stop Smoking* (Bridge, 2005), for further exploration of this matter and for a way to give up.

Alcohol and drugs

I look at alcohol and drugs in more detail in Appendix A, but in line with all I have said about caring about the brain as an integral part of the overall physical self, it should be obvious that anything which impacts adversely on the body is going to adversely affect cognition and mental health. Relatively small quantities of alcohol, particularly red wine, have been shown to be beneficial for the heart. However, I know of no research that shows that cannabis, cocaine, opium and so on provide health benefits of either the physical or mental kind. There is indeed research which suggests that cannabis may be helpful in mitigating symptoms in cases of wasting diseases such as motor neurone disease and even Alzheimer's, but it is largely anecdotal and the findings may relate to the placebo effect as much as to anything else (Gilman et al., 2014).[6] Any claims made for the health benefits of other illicit drugs seem to be entirely spurious, and anyway would be offset by all the other negative effects they have on health.

My experience of working with those affected by substance use, either directly or indirectly, has led me to the conclusion that there is nothing positive to be gained by using drugs, unless medicinally (and not always then[7]), and that those people who claim that drug use has not affected or does not affect them are falling into the first trap laid by drugs – that of loss of self-knowledge.

One of the first things to happen when a person uses a psychoactive substance is that the orbitofrontal cortex, part of the executive prefrontal cortex, is negatively affected. Its usual function, which is to associate or gather together information from various

---

6   A study from the Northwestern University Feinberg School of Medicine in Chicago has shown that changes in two brain regions, the nucleus accumbens and the amygdala, can be seen even with 'light' cannabis use. This finding has serious implications with regards to brain function. However, the researchers make it clear the research is in its early stages and much still needs to be clarified. Even more recently, the University of Toulouse has suggested that cannabis use can lead to potentially lethal heart damage in young and middle-aged adults.

7   A New Zealand study (Read et al., 2014) found that anti-depressants, even when effective for purpose, have many unwanted side effects apart from weight gain and nausea. For example, out of a sample of 1,829 people, 62% had sexual difficulties, 60% emotional numbness, 52% depersonalisation, 39% cared less about others and 39% suicidal ideation – and this rose to 55% in the 18–25 age group. Hardly a ringing endorsement for any drug treatment that is not absolutely essential.

areas of the brain, begins to fail.[8] We start to lose our awareness of past events and states, current internal feeling states, physical sensations and intentions or goals, which together are essential to decision making. Psychoactive substances of all kinds affect these information circuits, resulting in the brain becoming inflexible and stubborn in the face of salient information. This leads to both a loss of self-monitoring and an inability to foresee the probable consequences of its own behaviour and choices. More significantly, it loses the ability to compare the relative value of choices it has made against those it has not made. In other words, it cannot see the true consequences of bad decisions because it cannot evaluate how things might otherwise have been had its decisions been different.

What these effects really amount to is a loss of self-awareness. This is both profound and long lasting, if not permanent. In cases of heavy substance use the effects are almost certainly permanent.

So what does the practice of good mental health finally amount to? Really it's much the same as the practice of good physical health.

We get out what we put in. GIGO, in the language of computing – garbage in, garbage out. We need to practise good brain hygiene and care for our brains as if they are the one and only treasure that really matters – which in a way, they are. We also need to cut them some slack because we are constantly demanding that they work overtime connecting everything up and making sense of the world. Because of that inherent hyper-connectivity, courtesy of the strange mutations that have taken place over the millennia, the brain's tendency, if allowed, is to over-associate things – looking for meaning in an arrangement of tea leaves or in a chance series of world events (the apocalypse is nigh). It is up to us, as owners and carers, not only to attend to brain hygiene but also to brain relaxation. We must occasionally ask our brains to stop trying to make sense of everything; to stop trying to find an epiphany in every narrative; to stop seeking out shape, sense, structure and meaning in every object, sensation or piece of incoming data that we are exposed to. We must allow that the universe does not demand that 'I, myself and me' should understand it all, or indeed anything whatsoever about it.

---

8   As ever, this is a simplification. As I said near the start of the book, there is no absolute 'function' for any particular brain region but this is a convenient way to explain things. For the real science behind substance use, go to the work of Schoenbaum et al. (2006), or read Darryl S. Inaba and William E. Cohen's *Uppers, Downers, All Arounders* (2000) to learn all most people would ever need to know on the subject.

Sometimes it's enough just *to be*. Many of us would be a lot happier and mentally healthier if we could simply accept that possibility.

One final point leads us quite neatly on to the next chapter which covers our need to feel we belong to a wider whole. This is actually the core message of this book. It is for the good of any individual's mental health that they must do everything possible to keep their focus away from the self and point it firmly at the world beyond the self. After all, we are social animals, and all the 'because you're worth it's in the world will not change that. We are only worth it in a social context. Deep down most of us acknowledge that; we feel ourselves lesser beings if we only take counsel from ourselves as to whether or not we are worth it. The more we try to persuade ourselves of our value to ourselves, the unhappier we seem to become. Like Narcissus, checking out our own reflection all the time, we miss out on what others can offer us – and, more to the point, what we can offer them. And that is the only truly psychologically rewarding way to be of value.

Chapter 14

Belonging to a Wider Whole

The practice of feeling we belong to a wider whole

The primacy of the individual and their feelings and perceptions did not really begin with Hamlet, or even with Jesus. All the same, in its writings and musings, the modern Western, largely Christian, world has made subjectivity something of a cause célèbre. Even so, we do not feel significantly happier or more fulfilled for this fixation on the individual inner life – on the individual sheep rather than on the larger flock. Perhaps deep down, in our primitive unevolved core, there remains more of an inclination to live like herd animals than our modern minds like to recognise.

According to psychologists from the Universities of Sussex, Leeds and St Andrews, 'social identity is a key factor in predicting positive emotions in crowds and that people's social identification with the crowd leads them to seek out and enjoy more dense locations'. In other words, even though we might like to think of ourselves as individuals, the more we identify ourselves with a group of people, the more sensory tolerance we become capable of; we feel less threatened, less crowded and less in need of personal space than when we see ourselves as separate and unique units. The research leader, Dr John Drury, added that it was wrong to assume we have only our own unique personal identity, saying, 'Our findings are part of a body of work that shows that we have multiple identities based on our group memberships' (University of Sussex, 2013; see also Novelli et al., 2013).

This finding might go some way to explaining why events like the Nuremberg rallies were so successful and even how otherwise decent individuals are capable of thinking and behaving like savage pack animals (especially when this knowledge is combined with what we already know about social groups and oxytocin). But taking a more positive view, it also shows that simply feeling we belong can help us to live outside our own sensations more – and so to avoid the dreadful experience of that girl in the canvas sack in Chapter 2 who was being driven mad by the feeling that she was living inside her head, imprisoned and unable to get out.

So how do we achieve this sense of belonging in the day to day, given that mass crowd events like Nuremberg (thankfully) or Glastonbury (sadly) don't happen all the time? I suggest that we need to conjure up imagined crowds, virtual crowds, to distract us from the idea that we are unique, special and different, and to help us commit to the idea that we are functional elements of a greater whole. We need to feel that it is as important to make the whole enterprise work as it is to make our little solitary lives have meaning.

What matters is our attitude to who we are and what we might be entitled to; if we expect to be special and different, to do everything 'my way', then we also must accept that we run the risk of greater unhappiness and more mental health problems. But if we allow that we are only ever a small element of the greater crowd, then we can benefit from lessened sensitivity to threats and from greater psychological and emotional protection.

Believing in the strength of the group, the residents of Balsall Heath, in Birmingham managed to turn their decaying inner-city suburb around. From being a place where crime was rife, where prostitution, litter and graffiti all combined to make it a thoroughly unpleasant place to have to walk through, it became one that is, only a few years later, a place that is 'an archetype of community regeneration, boasting clean streets and neighbours who look out for one another' (Angelini, 2014). Now there are flowers, shrubs and greenery everywhere, civilising and softening the look of the previously intimidating streets. A small number of residents, fed up with feeling so abandoned and alone in the mess – and presumably having some mental model for that virtual crowd – began the initiative by banding together. By working cooperatively and collaboratively with police, councils, schools, politicians and other locally involved bodies, they now have improved conditions all round, including facing off drug dealers. They have even managed to save money for the state providers. Equally importantly, they have personally gained a wealth of psychological and emotional benefits from belonging to the joint enterprise and from feeling that they are now significant parts of a greater whole. They no longer walk past litter thinking the problem belongs to someone else. They personally look after the planting of shrubberies and hanging baskets. As one resident says, 'It's all very rewarding. We wouldn't do this work otherwise.'

Similarly in Tetbury, in Gloucestershire – a much posher, less challenging environment – the residents stepped in when cuts in public spending meant that roundabouts and verges were about to be abandoned to their natural untended fate. The volunteer team, called Tetbury in Bloom (ages 30–70), works for an hour and a half twice a week to prepare, plant and weed twenty-seven flower beds and forty hanging baskets. This makes the area a delight to drive through and gives the volunteers a sense of purpose, community and fulfilment. As one volunteer said, 'It's been my therapy' (see Keen, 2013).

We don't literally have to be in a crowd to get its benefits. Many of these volunteers spend time working alone. We only have to believe that we are part of a crowd enterprise and that we are surrounded by and emotionally and morally supported by others. It doesn't matter if we are working on our own in absolute silence as long as we feel emotionally enclosed in the warmth of the community spirit around us.

Becoming stakeholders

Having a sense of ownership of, and feeling responsibility for, the area where we live is central to the belief that we belong to something bigger than the self. It's the same principle that Robert J. Sampson refers to in his Chicago research (Sampson, 2013a) which shows the benefits to an area of community self-monitoring and self-policing. It's for this very reason that I think that we need to make some adjustments to the way we bring up our children to think about their environments.

For quite a few years now, often through the influence of schools and TV, children have learned about the importance of the environment and their responsibility for it, but this has not been seriously or sufficiently equated to their own particular environments. Many a child who pontificates to adults about the state of the planet fails to recognise that their bedroom (and their house/street/town) is also a part of that very same planet. For too long, many children have been allowed to grow up believing that they are doing some kind of favour to their parents if they carry out any work around the house, and that they should be specially rewarded for doing what should be natural – taking care of what is, essentially, their native habitat.

Let's see our children as 'stakeholder kids' who have an interest in and responsibility for the planet and for their own local area. We can encourage them in understanding that they *belong*, not just to their peer group – as that way trouble may lie – but also within the whole muddled crowd around them. Their responsibilities will then extend to that whole muddled crowd and beyond their narrow subgroup of friends (narrow, even if the subgroup does incorporate several thousand social media 'friends').

It's not necessarily going to be an easy ask. I know this because I once made the suggestion to an audience of parents at a very reputable public school. I was as appalled as I was amused by the father who responded by standing up and saying, 'But I don't pay Filipino servants so that my children can clean their own rooms!'

And then there was the recent newspaper report (Hurst, 2014) about the young boys at an exclusive London prep school (once attended by the royals and even Hugh Grant) who were witnessed being horribly impolite to both their driver and their nanny, although they were normally considered to be well mannered boys among their equals. What does that story tell us about their sense of belonging and inclusiveness?

Turning wider social responsibilities into niche markets, best served by specialists and professionals, has been bad for our sense of community and personal responsibility. This has led both to neglect of the vulnerable and disempowerment of the many. Equally, allowing our young people to see themselves as niche products destined for special status and special consideration has worked against them, preventing them from realising that they are part of the greater whole and significant players in the way society functions. To that end, they need to have a vested interest in how well it functions.

Getting the balance of childhood right is hard. On the one hand, children around the world are capable of maturing fast enough to be out at work at the age of 6. On the other hand, the way we (in Western societies) treat our young people often keeps them artificially incompetent, and they do not mature because childhood is seen as a special place best protected from a difficult and complex world. The danger is that by emphasising their special and different status, we risk having them come to believe that they are only valued for their gifts, their academic successes, their cuteness, their prettiness, their ability with a football, their amusing backchat and so on. When really, in terms of their long-term interests, they should feel that they are of at least as much value for their evolving ability to be successful parts of the bigger jigsaw of humankind, able to act sociably and look out for others as well as for themselves, able to see beyond their own needs of the moment, and able to value themselves for the contribution they make to the wellbeing and smooth running of the whole.

For example, children need to be taught from the start that there are places where shouting and screaming are valid outlets of energy and places where they quite simply are not. They must learn that theirs are not the most important considerations at all times, and not only that other people around them have rights and needs too but, perhaps more usefully, that the whole jigsaw that is social life would fall apart if individual pieces refused to sit comfortably and agreeably with the rest.[1] Children need to understand that they are expected to care for amenities created for their use. Special facilities, such as playgrounds and skateboard parks, should come with the expectation that these facilities are, in part, the responsibility of the users and their families. And if we, other disinterested adults, simply accept that such expensive facilities are bound to be vandalised and will require ever increasing amounts of cash to maintain them, then we are failing in our duty to society.

Young people should have a stake in the place they call home. As well as calling some of the shots they should be expected to help maintain them – for example, they can help to produce and prepare some of their own food, maintain the family car(s) and do their own washing and ironing as soon as they are physically capable. They can also carry out general organisational stuff, like working out timetables for activities, checking journey routes (yes, I know satnavs will do the job but, remember, it's good brain exercise) and helping younger siblings to get ready for the day.

If this approach is taken in the home, then there should be a knock-on effect leading to higher expectations of children's abilities, especially in schools. Hopefully, people will have more confidence in their right, even, dare one say it, in their duty to help other children develop – initially, by refusing to tolerate anti-social behaviour and then by praising children more for their pro-social behaviour than for being cute, cheeky, mini-princesses, mini-monsters or any of the other things that sentimentality and commerce have deemed somehow desirable (not to mention highly profitable).

---

1   Baumeister and Tierney (2011: 130–132) describe an experiment in which students tried to build up their self-control. Of a number of different approaches, the one that worked best to achieve improvements across a range of other unrelated behaviours was asking them to force themselves to spend time each day concentrating on their posture – in effect, doing nothing more sophisticated than just sitting up straight. They decided that it was the 'making yourself do something consciously different' aspect that was so effective. In other words, self-discipline is a habit that can be trained to good effect. Perhaps modern schools could take a lesson from the past.

Maintaining our stake

This is both a policy matter and a private matter. Feeling that we are part of the bigger world in multiple ways on an ongoing basis starts with childhood, inculcating the right attitudes from the beginning. We need to be constantly and consistently sending out messages that communicate, 'Yes, it does all join up, and, yes, we're all joined up too.' This way, no one feels that they're out there on their own.

Policy wise that means more joined-up thinking on matters such as sharing information among service providers and increasing public participation in many more aspects of decision making and the subsequent implementation of, and responsibility for, the decisions that are made. For example, the people who run social housing may well have contracts in place with their tenants but often seem reluctant to enforce some of the conditions regarding the standards of behaviour which would make large urban estates, and even small village enclaves, more pleasant and less threatening places. There has been a slow evolution from a time when tenants were inspected for standards of cleanliness, never mind pro-social behaviour, to the present day, when many tenants, who are in receipt of a great financial benefit, are simply never required to offer any evidence that they are taking care of, or responsibility for, the places where they live. This is in contrast to private tenants who, while paying massive rents, may still have to undergo regular inspections that itemise such details as cleanliness of light switches and door handles. This double standard is no way to encourage errant social housing tenants to feel involved in the bigger enterprise; it could be said to be both discriminatory and patronising.

Although well intentioned, Neighbourhood Watch schemes tend to pit people against each other. Therefore, would it not be better to replace them with Neighbourhood Care schemes which would be more positive and affirming? These would have the aim of involving all residents, whatever their residency status, in the beautification and socialisation of their area. Such an aim, apart from helping to reduce crime, would have the added benefit in this hyper-mobile age of helping newcomers feel more immediately engaged with the place they have moved to, and would possibly lead to more stable populations, given that people are likely to remain longer in places where they feel they have a stake.

Altruism and volunteering – which my Neighbourhood Care idea would encourage – are known to be good for people's health. But not everyone feels as motivated to do good as, say, the 500,000 publicly spirited people involved in the UK Biobank (www.ukbio-bank.ac.uk). They have volunteered to be questioned and tested about their health on an ongoing basis throughout their lives, for no obvious personal health benefit at all, but simply to provide a national resource for scientists and health professionals who are working to understand and eliminate diseases and disorders. Ideally, we would all feel as committed to the overall good as they do, but we need to face the reality of those of a less pro-social persuasion and engage in a bit of slightly forceful nudging to help them recognise their responsibilities and so access the psychological rewards that come with doing good and becoming involved. It's here that some of those professionals (whose involvement – aka 'interference' – can seem so unhelpful) might come into their own, if they would be prepared to nudge people on benefits or with long-term mental health problems towards volunteering in the local park or helping to maintain street furniture.

I say this because I have worked in too many public sector workplaces stuffed full of professionals working in wholly unimaginative and constrained ways. They ignore opportunities for promoting engagement and wellbeing in their clients and seem fearful of engaging with other professionals themselves. Frequently they will not share information with others, either for personal political reasons or for reasons that are more to do with professional kudos and fears over funding, or, quite simply, because they have never thought beyond the immediate requirements of their narrow and unambitious job description. In a joined-up world public officials should be sharing information between services (if public safety is not involved). There should be no justification for professions and service providers to close ranks and work in silos when they should be seeing the bigger picture, recognising their roles within it and then working to promote opportunities to work harmoniously with others. For example, the enterprising farmers who go into intimidating city centre estates to set up links that ensure the direct supply of fresh produce at affordable prices to poor and vulnerable people should not be working alone.

Where are the town planners? The police? The housing association staff?[2] And the well-paid heads of policy who want to see our children having access to better nourishment in their early years? There are already many enterprising and well-intended people like

---

2   Too often in bunkers behind metal grilles – and who can blame them? Except that when they go home at night they leave the vulnerable and the old to tough it out without recourse to such protection.

those farmers out there trying to get involved, but they would appreciate feeling supported and protected as they do their best to provide a vital and life enhancing service. People need confidence to do the things that many are already persuaded need to be done. They need confidence that they will not be exposed to actual danger and a conviction that they're not alone, singing in the wilderness.

What is required is a change in thinking. It would be helpful if more things in public life encouraged us to feel we belonged to a wider whole – for example, promoting greater pro-social thinking by judiciously tweaking the way we talk about our public activities. The driving test, for instance, does not entirely prioritise what might be thought of as pro-social driving. Its implied rationale is to promote both safety and traffic flow (which should necessarily depend on awareness of others), but the principle that we're all part of this big interdependent dance could be better addressed and communicated in a much more significant way. And then maybe, just maybe, fewer people would pass their driving test yet still drive as if they had ownership of any particular traffic lane.

Now that few of us attend any kind of religious service we miss out on regularly being asked to focus on social and personal values that could encourage a sense of belonging. However, one small Surrey primary school is doing its bit by the next generation by producing a regular news sheet that encourages these young children to think about some quite sophisticated concepts to do with the interconnectedness of personal behaviour and the greater good. This is taken from the modestly titled *Tadworth Times*:

This month's value is *dependability*. It's a value that comes up many times in our daily life. Someone who is dependable does what they say they will do (like meeting you when they said they would). They are organised, self disciplined and truthful too. Life goes smoother [*sic*] because of dependable people: the school is open on time because someone unlocks the doors every day; rubbish is cleared and mess cleaned up because of reliable cleaning staff. You have lunch because dinner staff turn up every day … And you get to enjoy play dates because your friends and their parents make arrangements and follow through as they promised. Some may think that being dependable is boring, but it's a key value for anyone who wants friends and wants to be trusted to do fun things. In time, being dependable may even land you a job you really want.

How dependable are you?

It signs off its consideration of the great life web that is woven out of attitudes, behaviours and outcomes by focusing on the individual child and their contribution to the concept of the whole – quite simply brilliant!

At least these future adults will have a better understanding than many of their parents may have done that we all belong to a wider whole and that our personal actions can either support that whole or undermine it. In addition, that actions and attitudes which support it will not only result in the general good but may also lead to some improved personal outcomes. It's going to be a win-win situation for them.

The practice of significance

How do we enhance the feeling that we matter as individuals and that life, itself, matters? If we already feel that we belong then we have a head start in the race to significance. The earliest form of belonging is the sense of belonging to the mother (see Chapter 3). This is essential to a child's developing sense of self and feeling of wellbeing, but there is more to having a sense of personal significance than simply having had the benefit of the best kind of upbringing. This is just as well, otherwise it would be like saying that if you weren't born with a silver spoon in your mouth there's no point in trying to make your own fortune.

We *can* make our own destiny, up to a point, and we *can* create a sense that we really do matter. However, there may be more work involved than if you were born lucky. And it is through effort that we gain an even greater sense of personal satisfaction.

Feeling significant is a state associated with dopamine levels. These, as we saw earlier, appear to have a default baseline which is set at birth. It's partly influenced by genetic factors and partly by environmental ones (some of which may be *in utero* conditions). Dopamine is the chemical for and of significance. To a very large extent it appears to work in relationship with the anterior cingulate cortex. Together they direct our attention on to things that matter, either inside or outside our own heads.

When John Donne wrote, 'Be thine own palace, or the world's thy jail', he touched on the anomaly at the (mutated) heart of being human. We can feel that the inner life is the only truly rewarding one but, equally, like the girl in the canvas sack, we can feel that the inner life is truly hellish. In both cases our attention is probably being overly directed inwards by the dopamine/ACC nexus to the world of the mind. If what we find there is a world full of lightning strikes of inspirational ideas, sudden clear-eyed perceptions of the meaning of life and a sense that all fits together harmoniously in the best of all possible worlds, then we are very happy and feel totally at one with life – we feel *truly* significant. If, on the other hand, we experience our thoughts scurrying blackly and randomly through muck, like rats in a sewer, then we are very unhappy and feel adrift and *truly* insignificant.

Truthfully, both states are equally unhelpful with respect to feeling genuinely significant. The first is the outcome of excess dopamine in a fundamentally left-biased and creative brain, and can lead to over-inflation of one's sense of significance. This results in ideas of grandiosity, inflated and implausible ambitions and the pursuit of unrealisable dreams. It can lead students to be very certain that their every thought and belief is the right and only one, and politicians to berate parliaments with rhetorical flights that they believe should become the foundation of true and noble policies. The risk of being caught out, or found out, in these states of excess comes with the territory and is fraught with possibilities of breakdown, bankruptcy (of finances and endeavour) and even suicide. The second state may also be the result of excess dopamine acting on the ACC but in a fundamentally right-biased brain which has a tendency towards negativity. The overall effect is to lock attention on to negative thoughts which proliferate, without the damping and rationalising input of the prefrontal cortex.

Too much dopamine, acting irresponsibly, is likely to encourage the brain to see significance where there is none – even inside itself (strange beings, humans). And that significance can go either way, positively or negatively. Beware the overly excited thinker and beware the overly depressed thinker. They are both likely to be too full of themselves.

But a brain that can step outside itself, that can look back at its own functionality and assess the part it plays, is one that can value itself in a more long term and healthy way than one that approves of itself instantly and besottedly. It generates a true and functional feeling of significance, and this offers the greatest practical chance of creating relationships that help support a sense of personal significance.

Rosa (met with in Chapter 9), who needed to be loved regardless of the quality of the lover, was not able to evaluate herself in any realistic way, never mind value herself in any meaningful way.

Swinging between believing she was a strong, capable modern woman ('Leave it to me', 'I know how to bring him round') and feeling utterly bereft on her own, she found herself in a relationship with a brute. Had she been able to move on from the rejection of childhood and learn to look at herself in a more objective way, she might have been able to recognise what it was that she really had to offer the world (apart from the obvious physical, sexual offer) and to work on promoting it and offering it in good faith, without game playing, to someone who was equally ready to value it and to treat her as an individual of significance rather than as some totem. Then she might have felt truly significant. (This is somewhat different from believing in a product 'because you're worth it'. Marketing does little to help our cause, implying that products costing a few pounds could help buy off a deep sense of inadequacy.)

Genuine significance is not about feeling superior to the rest of the world and wanting to give it the cold shoulder by endlessly intoning, 'I did it my way.' Nor is it about feelings of entitlement, be it to specialist products or to specialist treatment. Significance is about brains that had evolutionary spurts of hyper-connectivity and now need to make links between all sorts of things, specifically links between the self and the world beyond the self. In this way, they confirm that their way of joining things up has validity and that both their existence and their perception of their existence actually matter.

It's mere courtesy to extend that sense of mattering to others because, when all's said and done, it's only a delusion, but a delusion which needs to be shared in order that everything works as well as possible. So, we should all feel we have a part to play in the practice of helping others to feel significant, if only to prove to ourselves that we're big enough to do it.

It's not just blanket approval of people, though, that makes them feel significant. It's recognising all their individuality, including their negative bits, that does the trick. You won't make the average prisoner feel significant by telling them that they are really all lovely and cuddly behind that mask of hardness. They're not going to buy that. You do it by listening to what they're saying – about their lives, their experiences, their feelings – and by showing them how they and their particular circumstances could be made much better with your support but their effort. Give people respect by recognising the individuality of their existence and by believing in their capabilities and that will demonstrate to them that you think they are agents in this world, not just pawns – in effect, that they matter.

This is the opposite of adopting the patronising attitude that suggests someone is not as capable as the next person of competence, decency, kindness, honesty or whatever, and going on to insist that they must be dealt with as a special case, while all along implying that they are actually less than fully fledged members of the human race. Treating someone as if they matter (however flawed they may be) is also the starting point on the road to a necessary recognition that we are all 'in it together' and that even the hardest among us needs others for survival. We gain nothing by setting anyone apart from the rest; we gain everything by esteeming the fact of each other's equal existence.

To summarise: the practice of personal significance is a two-way affair. First, if we weren't lucky enough to have an upbringing that made us feel we were naturally wonderful and valuable, we may have to ask others for help in defining what we really have to offer the world (ignoring the emotionally atavistic murmurings of, 'I'm unattractive', 'I'll never amount to anything'). What are our capabilities, skills, physical and mental attractions? We can then either be satisfied with what we have to offer or we can make adaptations in line with *rational* aspirations for ourselves, and be pleased both with our own adaptability and with the outcome.

We can follow this up by looking for a suitable fit with our new understanding of who we are, when looking for jobs, partners, activities and so on. It's all very well aiming for the stars, but if we aim too high the result can be endless put-downs and fruitless attempts to live up to other lifestyles, career demands, expectations of appearance or whatever. It's too easy to fall into the trap of trying to live up to some notional status as the right kind of employee or as a multitasking success story, and then finding yourself putting in long hours or making exceptional efforts to try to prove the point. A really good job match or a truly effective life should demand human, not superhuman, input. The latter suggests a desperate need to find validation and significance.

Aiming too high and unrealistically can be both exhausting and have a very designificancing effect on a person. Equally, aim too low and that can result in feelings of resentment and a sense of selling oneself short – which hardly values the significance of Other in an endorsing and positive way and also leads to a designificancing of self. Ideally, we need to look for people/jobs/activities that match our own realistic and never negatively framed appraisal of self. That way should lie a lifetime of contentment. In doing so we will see ourselves mirrored appropriately in Other and, hopefully, approved – just as we should have been when babies.

The second part of the practice of significance is in line with wanting to see ourselves as engaged members of a wider whole. This means promoting other people's sense that they are significant. It does not mean puffing them up unrealistically or telling thieves that they're just suffering from low self-esteem or anything like that. What it does mean (in line with desired principles) is that we should feel some responsibility towards others and their behaviour, supporting their realisation that we are affected by what they do – that their existence has made its mark – and that they are of consequence. We're usually quick off the mark when it comes to grumbling about services that have let us down or our perceived loss of rights and entitlements, but how many of us are as quick to send an update and a 'thank you' to the doctor who treats us and helps us to get better or a commendation to the MP (yes, they're real people too), civil servant or worker on the ground who helps to keep the great fairground ride of public and community life spinning? We don't have to wholeheartedly approve of every aspect of other people or their behaviour, but we do have to endorse their reality, which is why the escalating trend of refusing to recognise even the slightest acknowledgement of another's communication is so deeply unhelpful. So, let's do more to show we know Other is out there. Because, after all, we're their Other.

Finally, personal significance is not about getting even, treating someone as if they're special (in a good or a bad way), wanting to be best, first, richest or any of those things. Personal significance is about recognising that we're human only because of all the connectivity that led to us needing to find meanings in inner and outer life, and so, ultimately, it is about keeping a useful and shared delusion alive – that people *matter.*

Chapter 15
Life Itself

Does life have meaning? Does life matter?

We ask such questions largely to keep our brains entertained because, at one level, life doesn't matter or have any meaning at all. If none of us were alive who or what would care? However, as self-important (not to say self-obsessed) creatures, we filter such questions about whether life has meaning through our own exquisite sensibilities and therefore they have to be dealt with on that basis. We mutated creatures need a reason to be alive, whereas, presumably, most of the other creatures on the earth just get on with the business of living. Querying the purpose of life, wondering what great cosmic plan can be in action and all other specious speculations plausibly prompted by jumping genes and genetic mini-me's only serve to emphasise how very, very self-referential life has become for us.

We can, however, use that recognition to good purpose. Like all animals, we want to survive, and so we should treat this need to understand it all as a survival need, as pragmatic rather than metaphysical. Knowing that we have this strange requirement of life – that it should have meaning – we can then work to create meaning in thoroughly straightforward (rather than mystical) ways by purposefully investing achievable, sustainable and concrete outcomes with meaning – and all in our best possible long-term interests.

Should we fail to see the attractions of such a solid yet unromantic reality, we risk chasing shadows, of making ourselves feel comprehensively dissatisfied and placing our very survival in danger. The fact that we haven't got there yet is largely down to the strange allure of some ghosts in our grey matter.

Anticipation

'Well,' said Pooh, 'what I like best–,' and then he had to stop and think. Because although Eating Honey *was* a very good thing to do, there was a moment just before you began to eat it which was better than when you were, but he didn't know what it was called.

A. A. Milne, *The House at Pooh Corner*

Winnie the Pooh, arguably one of life's greatest philosophers, manages to sum up this puzzle inside us better than most. Our ability to inhabit an imaginary yet well-realised and enticing future motivates us to want things and to strive to achieve them. However, the reality of achieving our goals sometimes pales in significance compared to the dream we had. It's often the case that the fantasy is more satisfying than actually getting what we thought we wanted. This originates with our old frenemy, the anterior cingulate cortex. The ACC makes it more thrilling and fulfilling to dream than to act. Consequently, we are often not prepared to settle for the rational and mundane while we still have such peerless prospects in the mind's eye.

We might call it anticipation. It's what makes it better to travel hopefully than to arrive, or better to dream of romance than to live with smelly socks or leg hair in your razor. It's much the same thing that a smoker or alcoholic experiences on a continual basis. The craving sensation (which is about anticipation) is usually more satisfying than the actual experience – at least after the first gasp or slurp. Similarly, what could be described as an unextinguished anticipation effect sees addicts returning to their old habits sometimes many years after they think they've given them up.[1]

We often imbue anticipated outcomes with more meaning and validity than any clear-eyed observation or knowledge of the past should allow. It's not just poets and dreamers who do this but those supposedly objective and unbiased scientists. They set up expectations, based on some unrecognised but still formative and influential set of cultural standards, and then find scientific evidence to support their suppositions (they might deny this but science tends to fit the times – chicken or egg?). But real life curves and dives; it's an unpredictable arrow and it defies anticipation's targets.

This was the case when social scientists predicted that women (being empathic and non-hierarchical by nature) would, once

---

1   The world of addiction has an expression, 'euphoric recall', which refers to addicts' tendency to remember only the positive, pleasurable aspects of their using behaviour and rarely the horrors. It extends, of course, to other matters – lost loves, our childhoods (those 'lands of lost content') and many other things most of us love to regret. However, in addiction, euphoric recall works hand in hand with anticipation to produce a perfect storm of longing, which allied to related loss of what we call 'executive control' tends to result in the person using again.

promoted, make much more cooperative and democratic managers than men. But according to research at Harvard University (Benenson et al., 2014), things have not quite turned out that way. They found that – at least in the admittedly confined world of academia – women were less willing than men to work with those they considered beneath them and less likely to share the kudos of co-authorship of papers. Flawed science or flawed anticipation – that phantasmagoria coined in our shape-shifting brains – which is to blame? Because our brains, moving rather faster than our conscious selves, will obligingly fill in the things we're hunting for.

If we want to avoid not only the sheer embarrassment of making fools of ourselves but also the endless frustration of querying the validity of life, our contribution to it, to be or not to be or even whether forty-two is genuinely the answer, then a better answer might be to sign up to accepted codes of meaning that are achievable, sustainable and concrete. These are all much more likely to lead to the feeling that there *is* a point than the search for the perfect love, the solution to ageing or even whether the bare bodkin is in fact it and, ironically, more likely to result in happiness.

I suspect that it was an intuitive understanding of this principle that led Winston Churchill to join the Amalgamated Union of Building Trade Workers and say that his ideal day would include 'the laying of hundreds of bricks' – literally achievable, sustainable and concrete. Churchill possibly had undiagnosed bipolar disorder. He showed many of the symptoms including 'black dog' – all that manic energy and a clear need for life to have purpose. In addition to all his other absorbing and time-consuming activities, he felt what almost amounted to a compulsion to fit in such a strictly unnecessary one as bricklaying, something not naturally belonging to the life of an aristocrat and statesman. But given the inevitable frustrations of trying to save the world and convince others of your dreams of how it might and should be, what could be more grounding and reliable than engaging in a practical physical activity? Regardless of what else had worked out that day, having laid hundreds of bricks you could still look at your achievement and see the evidence of a day that had had purpose.

A practical life

In a recent survey on job satisfaction both vicars and farmers were in the top ten (publicans came in the bottom ten which must say something about the company they keep and the philosophising they're exposed to!) (see Flanagan, 2014b). Apart from being alike in that both guard flocks, they both also spend most of their time in very practical ways. Not for the average modern vicar a life full of numinous speculation, counting angels on pin-heads. They are more likely to share with farmers the same long unregulated hours, reams of paperwork, tedious accounting procedures and wellbeing and health-related issues, not to mention the physical graft and maintenance relating to buildings at the heart of the job. Although their input is massive and the financial rewards mostly slight, the big benefit for both groups is that they know why they're doing the work they do. They know its purpose and what their motivation is for doing it. They know that there are achievable goals within the job, whether that's holding an Easter service or helping a cow give birth; they know that the work has a long track record of being sustainable and is likely to continue into the future and be validated by society. It is concrete work that sets specific tasks which can be seen to be completed – unlike in a call centre, say, where workers will never see through a full process.

A practical life isn't necessarily limited to simple physical labour (floor tilers come low down in terms of job satisfaction). It is much more to do with being fully engaged in the fundamental aspects of life and work rather than in the procedural, peripheral or ceremonial. Years ago, before *The X Factor*, before TV at all, people weren't as exposed as we are to what might be called 'the grand finale effect', which demands that every undertaking reach a single moment of fruition, a consummation of the relationship between endeavour, purpose and publicly and culturally approved assessment. Before this constant triumphalism became normalised, most people would have seen life in a more nuanced way, as a work in progress rather than as a compilation of competitive highs. They would have played the piano to give pleasure to themselves and others rather than to pass exam grades 1 to 6. They would have walked to work or around their neighbourhoods for exercise and to learn the news rather than to tick an 'arduous ten miler' off the list. And they would have grown, prepared and cooked food because these were the necessities of life rather than the ingredients of a confected, competitive TV game show. They were fully engaged and therefore lived much more in the moment than many of us do now – which, ironically, is the principle behind the popular and burgeoning practice of mindfulness.

Being mindful is about living less in the some-place, sometime else that our brains conjure up, and more in the reality of our own embodied, physically present existences. Life lived in this way, predicated on the realistically achievable and on absorption in the demonstrably useful task in hand, increases the probability that we will feel that day-to-day life has a point, a meaning. Much more so than if we chase dreams, expect someone/something else to provide meaning for us, or rely on the constancy of social or cultural factors to continue to satisfy our sense that things matter because 'they' carry on saying they do.[2]

Bottom line

This chapter has moved on from focusing on the search for personal significance to look at the increasing need for us to prioritise socially aware principles and community goals over the subjective agenda that would be dictated by an unmitigated pursuit of personal significance. Such principles and aspirations are necessary for the long-term survival of society. They are predicated on us being stakeholders in something bigger than the merely personal and on us focusing more on what is grounded and practically achievable.

The behavioural fundamentals of the life we should be aiming to live to achieve this desirable state include the best possible physical health for all, the best possible mental health for all, the creation of a sense of belonging to a wider whole and the establishment of feelings of genuine significance. These feelings should be both subjective and objective – the latter meaning that we feel there's a point to life.

My purpose in putting together a checklist of aspirations for surthrival was not so much to create an exhaustive resource for oddball students of the arcane, but to develop a kind of framework or shuttering into which could be poured that mix of behavioural ingredients (in other words, the *practice* of doing the things) most likely to achieve outcomes which I see as being essential to (or the

---

2   One of the great frustrations of getting older is that social and cultural goalposts shift so much that what seemed important or a moral/ethical 'given' gets given short shrift by the next generation, leaving those who depended on social and cultural certainties feeling cast adrift, marginalised and purposeless.

foundation of, to continue the metaphor) human wellbeing in the long term.

Although our self-referential delusional brains may be brilliant at devising abstract principles, we have become rather less efficient at the practice of seeing them through on the ground in real time. Therefore, it's the practice of things that have already been seen to work that we will be turning to next, *pour encourager les autres* (i.e. the rest of us).

Unlocking the door

There is little point in having a key, even a magic key, unless it has something to unlock. The magic Cinderella key, Significance, has the specific function of unlocking the cells in our imprisoning brains. It does that by helping us to see significance more or less everywhere, expanding our universe, but simultaneously making it so vast, so infinitely capable of interpretation that for many this outcome is more lunacy inducing than liberating. Especially so when the focus for significance is the inside of our own heads because then the self knows no bounds. Result: infinite despair/delusion regarding one's place in the universe.

In earlier chapters I have described the key as both 'unlocking cells' and 'unlocking the door to the lives we live today', but I did not say anything about it freeing us. Cell doors can be opened but we might remain in prison. Modern life does not always feel as free as we might wish. Final freedom, or the closest thing that we can find to it (because freedom is as illusory as everything else about human experience), will not be found through the search for significance itself, but through the liberating realisation that it *is* a delusion, and it is at its most delusory when the spotlight and the search are centred on the self.

This final chapter is about finding that freedom. It is also about the actual practices and behaviours most likely to achieve outcomes essential to long-term human wellbeing or surthrival. Funnily enough, they might just turn out to be closely related.

The Whiteladies Road[3] assumption

A prisoner was once excusing himself from the effort of having to avoid drugs on release by telling me that I didn't 'know what it's like' – 'I can't walk down the Whiteladies Road without someone offering me drugs.' I pointed out that I didn't have that problem when I went there. After he'd finished laughing, we set about deconstructing my comment in a more positive mood. He agreed that it was possible for a middle-aged middle-class woman to take drugs so the problem didn't lie there. Put on the spot, he was able to work out for himself that the problem was in the way I walked, looked and related to the world around me – my gait, gaze, dress and body language. They just weren't up to the job of hooking in a drug dealer. Never have been.

It came as quite a revelation to him that he had such a closed mindset around his own competences and capabilities that he had never thought to *change his behaviour* in order to change his life – behaviour as simple but fundamental as ways of standing, walking, looking around, talking, dressing and grooming. Therapies are usually very hot on things like self-love, rebalancing the masculine and feminine, healing the trauma and so on, but very few ask clients to change the way they present themselves to the world because their current way is simply not working for them. As with the practice of sitting up straight, the practice of acting differently is a form of re-engineering of the self.

It's what we do that counts

Here are some 'to do' ideas that seem to work for people:

- Do housework, farming and gardening throughout your life. Walk everywhere, preferably up and down hills. Never retire but take a siesta every day. Eat meals packed with olive oil, pulses, green veg and fruit. Avoid red meat. Drink herbal teas morning, noon and night, and goats' milk every week. Don't wear a watch and surround yourself with friends. This is what the inhabitants of Ikaria, a tiny Greek island, do (see Larson, 2012). They have the longest lifespans in the world; one in three makes it into their nineties. They also overturn the theory that

---

3   A vibrant road in Bristol.

poor health and depression are correlated with poverty. By Western standards these people are poor. Luckily for them, though, they do not live by Western standards (or read the works of Western sociologists) and so they are both extraordinarily healthy and extraordinarily cheerful.

- Keep well, get a job and get married. According to the Office of National Statistics, health and employment are the first requirements for a happy life (see Swinford, 2013). Next in line, marriage makes people happier than having religious beliefs, six-figure salaries or children – it is twenty times more important to a person's wellbeing than their earnings and thirteen times more important than owning a home. Also, according to other studies, marriage cuts rates of criminal recidivism in half (Sampson and Laub, 1993). On the other hand, getting divorced has a terrible tendency to counter all those benefits.

- Act the part. It doesn't matter what is going on inside if you adopt behaviours in line with how you'd rather be. Feeling down? Smile. Your neural circuits will hardly know the difference and you'll feel instantly happier. Feeling like a slob, out of control, your life's a mess? Put on your best clothes, walk tall, walk purposefully – and your head will believe you're in charge; you will feel instantly more controlled. You really can't change your feelings by thought alone – but you can turn thought into action, and it's the action that will change the feelings.

- Have a plan, a goal, a target – not just a dream. There is a big, big difference between the anticipation of a fantasy future and the reality of setting an achievable goal. Apart from providing a necessary sense of purpose, goal setting, even on a small scale, prompts us to plan and make lists – a very functional thing to do. I know someone with a poorly functioning memory who, rather than live with the sensation that there's a bulging loft inside her head that desperately needs clearing, immediately writes things down on her to do list. She then does them, tidily ticking them off as she goes. It doesn't matter to her how immediately she attends to them. What counts is removing anything annoyingly insistent in her brain by doing what's on the list. That way lies a sense of achievement, self-control and regulation – resilience, in fact. A great outcome from something so simple.

- Subtle behavioural changes can make a huge difference. Simply getting patients to write things down could help to reduce the NHS's financial difficulties. Every no-show costs time and money. An initiative in Bedfordshire (Adams, 2011) cut the number of no-shows by up to 30% just by getting patients to write their appointment times down for themselves. They were then asked to repeat the information back to the receptionists – job done. Either the haptic effect was at work,[4] or being asked to take on a smidgeon of responsibility made patients feel more accountable for their overall behaviour. Whichever, the message stuck, costs were cut and patients presumably were made better, faster. Such strategies could help us all to engage more in society as well as boosting memory skills.

- Train for something: a marathon, a long cycle ride, a music recital, whatever. This is not for the grand finale effect or the finishing line but about rehearsing behaviours that get results by focusing on proven step-by-step guidance. This is a good model for any enterprise, especially with respect to delaying gratification and focusing on the practical. As they say about the basic simplicity of running marathons, 'Just keep on putting one foot in front of the other' (and don't forget nutrition, fartlecking and your water bottle). Training involves giving up the personal autonomy of making your own decisions. It's all about losing yourself in the endeavour and the process, morphing yourself into what Buddhists might call 'anatta' – no self. When the self is largely removed from the equation there is less of the significance-related peripheral stuff that obstructs progress and more of the pragmatic 'do what works to get where you've got to go' stuff. It's different at the very top (where ego isn't entirely unknown); I'm talking about 'every (wo)man' training, where training tends to result in lowered ego and heightened resilience.

- Team games and activities such as traditional dancing and singing in choirs encourage people to behave harmoniously and cooperatively with others, and to be alert and responsive to pressure from external forces such as the opposition, choirmasters or referees. They (team games especially) also promote resilience in the face of failure, something which many children have had little experience of and have acquired almost

---

4   Haptics: non-verbal communication relating to touch. Handwriting, a tactile form of communication, has been shown to 'impress' ideas on the mind better than simply reading them off a screen. Hence the old-fashioned notion of copying off a board was not such a bad one after all.

no tolerance for. The ability to demonstrate grace in defeat may not attract the same kudos as winning a gold medal but it may be better training for life.

- On the flip side, if a person really, really does want to go to the top – they should practise, practise, practise – according to geneticist David Shenk (Shenk, 2010). He quotes the marshmallow studies of Walter Mischel (Mischel and Ayduk, 2004; see also Chapter 7) and shows how that ability to delay gratification is fundamental to self-discipline, which, in turn, is what it takes to improve at anything. He also discusses self-limiting thinking (essentially the Whiteladies Road assumption – see above) and emphasises how important it is to identify (perceived) limitations and then ignore them in order to go further than you ever thought you could. Support for his theories comes from K. Anders Ericsson at Florida State University who believes that the performances of many of the elite in a whole variety of fields, from sporting to musical, probably depend more on focused practice than on any innate talent (Ericsson, 1996). These academics are giving us the very positive message that we *can* grow, but I would add the proviso that we must have realistic expectations; positive thinking is not sufficient. The goals we set ourselves have to be achievable. Practice is an essential behaviour but not a panacea; even after centuries of trying we still can't turn sows' ears into silk purses.

- Creativity, often seen as being a gift from the gods, is also affected by our behaviour. David Strayer, professor of psychology at the University of Utah, and his team found that modern technology and multitasking could place so many demands on what he calls our 'executive attention' (ability to concentrate and inhibit distracting thoughts) that it becomes less effective, whereas time spent in nature could restore its function (Atchley et al., 2012; see also University of Utah News Center, 2012). The study, which involved fifty-six people spending from four to six days hiking in the wilderness without their mobile phones and other electronic devices, found that they increased their creative problem-solving skills by 50%. Although the researchers were unable to say definitively whether the outcome was due to increased exposure to nature per se, the decreased use of technology or to a combination of the two, the 50% improvement in creative problem-solving skills was irrefutable.

Other 'to do' activities that could be added to this list are things like maintaining routines and establishing simple rituals. These help us to be less obsessive about gratifying our fleeting personal preferences while satisfying our fixation on significance (without making too much of a meal of it). There are many other possible contenders, but the principle behind the list is that behaviour makes us who we are. It's what the outside world sees of us (how little they know about the fabulously rich content of our heads!) and, as we have seen, it is behaviour that has the potential to radically affect the ways in which we see and feel about ourselves.

If we wish to become better people ourselves or, more grandiosely, make the world a better place, then it's the behaviour that will be in charge, not the beliefs. What works best in protecting both our own brains and the wellbeing of our species is behaviour that is not focused on the self but on the world and others in it.

Freedom from self and from the alluring tyranny of significance

We live in an age when banal jottings about the mundane goings on in journalists' lives are deemed suitable content for once august journals. This principle extends from printed newspapers to the ephemera of Twitter, Facebook and other social media. Wanting ever more of other people's trivial and self-absorbed musings makes us our own worst enemies when it comes to discouraging a focus on the self. So it may take a hefty shove, rather than the 'nudge' so beloved of behavioural psychologists, to get people on to a less egocentric track.

Many see nothing wrong with lives centred purely on the self and on finding meaning through pursuing things that massage and gratify that self. But they also fail to make the link between those terrible headlines at the start of this book and the lifestyles they admire. Two recent news reports perhaps should have made people think more critically about the relationship between our absorption in the search for significance within the self and those headlines. One of those reports read: 'Depression top cause of illness in world's teens, World Health Organization reports' (*Sydney Morning Herald*, 15 May 2014). The other read, 'Cancer charity fundraiser Stephen Sutton dies aged 19' (*BBC News*, 14 May 2014).

Both, of course, are terribly sad, and the first went on to say that suicide is the third biggest cause of death in adolescents. Stephen

Sutton, who died at 19, lived the last four years of his life with terminal cancer. His dedication to fundraising became a phenomenal worldwide success thanks to social media sites (their upside). He said that he wanted people not to take life for granted, adding that he didn't know how long he had left to live because he hadn't asked – because it didn't matter: 'I don't see the point of measuring life in terms of time anymore, I would rather measure it in terms of making a difference, which I think is a much more valid and *pragmatic* measure' (my italics).

By any standards Stephen was a remarkable young man; his own words convey all the meaning I could possibly want. But it may still be worth emphasising that for him life was worth living even though his future literally held no meaning. For Stephen, it was simply about what you did and how beneficially what you did affected others. He didn't ask life to hand things out to him, he handed himself over to life. Nor did he demand that any of it should be easy or that there should be any let-up of pressure to perform. No lying back and feeling sorry for himself at all.

Stephen is just one example of many other remarkable people who have faced a variety of challenges with the same sort of spirit (and behavioural approach). Another was Gill Hicks, who lost both legs in the 7/7 King's Cross attack. Rather than focusing on what she lost, inquests into the past or revenge against the perpetrators of the attack, she has actively sought to remember the love shown to her by those who saved her life and the euphoria she felt when she finally knew she was going to survive. She has learned to value her new, differently powerful body, honouring its reality by feeding it well and treating it with respect. She has said that she feels fortunate to have all that she does, and that she has made a *conscious decision* to bring positives out of 7/7 (my italics).

Entrepreneur Richard Branson tells of the freedom and challenges he experienced in his rural childhood in deepest Sussex, how he and his brother were left pretty much to their own devices. They were even allowed to go to France, cycling and camping for two and a half weeks all on their own. In his autobiography, *Losing My Virginity* (2009), Branson recounts the story of how his mother stopped her car one day when they were still a few miles from home and made him complete his journey across the fields on foot and alone. He says he was just 4 at the time; his mother Eve says he was about 6 and it was only one mile (Branson, 2013: 43). According to Eve, he suffered from crippling shyness and wouldn't talk to adults. Believing that shyness was being 'introverted and thinking only of yourself', Eve says she let him out of the car with the message, 'You will now walk home. You will have to talk to people to find your way home.' Branson says it took him around ten hours but he eventually made it. After this experience he started to interact with grown-ups much better. Although there appears to be some familial confusion (delusion?) around chronology and distance, the episode clearly led to an improvement in resourcefulness and resilience.

In line with the tough love behaviour of Eve Branson are the attitudes and behaviours of many of the parents of successful Paralympians (see Rumbelow, 2012). One, Elizabeth Brown, mother of archer, Danielle, says of the time Danielle was struggling to complete a thirty mile Duke of Edinburgh's Award scheme walk: 'I did get upset about it, I didn't want to see her struggling but she has to live and it has made her the person she is.' Another, Darrell Hynd, father of two swimmers, Sam and Olly, says, 'It is always hard when you get a diagnosis, but having a disability, it does teach you to get on with it. That's the attitude we've encouraged. What you've got is what you've got [note: no delusional fantasies there]. I think children with disabilities do tend to work on getting a more positive disposition'. Their parenting style, across the board, was resolutely anti-mollycoddling.

Should we conclude that the worldwide toll of depressed but otherwise healthy and able-bodied teens is the result of worldwide mollycoddling? If more young people were challenged and expected to actively and positively engage with the wider world, focusing on it rather than on themselves, would their lives be significantly improved? It's a tantalisingly attractive proposition, not least because it provides a clear and doable solution to one of humanity's most unnatural seeming and upsetting disorders.

One final curio to add to my gallery of evidence suggesting that this might indeed be the way forward. Maya Van Wagenen, an adolescent girl in Texas, was feeling bullied and outcast at her tough new school. Instead of seeing herself as a victim, she decided to see herself purposefully as part of her own project. She spent the whole of the next year following the advice of a 1951 self-help manual, step by step. The manual she followed was *Betty Cornell's Teen-age Popularity Guide* (2014), and it must have worked, inasmuch as she is now one of the most influential (not to mention wealthy) teenagers in the United States. The book of Maya's story (Van Wagenen, 2015) covers so much that it's impossible to pick out any single factor that worked best for her. Curiosity and confidence may both have played their part in her gradual acceptance in her school. But she also followed a plan, took a positive proactive approach (the bull by the horns) and adapted her behaviour to become who she wanted to be (the Whiteladies Road effect again). It didn't matter that the particular version was an anachronism. As she says, 'Here I am, I am the character of this story, and I will act accordingly. I will be the person that I found at the end of eighth grade' (see Hodson, 2014). By changing her behaviour and by focusing on the external effect of it, she changed her status in life from victim to vanquisher.

Conclusion

The question I posed at the very start of the book was: is life enough? And the answer is yes, providing we achieve freedom from self and from the alluring tyranny of Significance.

Perhaps I should just stop here. Is there anything else to say? But we have covered a lot of territory and as it seems a long way from there to here, maybe a gentle round-up and a few final comments could be helpful.

I began by suggesting that there was something I had discovered which seemed to lie behind all the dysfunctional thinking and behaviour I had come across. I called this the magic Cinderella key.

I also pointed to a danger inherent in our DNA which made our species strangely vulnerable to a failure to thrive. I then looked at how our brains may have evolved, especially at the strange mutations which seem to have played such an important role in our development as a symbolic species, such as jumping genes and genetic mini-me's, which appear to have impelled us to associate things ever more wildly until connecting things up and creating meaning became our *raison d'être*. As we came to depend ever less on external information and ever more on the ways in which our brains filtered and processed it, we have ended up living in a permanently delusional state.

I suggested that our lives had become predicated on the ultimately delusional search for Significance (the perfect storm of connectivity), and that the magic Cinderella key had become both our incentive for living and a shackle on our ability to live easily and naturally.

I moved on to look at the ways in which our sense of personal significance might be compromised by an imperfect upbringing, leading (in this world which prioritises significance) to all manner of problems from which cats and dogs presumably do not suffer. I looked at some of the problems through the stories of kaleidoscope people, bamboo men, voiceless girls and others, and I considered the part played in some of the disorders by brain chemicals such as dopamine and oxytocin. Never forgetting my occasional mention of the amazing anterior cingulate cortex!

Bizarrely, a lack of sense of personal significance seems to lead to more rather than less focus on the self, so I dwelt on the dangers of an 'I, myself and me' fixation, and looked at the role of language in producing associated thoughts, attitudes and moods. I also considered how the search for self can lead to an increase in cases of extreme individualism and an abandonment of personal responsibility. Whereas, if we want good mental health, we should be connecting more with others and taking on more, not less, responsibility for them.

I told a cautionary tale of what can happen to human society when a pursuit of the personal leads to a breakdown in community, using the examples of San Gimignano and Siena, and showed how, even though all significance is a delusion, we have at least to share a delusion, otherwise people will start sticking heels onto the toes of boots and believing they're more important than God (or everyone else).

I suggested that as crises were times when people tend to be less self-absorbed and pull together much more, maybe what was needed now was a sense of crisis, even an engineered one, to make us work harder to achieve 'collective efficacy'. But first, as individuals, we would have to recognise any spurious significance agenda that we might have, so that we could repudiate and overlook it should it get in the way of working towards that collective efficacy and the common good. I suggested a list of possible contenders for the category of 'spurious significance', from romantic love to self-harming and from ceremony to secrets.

I also investigated the fundamentals of what I call the 'silo mentality'. This is more a social force than spurious significance, but it's equally responsible for sidetracking us from the recognition that we are a single species, one that currently needs to behave more like a species (and an endangered one at that) and less as a bunch of individuals with separate and special issues. If we do not recognise this need there are going to be mental health problems – and some very bad driving habits (what do I mean, 'going to be'!).

Having looked at what was not working well, I explored the 'desired principles' that would lead to a more collective, socially responsible life and examined how they could be implemented in practice.

Having worked through the aspirations, principles and practice, check-listing health (physical and mental), a sense of belonging and a sense of significance, I then looked at a whole host of things we can and should be doing if we want to improve our wellbeing, our connectedness and, ultimately, our resilience.

The whole shebang culminated in the behaviours we should be aiming for if we finally want to use the magic Cinderella key to unlock the cells and (with one bound) set ourselves free. These are all based around the liberating idea that if all is a delusion, and nothing has absolute meaning, then to set out to achieve the achievable (especially if it is at the same time pro-social) is a far, far better thing to do than we seem to have done before.

Ever since humankind came out of the swamp and those genes mutated, people have been looking for the meaning of life. First they looked to the heavens and built implausibly tall structures to glorify their findings (at a time when most life had to be lived rather closer to earth); now we search the labyrinthine structures of our brains and hope for lightning flashes of dopamine to illuminate the mystery where neuron meets neuron. We keep on believing, against all the apparent evidence, that there is something out there (or in there, as the case may be) which will explain it all and take the onus off us to make it meaningful for ourselves – by the simple expedient of living it well.

Even when exposed to the obvious, as was Kurtz in Conrad's *Heart of Darkness*, rather than see how liberating the unveiling was, he could only react to 'the horror' of it, because deep down he still thought that there *ought* to be meaning. He was like a child suddenly deprived of a favourite toy. Feeling, like him, that there ought to be purpose and meaning, we fill every ounce of space, every minute of time, with bigger and bigger structures and more and more stuff and ever increasing work and play loads, to block out the possibility that we, too, might be faced with that same 'horror'.

What's it all about? Our refusal to accept how very *unimportant* we all are?

How deluded we have all been. Life itself *is* enough. It's all we have. Let go of the tyrannical hold of Significance (once we have, pragmatically, done all we can about it), then we can stop worrying about Life and what we're missing out on.

We can start to *live*.

Appendix A
Addiction

> If I had a thousand sons, the first humane principle I would teach them should be, to forswear thin potations and to addict themselves to sack.
>
> ### *Henry IV, Part 2*, **IV. iii**

What is addiction? What do we mean by addict? The perception of addiction is so vague and has become so encompassing that it's even used to 'big up' a love of confectionery: 'I'm positively addicted to Creme Eggs/Mars Bars/Kit Kats' and so on. But what do we really mean by these terms?

Shakespeare's Falstaff, his most famously raddled toper, uses the term 'addict' when he says he would want his sons (if he had them) to avoid weak drinks and take to the stronger sack (sherry) instead. Even though it seems such an appropriate association, Falstaff actually means something a little different from us because historically 'addict' meant 'to sign up to', 'to commit to'. Perhaps it's not too big a leap from that to a greedy love of chocolate. But that's not what we really mean by it.

Turning to Alcoholics Anonymous, Narcotics Anonymous or any other 12-step movements, we discover addiction used in a more passive form. To be addicted to means to be in thrall to a disease over which one has no control. However, psychologists see addiction as a persistent, compulsive *dependence* ('dependency' is now frequently preferred over 'addiction' as a label of choice) on a behaviour or substance, regardless of the adverse consequences of doing or using.

I prefer the definition given by a client, one who had tried a number of ways to rid himself of his addiction. He described people like himself in this way: 'Addicts are people who can't sit with themselves. The substance or behaviour is a red herring.'

'Can't sit with themselves' – in other words, can't manage their inner sensations. If I were pushed to enlarge on that, I would add that I do think a substance is material to the problem but that it is not an exogenous (external) one but an endogenous (internally generated) one. And that if we are ever addicted to or dependent on anything in particular, it is this one thing alone that is the star of the show. We've met it before – dopamine.

Dopamine, that motivating but not necessarily moral neurotransmitter, now looks like the protagonist at the heart of the drama to which so many people seem to be in thrall. As we've already seen, dopamine is necessary for many processes in human behaviour, from motivation to motor function and from language to learning and memory. But regulation of dopamine production is also vital to most of these same processes. Too little dopamine is implicated in diseases like Parkinson's; too much in forms of schizophrenia and bipolar disorder; but both too much and too little appear to be associated with addiction, especially when they happen in quick succession within any one brain.

Basically dopamine is part of the brain's reward system. The reward system circuitry involves a number of brain areas, including the nucleus accumbens (sometimes called a pleasure centre), the ventral tegmental area (which produces dopamine) and the prefrontal cortex including, of course, the anterior cingulate cortex. The exact relationships involved are complex, as is the balance between neurotransmitter production and behavioural outcome, but it seems that dopamine is produced not so much when pleasure is actually being experienced but rather when it is anticipated. This is in line with its description as a motivational chemical – it keeps our endeavours up to the mark. We want to get to the reward more than we want the reward once we have it. This excited anticipation forms a reward of sorts in itself, as it is stimulatory and makes the whole experience of life more intense.

So dopamine is produced in advance of a pleasure and it stimulates learning around its own production – that is to say, we remember what it feels like to have that pleasurable feeling of anticipation. Then, when we add the substance/behaviour of choice, we get another brief stimulation of the reward circuit, before there is a numbing of the pleasure response brought on by overstimulation of all the areas involved. There is also, courtesy of the effect of both endogenous and exogenous chemicals, a damping down of the inhibitory strength of the prefrontal cortex which might otherwise bring more rational considerations to bear on compulsive and negative behaviours (the jury is out on whether prefrontal cortex function is already more compromised in so-called addictive personalities).

All very interesting, but what evidence is there that dopamine plays such a central role in addiction? There are two very strong pointers here. The first is the D2R2 allele (an allele is a variant of a normal gene). This prevents dopamine from acting on the reward pathways of the brain – so reducing the pleasure rush and reinforcement that usually comes when people eat, drink, have sex, take risks and stimulate their senses in all sorts of ways – and it seems that this particular genetic party pooper is to be found in between 50–80% of substance-dependent people. This is distinctly suggestive of what has been called a 'reward deficiency syndrome' which plays a large part in satisfaction-seeking behaviour.

The second pointer comes from a seemingly unlikely source, the treatment of symptoms in Parkinson's disease. In Parkinson's, brain cells responsible for dopamine production die off, leading to the characteristic loss of physical and psychological motivation. Drugs which mimic naturally occurring dopamine by reactivating the dopamine receptors are often used to treat the symptoms but may end up over-treating them, with the result that there is greater than normal dopamine activity. A number of patients who previously had no association with gambling and only normal levels of sexual activity have ended up as either problem gamblers or hyper-sexualised. Not an outcome that anyone had predicted. Research has shown that patients taking these dopamine agonists are three times as likely as other people to become problem gamblers (Kelley et al., 2012). So it seems it is actually possible to manufacture this 'disease' of addiction.

Ergo it would appear that dopamine is the number one chemical suspect in dependency. If any other evidence were needed to show it is not the presenting substance/behaviour that is the real root of the problem (that, as my client says, is a red herring) then cross addiction should seal the case. Cross addiction is when a person once dependent on a particular substance moves – often quite seamlessly – on to another substance or 'compensating' behaviour. As I've witnessed only too often, people in recovery from say alcohol or crack will (sometimes while in rehab; occasionally with the complicity of rehab) mainline coffee, sweets and nicotine, then become compulsive bodybuilders or runners who run themselves into the ground. But rarely will they recognise their unchanging attitude which assumes that the need for self-gratification is somehow die-stamped through the human soul.

But chasing after that particular dragon-tail of dopamine gratification is akin to chasing an *ignis fatuus*. Overly high levels of dopamine, whether produced endogenously or exogenously, lead to the rapid depletion of it and feelings of emptiness and depression after any initial high. It really doesn't matter whether you are addicted to stimulants (uppers such as cocaine, Ritalin and even caffeine) or depressants (downers such as heroin and alcohol), or miscellaneous things such as nicotine, marijuana, gambling, shopping, porn, eating or video games, you are always chasing an ever-decreasing possibility of satisfaction. More soon becomes less, and will be increasingly less as time goes on.

Yet, with exquisite alertness to irony, the anticipation will be greater and greater. Cravings are nature's way of keeping substance manufacturers happy. Cravings, and a corrupted dopamine system, bipolar in its ups and downs, keep the focus on a memory of the anticipation of what has gone before. The person who can't 'sit with themselves' feels they can't bear all that ramping up of wanting (or as many prefer to put it, 'needing') and so they will put all other considerations aside. They allow their reward systems to override their prefrontal ones, and family, work, finances to go hang as they satisfy their urge to gorge on dopamine.

You can discover all the horrid effects of substance abuse elsewhere: the rotten teeth, the damage to hearts and livers, the lung diseases and the pains of withdrawal. Although much complained about, these last are mostly not in the least bit dangerous, the main exceptions being withdrawal from alcohol (which can be very dangerous without supervision) and from benzodiazepines.

Although that sort of information is sometimes the only material covered in educational training courses, this appendix aims to be more incisive. It is looking at the mechanisms behind dependency, commonly known as addiction, and hopes to divert attention away from the curious romanticism of films like *Trainspotting* and towards an understanding that dependency is actually about quotidian factors such as genetic susceptibility, the supernormal stimuli that are easily available to all of us on a daily basis and psycho-emotional attitudes (partly cultural and partly individual) that encourage a person to believe that they cannot, or should not have to, tolerate uncomfortable sensations such as unfulfilled appetite, sadness, emotional pain, loneliness and so on. And, given the main message of this book, naturally the other thing they cannot tolerate is a sense that either they or their lives have a significance deficit in some way.

Ultimately, although there are many additional substances that show promise in terms of dependency treatment, the long-term solution will always be for a person to sit more comfortably with their inner sensations – however they are experienced.

We have reached a tipping-point in attitudes to physical health and have come to accept that resting is usually not the answer to much physical discomfort such as aching joints, cancer treatment and so on. Perhaps the time is also ripe to challenge feelings in the same way and become much more muscular in our dealings with them. We can have feelings, indeed should recognise them and their origins, but absolutely we do not need always to believe in their reliability, supremacy or power over us.

The Autistic Spectrum

For people on the autistic spectrum (usually referred to as ASD or autism spectrum disorder) everything is different. (There is a great deal of information on the National Autistic Society and other similar websites.) This is what the National Autistic Society has to say about how the condition affects people:

> Autism is a lifelong developmental disability that affects how a person communicates with, and relates to, other people. It also affects how they make sense of the world around them.

The spectrum covers a range of different levels of impairment and social functioning, from low level where individuals may not be able to speak, to high level such as Asperger's syndrome – a condition in which there is relatively high (often very high) intelligence, fewer problems with speech as such but still many differences in language processing.

Essentially, there is a triad of impairments that affect people wherever they are on the spectrum:

- Difficulty with social communication.
- Difficulty with social interaction.
- Difficulty with social imagination.

For them, life is an ongoing challenge as they try to make sense of the world and the people in it. This usually results in high anxiety levels.

I want to look at some of the underlying factors in ASD, in high-functioning autism and Asperger's in particular as these provide some useful insights.

ASD is an area of much debate and much controversy, so I cannot say, 'Here is the explanation; now for the treatment.' No one is yet in a position to offer either with any confidence. It's not even clear if any truly contributory factors have been identified. Studies of twins suggest a genetic component and it does appear to run in families, especially on the male side. It is identified in males four times more often than in females (possibly because females, even ASD females, have innately superior social skills which mask some of the symptoms). Both testosterone and older fathers have been implicated but no absolute evidence has been found for any one specific 'cause'. Most likely, multiple factors are involved.

Certainly there are multiple presentations of the syndrome, and part of the difficulty in diagnosis is down to historic ways of explaining and identifying it. These have not only proved to be wrong but have misled/misdirected both research and diagnostic approaches. For example, for a long time it was believed that lack of eye contact, lack of empathy, lack of either sense of humour or understanding of wordplay (puns and metaphors) were good indications of autism. However, it is now recognised that many people on the spectrum are capable of these subtle behaviours, although they can seem slightly rehearsed and/or one-sided at times. For example, Asperger's people may produce very colourful writing but may also be less than proficient at understanding other writers' literary tropes.

A current focus of research (appropriately) is on eye-tracking by infants. It is thought that babies who focus less on carers' eyes and more on carers' mouths or on their surroundings show early indications of autism. This can then be picked up and treated early (good if it's true). However, some children who focus on mouths may do so for other reasons, and it seems that this could be yet another misdirection for confused parents and caregivers. (I personally focus more on mouths than on eyes when interacting, but I don't think that I fulfil other requirements of ASD.)

As with addiction, it is not so much the specifics of behaviour that determine the problem, but more the underlying patterns, and it is those that we need to get at.

One small boy, who many decades later would be identified as Asperger's, typically demanded a lot of attention and reassurance from his parents, but was unable to comprehend that they were essentially separate from himself. As they sat silently at night, no doubt hoping he would finally go to sleep, rather than infer silent but human parents, he assumed that they were machines, previously active things that had been 'switched off'.

Not understanding Other (known as 'theory of mind' when Other applies to people) also leads to an inability to take comfort from others. It makes sense that a lack of fellow feeling would result in lessened ability to understand comfort at a purely emotional level. So that small boy when grown up, having witnessed the physical behaviours in action, was more than capable of offering hugs, kisses and soothing words to others, but never seemed to get any comfort from receiving them himself. In fact, such gestures appeared to be irritating to him.

This indicates not just an emotional deficit but an inability to switch perspectives. Think torches. If on a dark night you give an autistic child a torch, they are more likely to switch it on when they need to see rather than when they need to be seen (see also my comments on modern driving in Chapter 10). They do not realise that for safety other people need to be able to see them. Just because they themselves can see does not mean they are visible to others. If they are to be taught appropriate behaviour they need to have listed all the times when the torch must be switched on – and not told *if* such and such happens but *when*, as they will not be able to extrapolate from one specific and apply the principle to other situations. To do so would be to link and cross-reference, and that is where the deep problem lies.

The neural circuits which ASD brains employ are very different from the ones neurotypicals (NTs) employ. Where an NT brain can make a continuous journey across the landscape of past, present, future, autobiographical self-knowledge, continuous narrative and all related spurs and byways, the ASD brain hits lots of dead ends instead. When wandering about in their own brains, theirs are never continuous, narratised journeys. To use another metaphor, they have islands of remembered but not contextualised information or biography which will bob up in seas of irrelevance or confusion. This can lead to confabulation, when plausible explanations are generated to explain away an image that might have arisen or a word that might have intruded without apparent purpose. Early attempts to define ASD people claimed they were always ruthlessly truthful, but that is less than accurate. Some may be, but truthfulness is not by any means universal.

In fact, depending on things always being a particular way in ASD is rarely a good idea. I like the self-description of one Asperger's client who, at an intellectual level, was capable of recognising (I won't say understanding) how infuriating his behaviour could be: 'It must be awful. People can't even depend on me being reliably unreliable.'

He had a point. Looking at the available evidence, his comment is quite illuminating. In any given situation, neural circuits in all brains fire up. For most of us they are complex and interconnecting circuits that subtly adjust and rewire themselves on an ongoing basis. In ASD people it's as though they have to depend on a limited number of operations based on discrete circuitry which is not inter-connected in the same way, much like postal systems before the cross posts of the eighteenth century. For ASD people, as for anyone else, one set of circuits may fire up in response to certain stimuli. Given the same situation and stimuli, for most NTs pretty much the same circuits – with a few adaptations – will fire again. However, this may not be the case in ASD brains as things are not associated or linked together in the same ways. Because they are more dependent on concrete rather than symbolic connections, different circuits are likely to supplant rather than slightly amend earlier ones.

Take the case of the autistic artistic savant, Nadia Chomyn (1967–2015). At age 5 she could draw exquisitely realised perspec-tive images of horses and riders (the animal faces being more credible than the human ones, interestingly) but she could not speak. To help her overall development she was given intensive lan-guage training. However, as her ability to communicate linguistically improved, her preternatural visualisation abilities declined. It could be inferred that the two brain systems were incapable of working interactively, so one had to give way to the other. The visual thinking that humankind shares with the animal world was covered over by language.

For most people the practice of cross-referencing these and other abilities involves the narrative thread that is also protective of men-tal health (it has been suggested that soldiers who can keep the narrative thread active in the throes of combat are better protected against post-traumatic stress disorder than those who can't). Without that narrative the world is a much more disjointed, inexplicable place, though maybe visually more interesting and sophisticated. ASD people experience life as a series of unrelated inputs, fast and furious, as so many brickbats being hurled at them by an unknow-able cosmic force. And the weirdest things can be brickbats. I have known ASD people so fearful of things as diverse as the moon, sandals, toilet roll covers and shiny fabrics that they become violent!

In 2009 I wrote an article in *Addiction Today* suggesting there are links between autism, addiction and criminality – not implying any-thing causal but noting that autistic people with an 'addiction' may well be having a very different experience from NT people. As they seem unable to daydream in normal ways, so they do not appear to have cravings (cravings being essentially symbolic and connected-up happenings) or euphoric recall in the way dependent people usually do. Nor do they respond well to talking therapies based on expressing feelings. Such things depend on activity in parts of the brain which are underactive in ASD people – particularly the anterior cingulate cortex.

Addicts and criminals also have underactive ACCs, hence the connection. Although aligned, the effects are rather different. One major function of the ACC is to take in information, then discount or override it in favour of an alternative (sometimes more symbolic, sometimes updated) interpretation of its meanings or possibilities. It does this with novel noun/verb combinations. Once the combination is accepted – becomes a habit – the insula cortex takes over the task. It may well be this area of the brain that takes on the 'job' of addiction in an ASD person. Theirs could be a habit rather than what might be called a classical addiction. They are certainly more likely to quit for good once they have stopped using, which is in line with their typical switch on/switch off model of behaviour and thinking. ASD people are also renowned for treating people the same way – on them or off them, with few shades of grey.

All of this links to the previously mentioned differences in language processing in ASD. If the ACC is necessary for juggling possibilities in linguistic combinations, but is less active in ASD, then it sort of follows that there will be less flexibility and evaluation of possible alternative networks associated with any word. Word use will be either more concrete or (courtesy of the possible insula involvement) more habitual. There is much evidence for this. Single words get used again and again, as if stuck. Limited associations lead to other people's pragmatic meanings getting lost and misunderstandings arising. When ASD people use humour in relation to language it is more likely to involve the less labyrinthine, more aural associations involved in puns.

If ASD people are in the vicinity of an argument, given that they have a more concrete agenda, they pick up on the anger in the voices and feel it's directed at them. Whereas NTs understand the context and realise that there is no actual causal association between themselves and the emotion being expressed in their presence.

'Self' is a construct, formed out of wiring, chemicals and experience. No two selves are alike (even identical twins) but most share some things, such as an idea that self is inside, is on both the receiving end and the delivery end of experience, is both vessel and agent of intention and is quite distinct from Other. The word autism, originating in Greek, actually refers to self. The irony for ASD people is that a genuine sense of self is what is missing. Boundaries in general are much hazier and it is harder for ASD people to differentiate between themselves and others.

This goes back to my description of them as kaleidoscope people. They keep presenting with different versions of themselves, and there may be little cross-referencing or referring back to previous encounters they've had with others. This has led some close associates of high-functioning ASD people to think they are going mad, given the lack of coherence, congruity and core validity in what ASD people say and do.

The reasons for this are to do with that sense of self, without which we cannot properly have a continuous thread running through our being and our doings. As mentioned in the footnote on page 251, it has been shown that the posterior cingulate cortex (an area closely related to the ACC) is activated when people understand their own intentions. However, it has also been shown that this area is not activated in ASD people, even if high functioning. The inference is that in lacking self-knowledge and understanding, ASD people are unable to presume other people's intentions (or even that they have them) as they have no model of their own processes on which to base the necessary understanding of humans in general.

Although they may recognise that in such a situation this is what someone does, not understanding that there is an intentional self behind the behaviour means they cannot possibly understand motivation or intentional forms of causality. An ASD person may seem very well informed about someone (as they will have large stores of information in general) but they will not understand them in the usual sense of the word, nor infer much from their behaviour. All of which makes living and dealing with someone on the spectrum extremely challenging, especially given the lack of emotional validation.

As a society's cultural norms are less well understood by people from other backgrounds, high functioning, clever, seemingly relatively successful ASD people may sometimes marry foreigners who do not at first spot the differences that others would. In fact, everything may seem fine initially, possibly because of the impact oxytocin will have on the ASD person, prompting more engaged and sympathetic behaviour that may later fade away (all part of the incomprehensibility that partners can feel).

This frustration isn't helped by the differences in language processing and use. For most people, language has forward meaning, indicating intention – in the way that pointing does – and suggesting abstract thought. But lacking that forward meaning and abstraction, stated ASD intentions may just stand alone without future consequence. 'But you said …' is just one red flag that marks the frustration of dealing with a person who does not do abstraction. However, ASD people will usually, sometimes obsessively, stick to appointments because they are concrete, but their spoken intentions, indicating probability, that something *might* happen, may prove unreliable.

All this may seem quite negative, even pejorative, but it should not be taken that way. I'm not an expert (no one knows enough yet to make that claim) but I and many of my clients have not found it useful to define ASD people in terms of being systematisers, having excess testosterone, or failures of empathy or theory of mind. Such thinking can be limiting. Parents experiencing children who open and close the same door for hours on end, partners living with chaotic individuals who can't seem to pay bills or keep themselves clean, or co-workers who are on the receiving end of extreme verbal violence, all feel there's something wrong somewhere. My wish is to indicate the threads connecting a whole host of possible behavioural differences – without specifically trying to define causation.

When a child with tears flowing says 'Eyes wet' but doesn't seem to grasp the concept of crying, or when an adult overwhelmed by social interaction sits slap-bang in the middle of an open space rather than hiding themselves away, they may well be on the spectrum. But identifying the specific behaviour, or interpreting it as lacking symbolism or theory of mind, is unlikely to add much to our ability to live comfortably with them. Or them with us.

A few final and hopefully helpful observations:

- ASD people are less likely to care about what others think about them than what they do to them.
- They are more likely to feel comfortable in controlled rather than casual social settings.
- Life for them is more stressful because it's less automatic and less buffered by understanding based on memory of past experience.
- However, much useful behaviour can be acquired by habit, especially if the process starts young. But habit has first to be ingrained by consciously practising life as role play: social skills and scripts can be learned (as for a stage play).
- Similarly language. This is an intellectual process, also learned as a series of scripts which have to be rehearsed. There are right and wrong scripts – 'I didn't know what I was supposed to say.'

- Extrapolation from the general to the specific, and vice versa, can be very difficult processes for ASD people.
- Not being overly concerned about what others think of them, ASD people are freer to be creative, without many of the usual constraints on what they allow into their minds.
- They suck up information like sponges.
- They treat more of what they see as information and less as supporting evidence for 'acceptable' theories.
- When free from anxiety and responsibilities they can be very creative in a number of fields: visual, maths and music, language.
- Many more 'free thinkers' than we realise may have been on the spectrum.

Bibliography and Further Reading

Adams, Stephen (2011) Writing own appointment cards could save NHS £250m, *The Telegraph* (27 July). Available at: http://www.telegraph.co.uk/news/health/news/8666403/Writing-own-appointment-cards-could-save-NHS-250m.html.

Agrawal, Rahul, Noble, Emily, Vergnes, Laurent, Ying, Zhe, Reue, Karen and Gomez-Pinilla, Fernando (2016) Dietary fructose aggravates the pathobiology of traumatic brain injury by influencing energy homeostasis and plasticity, *Journal of Cerebral Blood Flow and Metabolism* 36(5): 941–953.

Alcoholics Anonymous (2004) *Daily Reflections: A Book of Reflections by AA Members for AA Members*. New York: Alcoholics Anonymous World Services, Inc.

Alcoholics Anonymous (2013) *AA Service Handbook*. York: Alcoholics Anonymous.

American Psychiatric Association (2000) *Diagnostic and Statistical Manual of Mental Disorders, Fourth Edition* (DSM-IV). Washington, DC: APA.

Angelini, Francesca (2014) Sleeves up, bring in some real benefits, *Sunday Times* (9 February).

Armstrong, Jeremy (2006) Loss of fear went swimmingly, *Daily Mirror* (29 December).

Atchley, Ruth Ann, Strayer, David L. and Atchley, Paul (2012) Creativity in the wild: improving creative reasoning through immersion in natural settings, *PLoS ONE* 7(12): 1–3.

Aviva (2006) Driving is inherently visually demanding (7 April). Available at: http://www.aviva.co.uk/risksolutions/news/2006/04/07/sat-nav-makes-driving-more-difficult/.

Bandura, Albert (1977) Self-efficacy: toward a unifying theory of behavioural change, *Psychological Review* 82(2): 191–215.

Barrett, David (2014) Research reveals drivers' excuses for hogging the middle lane, and unveils England's top 10 lane hogging hotspots, *The Telegraph* (22 August). Available at: http://www.telegraph.co.uk/news/uknews/crime/11048800/The-reason-for-middle-lane-hogging-on-the-motorway-It-saves-me-changing-lanes-say-motorists.html.

Baumeister, Roy E., Smart, Laura and Boden, Joseph M. (1996) Relation of threatened egotism to violence and aggression: the dark side of high self-esteem, *Psychological Review* 103: 5–33.

Baumeister, Roy F. and Tierney, John (2011) *Willpower: Rediscovering Our Greatest Strength*. London: Penguin.

BBC News (2002) Sharing meals 'boosts mental health' (17

January). Available at: http://news.bbc.co.uk/1/hi/health/1763851.stm.

BBC News (2014) Cancer fundraiser Stephen Sutton dies aged 19 (14 May). Available at: http://www.bbc.co.uk/news/uk-england-27408818.

BBC News (2015) Are night shifts killing me? (27 July). Available at: http://www.bbc.co.uk/news/magazine-33638905.

Bell, Caroline, Abrams, Jolane and Nutt, David (2001) Tryptophan depletion and its implications for psychiatry, *British Journal of Psychiatry* 178(5): 399–405.

Benenden (2013) Study reveals small talk may be a thing of the past (23 May). Available at: https://www.benenden.co.uk/newsroom/research/research-archive/study-reveals-small-talk-may-be-a-thing-of-the-past/.

Benenson, Joyce F., Markovits, Henry and Wrangham, Richard (2014) Rank influences human sex differences in dyadic cooperation, *Current Biology* 24(5): R190–R191.

Bennington-Castro, Joseph (2013) The mystery of how identical twins develop different personalities, *i09* (9 May). Available at: http://io9.gizmodo.com/how-do-identical-twins-develop-different-personalities-497857032.

Bergouignan, Loretxu, Nyberg, Lars and Ehrsson, H. Henrik (2014) Out-of-body-induced hippocampal amnesia, *Proceedings of the National Academy of Science* 111: 4421–4426.

Bond, Michael (2013) Why are you? *New Scientist* 217(2905): 41–43.

The Brain: A Secret History (2011) *BBC4* (episode 3).

Branson, Eve (2013) *Mum's the Word: The High-Flying Adventures of Eve Branson*. Milton Keynes: Author House.

Branson, Richard (2009) *Losing My Virginity*. London: Virgin Books.

Bridge, Gillian (2005) *Stop Smoking: It's All in Your Mind*. Slough: W. Foulsham & Co.

Bridge, Gillian (2009) Guilty by association – autism, addiction and criminality, *Addiction Today* 21(120): 31–33.

Britten, Fleur (2013) Veiled emotions, *Sunday Times* (10 February).

Brown, Jonathan (2013) Is it rude to pay up while talking on your phone? Don't all call at once!, *The Independent* (2 July). Available at: http://www.independent.co.uk/news/uk/home-news/is-it-rude-to-pay-up-while-talking-on-your-phone-dont-all-call-at-once-8683927.html.

Cacioppo, John T. and Hawkley, Louise C. (2014) *Loneliness*. Chicago, IL: University of Chicago, Center for Cognitive and Social Neuroscience. Available at: http://psychology.uchicago.edu/people/faculty/cacioppo/jtcreprints/ch09.pdf.

Casinos Elite (2013) Psychologists find link between high risk gambling and loneliness (n.d.). Available at: http://www.onlinecasinoselite.com/post/psychologists-find-link-between-high-risk-gambling-and-loneliness.

Chabris, Christopher and Simons, Daniel (2011) *The Invisible Gorilla: How Our Intuitions Deceive Us*. New York: Random House.

Chiu, Pearl H., Kayali, M. Amin, Kishida, Kenneth T., Tomlin, Damon, Klinger, Laura G., Klinger, Mark R. and Montague,

P. Read (2008) Self responses along cingulate cortex reveal quantitative neural phenotype for high-functioning autism, *Neuron* 57: 463–473.

Chung, Cindy and Pennebaker, James (2007) The psychological functions of function words. In K. Fiedler (ed.), *Social Communication*. New York: Psychology Press, pp. 343–359.

Cojean, Annick (1997) The final interview [interview with Diana, Princess of Wales], *Le Monde* (27 August).

Compañ Poveda, E., Moreno, J., Ruiz, M. T. and Pascual, E. (2001) Doing things together: adolescent health and family rituals, *Journal of Epidemiology and Community Health* 56: 89–94.

Conrad, Joseph (1899) *Heart of Darkness*. London: J. M. Dent.

Cook, Gareth (2011) The Dark Side of Happiness, *The Boston Globe*, (16 October).

Cormier, Zoe (2013) Gene switches make prairie voles fall in love, *Nature* (2 June). Available at: http://www.nature.com/news/gene-switches-make-prairie-voles-fall-in-love-1.13112.

Cornell, Betty (2014) *Betty Cornell's Teen-age Popularity Guide*, reprint. London: Penguin.

Cossins, Dan (2013) The neurobiology of individuality, *The Scientist* (9 May). Available at: http://www.the-scientist.com/?articles.view/articleNo/35514/title/The-Neurobiology-of-Individuality/.

Cyders, Melissa A. and Smith, Gregory T. (2008) Emotion-based dispositions to rash action: positive and negative urgency, *Psychological Bulletin* 134: 807–828.

D'Esposito, Mark, Detre, John A., Alsop, David C., Shin, Robert K., Atlas, Scott and Grossman, Murray (1995) The neural basis of the central executive system of working memory, *Nature* 378: 279–281.

Da Mosto, Francesco (2006) *Francesco's Italy*. London: BBC Books.

Davidson, Richard J. (1998) Understanding positive and negative emotion. Keynote presentation at the Library of Congress/National Institute of Mental Health conference Discovering Ourselves: The Science of Emotion, 5–6 May, Washington DC.

Day, Jonathan, Savani, Soham, Krempley, Benjamin D., Nguyen, Matthew and Kitlinska, Joanna B. (2016) Influence of paternal preconception exposures on their offspring: through epigenetics to phenotype, *American Journal of Stem Cells* 5(1): 11–18.

Debette, S., Seshadri, S., Beiser, A., Au, R., Himali, J. J., Palumbo, C., Wolf, P. A. and Decarli, C. (2011) Midlife vascular risk factor exposure accelerates structural brain aging and cognitive decline, *Neurology* 77(5): 461–468.

Devlin, Hannah (2014) Exercise is essential to 'grow back your brain', *The Times* (18 February).

DeWitte, Sharon N. (2015) Setting the stage for medieval plague: pre-Black Death trends in survival and mortality, *American Journal of Physical Anthropology* 158(3): 441–451.

Duckworth, Angela L. and Seligman, Martin E. P. (2005) Self-discipline outdoes IQ in predicting academic performance of adolescents, *Psychological Science* 16(12): 939–944.

Duclos, Rod, Wen Wan, Echo and Jiang, Yuwei (2013) Show me the honey! Effects of social exclusion on financial risk-taking, *Journal of Consumer Research* 40(1): 122–135.

Elsevier (2010) Brain dopamine receptor density correlates with social status (press release) (3 February). Available at: https://www.elsevier.com/about/press-releases/research-and-journals/brain-dopamine-receptor-density-correlates-with-social-status.

Emmons, Robert A. and King, Laura A. (1988) Conflict among personal strivings: immediate and long-term implications for psychological and physical well-being, *Journal of Personality and Social Psychology* 54: 1040–1048.

Ericsson, K. Anders (1996) *The Road to Excellence: The Acquisition of Expert Performance in the Arts and Sciences, Sports and Games*. Mahwah, NJ: Lawrence Erlbaum Associates.

Faber, Johannes (2014) Die Chemie der Liebe, *Badische Zeitung* (24 October). Available at: http://www.badische-zeitung.de/bildung-wissen-1/die-chemie-der-liebe--93425255.html.

Farrer, Katherine E. (ed.) (2011) *Correspondence of Josiah Wedgwood, Vol. 2: Letters of Josiah Wedgwood 1772 to 1780*. Cambridge: Cambridge University Press.

Fernyhough, Charles (2013) Life in the chatter box, *New Scientist* 218(2919): 32–35.

Flanagan, Padraic (2014a) The Scilly Isles 'perhaps the most harmonious place in Britain', say researchers, *The Telegraph* (18 March). Available at: http://www.telegraph.co.uk/finance/property/10704950/Scilly-Isles-and-Fife-top-best-and-worst-locations-survey.html.

Flanagan, Padraic (2014b) Serving God beats serving pints for a happy life, *The Telegraph* (21 March). Available at: http://www.telegraph.co.uk/finance/jobs/10713990/Serving-God-beats-serving-pints-for-a-happy-life.html.

Forty, Adrian (1986) *Objects of Desire*. New York: Pantheon Books.

Frans, Emma, Sandin, Sven, Reichenberg, Abraham, Långström, Niklas, Lichtenstein, Paul J., McGrath, John and Hultman, Christina (2013) Autism risk across generations: a population based study of advancing grandpaternal and paternal age, *JAMA Psychiatry* 70(5): 516–521.

Freund, Julia, Brandmaier, Andreas M., Lewejohann, Lars, Kirste, Imke, Kritzler, Mareike, Krüger, Antonio, Sachser, Norbert, Lindenberger, Ulman and Kempermann, Gerd (2013) Emergence of individuality in genetically identical mice, *Science* 340(6133): 756–759.

Furness, Hannah (2013) Parents ruining children's lives by failing to teach them to sleep, Tanya Byron says, *The Telegraph* (12 March). Available at: http://www.telegraph.co.uk/news/health/children/9923378/Parents-ruining-childrens-lives-by-failing-to-teach-them-to-sleep-Tanya-Byron-says.html.

Gage, Fred H. and Muotri, Alysson R. (2012) What makes each brain unique, *Scientific American* 306(3): 26–31.

Ghosh, Pallab (2013) 'Love-test' identifies newly-weds true feelings, *BBC News* (29

November). Available at: http://www.bbc.co.uk/news/science-environment-25129117.

Gillespie, James (2012) 'Golden skirts' weaken business, *Sunday Times* (12 February).

Gilman, Jodi M., Kuster, John K., Lee, Sang, Lee, Myung Joo, Kim, Byoung Woo, Makris, Nikos, van der Kouwe, Andre, Blood, Anne J. and Breiter, Hans C. (2014) Cannabis use is quantitatively associated with nucleus accumbens and amygdala abnormalities in young adult recreational users, *Journal of Neuroscience* 34(16): 5529–5538.

Girlguiding (2013) *Equality for Girls: Girls' Attitudes Survey 2013*. London: Girlguiding.

Gmel, Gerhard, Mohler-Kuo, Meichun, Dermota, Petra, Gaume, Jacques, Bertholet, Nicolas, Daeppen, Jean-Bernard and Studer, Joseph (2013) Religion is good, belief is better: religion, religiosity, and substance use among young Swiss men, *Substance Use & Misuse* 48(12): 1085–1098.

Gobeske, Kevin T., Das, Sunit, Bonaguidi, Michael A., Weiss, Craig, Radulovic, Jelena, Disterhoft, John F. and Kessler, John A. (2009) BMP signaling mediates effects of exercise on hippocampal neurogenesis and cognition in mice, *PLoS ONE* 4(10): e7506.

Gothard, Katalin (2014) The amygdalo-motor pathways and the control of facial expressions, *Frontiers in Neuroscience* 8: 43.

Gruber, June, Mauss, Iris B. and Tamir, Maya (2011) A dark side of happiness? How, when, and why happiness is not always good, *Perspectives on Psychological Science* 6(3): 222–233.

Guardian (2014) Ofsted chief: reward good citizens who check why children are not at school (22 January). Available at: http://www.theguardian.com/education/2014/jan/22/ofsted-chief-michael-wilshaw-reward-good-citizens-check-children-school.

Hamilton, Jon (2013) How can identical twins turn out so different? *NPR* (9 May). Available at: http://www.npr.org/sections/health-shots/2013/05/14/182633402/how-can-identical-twins-turn-out-so-different.

Henry, Julie (2013) Shakespeare and Wordsworth boost the brain, new research reveals, *The Telegraph* (13 January). Available at: http://www.telegraph.co.uk/news/science/science-news/9797617/Shakespeare-and-Wordsworth-boost-the-brain-new-research-reveals.html.

Hodson, Heather (2014) How a 1950s guide to popularity changed a schoolgirl's life, *The Telegraph* (17 May). Available at: http://www.telegraph.co.uk/culture/books/authorinterviews/10836964/How-a-1950s-guide-to-popularity-changed-a-schoolgirls-life.html.

Horst, Jessica S., Parsons, Kelly L. and Bryan, Natasha M. (2011) Get the story straight: contextual repetition promotes word learning from storybooks, *Frontiers in Developmental Psychology* 2(17): 1–11.

Hurst, Greg (2014) Boys at exclusive school are told they must be nicer to their staff, *The Times* (3 April).

Immordino-Yang, Mary H., McColla, Andrea, Damasio, Hanna and Damasio, Antonio (2009) Neural correlates of admiration and compassion, *Proceedings of the National Academy of Sciences* 106(19): 8021–8026. Available at: http://www.pnas.org/content/106/19/8021.full.

Inaba, Darryl S. and Cohen, William E. (2000) *Uppers, Downers, All Arounders: Physical and Mental Effects of Psychoactive Drugs*, 4th edn. Ashland, OR: Paul J. Steinbroner.

Innes, Emma (2013) Why eating in front of the TV makes you fat: you consume 25% more LATER in the day without realising, *Daily Mail* (18 March). Available at: http://www.dailymail.co.uk/health/article-2295303/Why-eating-TV-makes-fat-You-consume-25-LATER-day-realising.html.

Institution of Mechanical Engineers (2013) *Global Food: Waste Not, Want Not*. London: IMECHE. Available at: https://www.imeche.org/docs/default-source/default-document-library/global-food---waste-not-want-not.pdf?sfvrsn=0.

Kappes, Heather Barry and Oettingen, Gabriele (2011) Positive fantasies about idealized futures sap energy, *Journal of Experimental Social Psychology* 47: 719–729.

Karama, S., Bastin, M.E., Murray, C., Royle, N.A., Penke, L., Muñoz Maniega, S., Gow, A.J., Corley, J., Valdés Hernández Mdel, C., Lewis, J.D., Rousseau, M.É., Lepage, C., Fonov, V., Collins, D.L., Booth, T., Rioux, P., Sherif, T., Adalat, R., Starr, J.M., Evans, A.C., Wardlaw, J.M. and Deary, I.J,. (2014) Childhood cognitive ability accounts for associations between cognitive ability and brain cortical

thickness in old age, *Molecular Psychiatry* 19: 555–559.

Keen, Mary (2013) Tetbury's roundabout teamwork is a blooming success, *The Telegraph* (26 August). Available at: http://www.telegraph.co.uk/gardening/gardenprojects/10259002/Tetburys-roundabout-teamwork-is-a-blooming-success.html.

Kelley, Brendan J., Duker, Andrew P. and Chiu, Peter (2012) Dopamine agonists and pathologic behaviors, *Parkinson's Disease*. Article ID: 603631.

King, Stephanie L. and Janik, Vincent M. (2013) Bottlenose dolphins can use learned vocal labels to address each other, *Proceedings of the National Academy of Sciences* 110(32): 13216–13221.

Klimecki, Olga and Singer, Tania (2012) Empathic distress fatigue rather than compassion fatigue? Integrating findings from empathy research in psychology and social neuroscience. In Barbara Oakley, Ariel Knafo, Guruprasad Madhavan and David Sloan Wilson (eds.), *Pathological Altruism*. Oxford: Oxford University Press, pp. 368–383.

Knapton, Sarah (2014) Older fathers have less attractive children, *The Telegraph* (24 March). Available at: http://www.telegraph.co.uk/news/science/science-news/10717694/Older-fathers-have-less-attractive-children.html.

Lamberg, Eric M. and Muratori, Lisa M. (2012) Cell phones change the way we walk, *Gait Posture* 35(4): 688–690.

Larson, Vanessa H. (2012) The Greek island diet you can eat forever, *The Guardian* (6 November). Available at: http://

www.theguardian.com/travel/
blog/2012/nov/06/
ikaria-greek-island-food-diet.

Lee, Syna Sze Wing (2007) A picture
is worth a thousand words? An
exploratory study in
self-disclosure using art and
writing among Hong Kong art
students. Unpublished paper,
Department of Applied Social
Studies, City University of Hong
Kong.

Lehrer, Jonah (2009) Don't! The
secret of self-control, *The New
Yorker* (18 May). Available at:
http://www.newyorker.com/
magazine/2009/05/18/dont-2.

Loftus, Elizabeth E. (2004)
Memories of things unseen,
*Current Directions in Psychological
Science* 13: 145–147.

Loudon, Andrew (1996) Parents'
plea to the girl driven away by
bullies, *Daily Mail* (27 March).

Lyubomirski, Sonia (2010) *The How
of Happiness: A Practical Guide to
Getting the Life You Want*. London:
Piatkus.

Maccari, Stephania, Darnaudery,
Muriel, Morley-Fletcher, Sara,
Zuena, Annarita, Cinque, Carlo
and Van Reeth, Olivier (2003)
Prenatal stress and long term
consequences: implications of
glucocorticoid hormones,
Neuroscience and Behavioural Reviews
27: 119–127.

Martin, Leslie R., Friedman,
Howard S., Tucker, Joan S.,
Tomlinson-Keasey, Carol, Criqui,
Michael H. and Schwartz, Joseph
E. (2002) A life course perspective
on childhood cheerfulness and its
relation to mortality risk,
*Personality and Social Psychology
Bulletin* 28: 1155–1165.

Martinez, Diana, Orlowska, Daria,
Narendran, Rajesh, Slifstein,
Mark, Liu, Fei, Kumar, Dileep,

Broft, Allegra, Van Heertum,
Ronald and Kleber, Herbert D.
(2010) D2/3 receptor availability
in the striatum and social status in
human volunteers, *Biological
Psychiatry* 67(3): 275–278.

Maslow, Abraham (1943) A theory
of human motivation, *Psychological
Review* 50: 370–396.

McCann, Jaymi (2013) Death of
small talk Britain: 'We have
become obsessed with social
media and haven't spoken to a
stranger for more than six
months', *Mail Online* (30 May).
Available at: http://www.
dailymail.co.uk/news/
article-2333298/
Britons-obsessed-social-media-
havent-spoken-stranger-months.
html.

McIntosh, Lindsay (2013) Volunteer
still working for the WRVS at
102, *The Times* (1 January).

McNulty, James K., Olson, Michael
A., Meltzer, Andrea L. and
Shaffer, Matthew J. (2013)
Though they may be unaware,
newlyweds implicitly know
whether their marriage will be
satisfying, *Science* (29 November):
1119–1120.

Miller, Alice (1978) *The Drama of the
Gifted Child: The Search for the True
Self* [*Das Drama des begabten
Kindes*]. New York: Basic Books.

Miller, Alice (1988) *Banished
Knowledge: Facing Childhood Injuries*
[*Das verbannte Wissen*]. New York:
Doubleday.

Miller, Alice (1995) *The Drama of
Being a Child and the Search for the
True Self*, rev. edn. London:
Virago.

Mischel, Walter and Ayduk, O.
(2004) Willpower in a
cognitive-affective processing
system: the dynamics of delay of
gratification. In Roy F.

Baumeister and Kathleen D. Vohs (eds.), *Handbook of Self-Regulation: Research, Theory, and Applications.* New York: Guildford Press, pp. 99–129.

Mohiuddin, Hafsa (2013) Connecting ideas: Shakespeare and Wordsworth act as brain boosters! *Journal of Pioneering Medical Sciences Blogs* (21 February). Available at: http://blogs.jpmsonline.com/2013/02/21/connecting-ideas-shakespeare-and-wordsworth-act-as-brain-boosters/.

Morelle, Rebecca (2013) Dolphins 'call each other by name', *BBC News* (23 July). Available at: http://www.bbc.co.uk/news/science-environment-23410137.

Mosier, Christine E. and Rogoff, Barbara (2003) Privileged treatment of toddlers: cultural aspects of individual choice and responsibility, *Developmental Psychology* 39(6): 1047–1060.

Nazroo, James and Matthews, Katey (2012) *The Impact of Volunteering on Well-Being in Later Life: A Report to WRVS.* Cardiff: WRVS.

Neubauer, Simon and Hublin, Jean-Jacques (2012) The evolution of human brain development, *Evolutionary Biology* 39(4): 568–586.

Newberg, Andrew B. and Waldman, Mark R. (2010) *How God Changes Your Brain: Breakthrough Findings from a Leading Neuroscientist.* New York: Ballantine Books.

Nisbett, Richard E. (2005) *The Geography of Thought: How Asians and Westerners Think Differently – And Why.* London: Nicholas Brealey.

Novelli, David, Drury, John, Reicher, Stephen and Stott, Clifford (2013) Crowdedness mediates the effect of social identification on positive emotion in a crowd: a survey of two crowd events, *PLoS ONE* 8(11): e78983.

Organisation for Economic Co-operation and Development (2013) *Development Cooperation Report 2013: Ending Poverty.* Paris: OECD. Available at: http://www.oecd-ilibrary.org/development/development-co-operation-report-2013_dcr-2013-en.

Pappas, Stephanie (2014) It got better: life improved after Black Death, study finds, *Live Science* (7 May). Available at: http://www.livescience.com/45428-health-improved-black-death.html.

Park, Stacy J., Walser, Tonya C., Perdomo, Catalina, Wang, Teresa, Pagano, Paul C., Liclican, Elvira L., Krysan, Kostyantyn, Larsen, Jill E., Minna, John D., Lenburg, Marc E., Spira, Avrum and Dubinett, Steven M. (2014) The effect of e-cigarette exposure on airway epithelial cell gene expression and transformation, *Clinical Cancer Research* 20: B16.

Paul, Marla (2014) Casual marijuana use linked to brain abnormalities, *Northwestern* (16 April). Available at: http://www.northwestern.edu/newscenter/stories/2014/04/casual-marijuana-use-linked-to-brain-abnormalities-in-students.html.

Pennebaker, James (2011) *The Secret Life of Pronouns: What Our Words Say About Us.* New York: Bloomsbury.

Pennebaker, James and Chung, Cindy (2011) Expressive writing: connections to physical and mental health. In Howard Friedman (ed.), *The Oxford Handbook of Health Psychology.* New

York: Oxford University Press, pp. 417–437.

Pennebaker, James, Mehl, Matthias and Niederhoffer, Kate (2003) Psychological aspects of natural language use: our words, our selves, *Annual Review of Psychology* 54: 547–577.

Pizzey, Erin and Shapiro, Jeff (1982) *Prone to Violence*. London: Hamlyn.

Policy Studies Institute (2013) New PSI research reveals the erosion of children's independence (press release) (13 January). Available at: http://www.psi.org.uk/index.php/site/news_article/851.

Priest, Alan (2011) Let's you and I talk, *Therapy Today* (December): 24–27. Available at: http://www.bacp.co.uk/admin/structure/files/pdf/15291_therapy%20today%20december%202011.pdf.

Priest, Alan (2013) You and I Listening To Me: Towards an Understanding of the Significance of Personal Pronoun Usage in Psychotherapy. Unpublished DPsych final project, Metanoia Institute/Middlesex University.

Prince's Trust (2015) *Youth Index 2015*. London: Prince's Trust.

Quinlan, Donald M. and Brown, Thomas E. (2003) Assessment of short-term verbal memory impairments in adolescents and adults with ADHD, *Journal of Attention Disorders* 6(4): 143–152.

Raichle, Marcus E., Fiez, Julie A., Videen, Tom O., MacLeod, Ann-Mary K., Pardo, Jose V., Fox, Peter T. and Petersen, Steven E. (1994) Practice-related changes in human brain functional anatomy during nonmotor learning, *Cerebral Cortex* 4(1): 8–26.

Raine, Adrian (2013) *The Anatomy of Violence: The Biological Roots of Crime*. London: Penguin.

Read, John, Cartwright, Claire and Gibson, Kerry (2014) Adverse emotional and interpersonal effects reported by 1829 New Zealanders while taking antidepressants, *Psychiatry Research* 216(1): 67–73.

Reardon, Sara (2012) The humanity switch: how one gene helped human brains become complex, *New Scientist* (3 May). Available at: https://www.newscientist.com/article/dn21777-the-humanity-switch-how-one-gene-made-us-brainier/.

Rudd, Matt (2011) At the next junction this sat nav will slow your brain, *Sunday Times* (24 April).

Rudin, Mike (2006) The science of happiness, *BBC* (30 April). Available at: http://news.bbc.co.uk/1/hi/programmes/happiness_formula/4783836.stm.

Rumbelow, Helen (2012) Paralympic parents: 'It's not about what they can't do, but what they can', *The Times* (30 August).

Salamon, Maureen (2011) Smoking, diabetes, obesity may shrink your brain, *Health Magazine* (1 August). Available at: http://news.health.com/2011/08/01/smoking-diabetes-obesity-may-shrink-your-brain/.

Sampson, Robert J. (2013a) *Great American City: Chicago and the Enduring Neighborhood Effect*. Chicago, IL: University of Chicago Press.

Sampson, Robert J. (2013b) *Neighborhood Effects and the Contemporary City* [video]. Available at: https://www.youtube.com/watch?v=rnKLIvyF0zc.

Sampson, Robert J. (2013c) When disaster strikes, it's survival of the sociable, *New Scientist* 2916 (17

May). Available at: http://scholar.
harvard.edu/files/sampson/files/
when_disaster_strikes.
pdf?m=1369336664.

Sampson, Robert J. and Laub, John
(1993) *Crime in the Making: Pathways
and Turning Points Through Life*.
Cambridge, MA: Harvard
University Press.

Sampson, Robert J., Raudenbush,
Stephen W. and Earls, Felton
(1997) Neighborhoods and violent
crime: a multilevel study of
collective efficacy, *Science* 277:
918–924.

Scherwitz, Larry (1989) Type A
behaviour assessment in the
structured interview: review,
critique, and recommendations.
In Aron W. Siegman and
Theodore M. Dembroski (eds.), *In
Search of Coronary-Prone Behaviour:
Beyond Type A*. Hillsdale, NJ:
Lawrence Erlbaum Associates,
pp. 117–148.

Scherwitz, L., Berton, K. and
Leventhal, H. (1977) Type A
assessment and interaction in the
behaviour pattern interview,
Psychosomatic Medicine 39:
219–227.

Schmidt, Elaine (2015) High-fructose
diet hampers recovery from
traumatic brain injury (press
release), *UCLA* (2 October).
Available at: http://newsroom.
ucla.edu/releases/
high-fructose-diet-hampers-
recovery-from-traumatic-brain-
injury.

Schoenbaum, Geoffrey, Roesch,
Matthew R. and Stalnaker,
Thomas A. (2006) Orbitofrontal
cortex, decision-making and drug
addiction, *Trends in Neuroscience* 29:
116–124.

Shamay-Tsoory, Simone G., Fischer,
Meytal, Dvash, Jonathan, Harari,
Hagai, Perach-Bloom, Nufar and

Levkovitz, Yechiel (2009)
Intranasal administration of
oxytocin increases envy and
Schadenfreude (gloating),
Biological Psychiatry 66(9): 864–870.

Shaw, Ben, Watson, Ben,
Frauendienst, Björn, Redecker,
Andrea, Jones, Tim and Hillman,
Mayer (2013) *Children's Independent
Mobility: A Comparative Study in
England and Germany (1971–2010)*.
London: Policy Studies Institute.

Shenk, David (2010) *The Genius In All
of Us: Why Everything You've Been
Told About Genes, Talent and
Intelligence is Wrong*. London: Icon.

Sherwood, Ben (2009) *The Survivors'
Club: The Secrets and Science That
Could Save Your Life*. New York:
Grand Central Publishing.

Silva, Stein, de Pasquale, Francesco,
Vuillaume, Corine, Riu, Beatrice,
Loubinoux, Isabelle, Geeraerts,
Thomas, Seguin, Thierry,
Bounes, Vincent, Fourcade,
Olivier, Demonet, Jean-Francois
and Péran, Patrice (2015)
Disruption of posteromedial
large-scale neural communication
predicts recovery from coma,
Neurology 85(23): 2036–2044.

Small, Ian (ed.) (2005) *The Complete
Works of Oscar Wilde*. Vol. II: *De
Profundis, Epistola, In Carcere et
Vinculis*. Oxford: Oxford
University Press.

Smith, Julia Llewellyn (2014) What
God does to your brain, *The
Telegraph* (20 June). Available at:
http://www.telegraph.co.uk/
culture/books/10914137/
What-God-does-to-your-brain.
html.

Swinford, Steven (2013) Living in
the countryside makes people
happier, ONS suggests, *The
Telegraph* (23 October). Available
at: http://www.telegraph.co.uk/
news/newstopics/

howaboutthat/10399019/
Living-in-the-countryside-makes-
people-happier-ONS-suggests.
html.

Sydney Morning Herald (2014)
Depression top cause of illness in
world's teens, World Health
Organization reports (15 May).
Available at: http://www.smh.
com.au/world/
depression-top-cause-of-illness-in-
worlds-teens-world-health-
organisation-reports-20140514-
zrd2i.html.

Tanaka, Yutaka and Bachman,
David L. (2000) The
pharmacotherapy of aphasia. In
Lisa Tabor Connor and Loraine
K. Obler (eds.), *Neuro Behaviour of
Language and Cognition: Studies of
Normal Aging and Brain Damage.*
Dordrecht: Kluwer Academic
Publishers, pp. 159–186.

Taylor, Gemma, Girling, Alan,
McNeill, Ann and Aveyard, Paul
(2015) Does smoking cessation
result in improved mental health?
A comparison of regression
modelling and propensity score
matching, *BMJ Open* 5: e008774.

Taylor, Gemma, McNeill, Ann,
Girling, Alan, Farley, Amanda,
Lindson-Hawley, Nicola and
Aveyard, Paul (2014) Change in
mental health after smoking
cessation: systematic review and
meta-analysis, *BMJ* 348: g1151.

Turkheimer, Eric, Pettersson, Erik
and Horn, Erin E. (2014) A
phenotypic null hypothesis for the
genetics of personality, *Annual
Review of Psychology* 65: 515–540.

University of Sussex (2013) In it
together: research reveals the joy
of the crowd, *Staff Bulletin* (15
November). Available at: http://
www.sussex.ac.uk/internal/
bulletin/staff/2013-14/151113/
crowds.

University of Utah News Center
(2012) Nature nurtures creativity
(press release) (12 December).
Available at: http://archive.
unews.utah.edu/news_releases/
nature-nurtures-creativity-2/.

Vallacher, Robin R. and Wegner,
Daniel M. (1989) Levels of
personal agency: individual
variation in action identification,
*Journal of Personality and Social
Psychology* 57: 660–671.

Van Kleef, Gerben A., De Dreu,
Carsten K. W., Pietroni, David
and Manstead, Antony S. R.
(2006) Power and emotion in
negotiation: power moderates the
interpersonal effects of anger and
unhappiness on concession
making, *European Journal of Social
Psychology* 36: 557–581.

van Staden, C. Werdie (1999)
Linguistic Changes During
Recovery: A Philosophical and
Empirical Study of First Person
Pronoun Usage and the Semantic
Positions of Patients as Expressed
in Psychotherapy and Mental
Illness. Unpublished MD,
University of Warwick.

van Staden, C. Werdie (2003)
Linguistic markers of recovery:
theoretical underpinnings of first
person pronoun usage and
semantic positions of patients,
Philosophy, Psychiatry & Psychology
9(2): 105–121.

Van Wagenen, Maya (2015) *Popular:
How a Geek in Pearls Discovered the
Secret to Confidence.* New York:
Speak/Penguin.

Wang, Z., Brandon, J. (1998) The
Prairie Vole: An Animal Model
of Behavioral Neuroendocrine
Research on Pair Bonding, *ILAR
Journal* 45(1): 35–45.

Wang, Hui, Duclot, Florian, Liu,
Yan, Wang, Zuoxin and Kabbaj,
Mohamed (2013) Histone

deacetylase inhibitors facilitate partner preference formation in female prairie voles, *Nature Neuroscience* 16(7): 919–924.

Wanjek, Christopher (2012) Your diet affects your grandchildren's DNA, scientists say, *Live Science* (27 July). Available at: http://www.livescience.com/21902-diet-epigenetics-grandchildren.html.

White, Jim (2013) Olympic spirit inspires the next generation of volunteers, *The Telegraph* (8 October). Available at: http://www.telegraph.co.uk/education/secondaryeducation/10337279/Olympic-spirit-inspires-the-next-generation-of-volunteers.html.

Wilson, David S. (2011) *The Neighborhood Project: Using Evolution to Improve My City, One Block at a Time*. New York: Little, Brown and Co.

Wilson, Robert S., Boyle, Patricia A., Yu, Lei, Barnes, Lisa L., Schneider, Julie A. and Bennett, David A. (2013) Life-span cognitive activity, neuropathologic burden, and cognitive aging, *Neurology* 81(4): 314–321.

World Health Organization (2015) *Mental Health Atlas 2014*. Geneva: WHO. Available at: http://www.who.int/mental_health/evidence/atlas/mental_health_atlas_2014/en/.

Yong, Ed (2012) Dark side of the love hormone, *New Scientist* (8 February). Available at: https://www.newscientist.com/article/mg21328512-100-dark-side-of-the-love-hormone/.

Zhu, N., Jacobs, D.R. Jr, Schreiner, P.J., Yaffe, K., Bryan, N., Launer, L.J., Whitmer, R.A., Sidney, S., Demerath, E., Thomas, W., Bouchard, C., He, K., Reis, J. and Sternfeld, B. (2014) Cardiorespiratory fitness and cognitive function in middle age: The CARDIA Study, *Neurology* 82(15): 1339–1346.

Index